AF818023

Marx, Engels, and Marxisms

Series Editors
Marcello Musto, York University, Toronto, ON, Canada
Terrell Carver, University of Bristol, Bristol, UK

The Marx renaissance is underway on a global scale. Wherever the critique of capitalism re-emerges, there is an intellectual and political demand for new, critical engagements with Marxism. The peer-reviewed series Marx, Engels and Marxisms (edited by Marcello Musto & Terrell Carver, with Babak Amini, Francesca Antonini, Paula Rauhala & Kohei Saito as Assistant Editors) publishes monographs, edited volumes, critical editions, reprints of old texts, as well as translations of books already published in other languages. Our volumes come from a wide range of political perspectives, subject matters, academic disciplines and geographical areas, producing an eclectic and informative collection that appeals to a diverse and international audience. Our main areas of focus include: the oeuvre of Marx and Engels, Marxist authors and traditions of the 19th and 20th centuries, labour and social movements, Marxist analyses of contemporary issues, and reception of Marxism in the world.

More information about this series at
http://www.palgrave.com/gp/series/14812

Tsuyoshi Yuki

Socialism, Markets, and the Critique of Money

The Theory of "Labor Notes"

palgrave
macmillan

Tsuyoshi Yuki
Graduate School of Humanities and Social Sciences
Saitama University
Saitama, Japan

ISSN 2524-7123 ISSN 2524-7131 (electronic)
Marx, Engels, and Marxisms
ISBN 978-3-030-78983-1 ISBN 978-3-030-80408-4 (eBook)
https://doi.org/10.1007/978-3-030-80408-4

Translation from the Japanese language edition: 労働証券論の歴史的位相 by Tsuyoshi Yuki, © Nippon Hyoron sha co., Ltd 2014. Published by Nippon Hyoron sha co., Ltd. All Rights Reserved.
© The Editor(s) (if applicable) and The Author(s), under exclusive license to Springer Nature Switzerland AG 2021
This work is subject to copyright. All rights are solely and exclusively licensed by the Publisher, whether the whole or part of the material is concerned, specifically the rights of reprinting, reuse of illustrations, recitation, broadcasting, reproduction on microfilms or in any other physical way, and transmission or information storage and retrieval, electronic adaptation, computer software, or by similar or dissimilar methodology now known or hereafter developed.
The use of general descriptive names, registered names, trademarks, service marks, etc. in this publication does not imply, even in the absence of a specific statement, that such names are exempt from the relevant protective laws and regulations and therefore free for general use.
The publisher, the authors and the editors are safe to assume that the advice and information in this book are believed to be true and accurate at the date of publication. Neither the publisher nor the authors or the editors give a warranty, expressed or implied, with respect to the material contained herein or for any errors or omissions that may have been made. The publisher remains neutral with regard to jurisdictional claims in published maps and institutional affiliations.

Cover image: © oxygen/Moment/Getty image

This Palgrave Macmillan imprint is published by the registered company Springer Nature Switzerland AG
The registered company address is: Gewerbestrasse 11, 6330 Cham, Switzerland

Series Editor's Foreword

Titles Published

1. Terrell Carver & Daniel Blank, *A Political History of the Editions of Marx and Engels's "German Ideology" Manuscripts*, 2014.
2. Terrell Carver & Daniel Blank, *Marx and Engels's "German Ideology" Manuscripts: Presentation and Analysis of the "Feuerbach Chapter,"* 2014.
3. Alfonso Maurizio Iacono, *The History and Theory of Fetishism*, 2015.
4. Paresh Chattopadhyay, *Marx's Associated Mode of Production: A Critique of Marxism*, 2016.
5. Domenico Losurdo, *Class Struggle: A Political and Philosophical History*, 2016.
6. Frederick Harry Pitts, *Critiquing Capitalism Today: New Ways to Read Marx*, 2017.
7. Ranabir Samaddar, *Karl Marx and the Postcolonial Age*, 2017.
8. George Comninel, *Alienation and Emancipation in the Work of Karl Marx*, 2018.
9. Jean-Numa Ducange & Razmig Keucheyan (Eds.), *The End of the Democratic State: Nicos Poulantzas, a Marxism for the 21st Century*, 2018.
10. Robert X. Ware, *Marx on Emancipation and Socialist Goals: Retrieving Marx for the Future*, 2018.
11. Xavier LaFrance & Charles Post (Eds.), *Case Studies in the Origins of Capitalism*, 2018.
12. John Gregson, *Marxism, Ethics, and Politics: The Work of Alasdair MacIntyre*, 2018.
13. Vladimir Puzone & Luis Felipe Miguel (Eds.), *The Brazilian Left in the 21st Century: Conflict and Conciliation in Peripheral Capitalism*, 2019.

14. James Muldoon & Gaard Kets (Eds.), *The German Revolution and Political Theory*, 2019.
15. Michael Brie, *Rediscovering Lenin: Dialectics of Revolution and Metaphysics of Domination*, 2019.
16. August H. Nimtz, *Marxism versus Liberalism: Comparative Real-Time Political Analysis*, 2019.
17. Gustavo Moura de Cavalcanti Mello and Mauricio de Souza Sabadini (Eds.), *Financial Speculation and Fictitious Profits: A Marxist Analysis*, 2019.
18. Shaibal Gupta, Marcello Musto & Babak Amini (Eds.), *Karl Marx's Life, Ideas, and Influences: A Critical Examination on the Bicentenary*, 2019.
19. Igor Shoikhedbrod, *Revisiting Marx's Critique of Liberalism: Rethinking Justice, Legality, and Rights*, 2019.
20. Juan Pablo Rodríguez, *Resisting Neoliberal Capitalism in Chile: The Possibility of Social Critique*, 2019.
21. Kaan Kangal, *Friedrich Engels and the Dialectics of Nature*, 2020.
22. Victor Wallis, *Socialist Practice: Histories and Theories*, 2020.
23. Alfonso Maurizio Iacono, *The Bourgeois and the Savage: A Marxian Critique of the Image of the Isolated Individual in Defoe, Turgot and Smith*, 2020.
24. Terrell Carver, *Engels Before Marx*, 2020.
25. Jean-Numa Ducange, *Jules Guesde: The Birth of Socialism and Marxism in France*, 2020.
26. Antonio Oliva, Ivan Novara & Angel Oliva (Eds.), *Marx and Contemporary Critical Theory: The Philosophy of Real Abstraction*, 2020.
27. Francesco Biagi, *Henri Lefebvre's Critical Theory of Space*, 2020.
28. Stefano Petrucciani, *The Ideas of Karl Marx: A Critical Introduction*, 2020.
29. Terrell Carver, *The Life and Thought of Friedrich Engels, 30th Anniversary Edition*, 2020.
30. Giuseppe Vacca, *Alternative Modernities: Antonio Gramsci's Twentieth Century*, 2020.
31. Kevin B. Anderson, Kieran Durkin & Heather Brown (Eds.), *Raya Dunayevskaya's Intersectional Marxism: Race, Gender, and the Dialectics of Liberation*, 2020.
32. Marco Di Maggio, *The Rise and Fall of Communist Parties in France and Italy*, 2020.
33. Ryuji Sasaki, *A New Introduction to Karl Marx: New Materialism, Critique of Political Economy, and the Concept of Metabolism*, 2020.
34. Kohei Saito (Ed.), *Reexamining Engels's Legacy in the 21st Century*, 2021.
35. Paresh Chattopadhyay, *Socialism in Marx's Capital: Towards a Dealienated World*, 2021.
36. Marcello Musto, *Karl Marx's Writings on Alienation*, 2021.

37. Michael Brie & Jörn Schütrumpf, *Rosa Luxemburg: A Revolutionary Marxist at the Limits of Marxism*, 2021.
38. Stefano Petrucciani, *Theodor W. Adorno's Philosophy, Society, and Aesthetics*, 2021.
39. Miguel Vedda, *Siegfried Kracauer, or, The Allegories of Improvisation: Critical Studies*, 2021.
40. Ronaldo Munck, *Rethinking Development: Marxist Perspectives*, 2021.
41. Jean-Numa Ducange & Elisa Marcobelli (Eds.), *Selected Writings of Jean Jaurès: On Socialism, Pacifism and Marxism*, 2021.
42. Elisa Marcobelli, *Internationalism Toward Diplomatic Crisis: The Second International and French, German and Italian Socialists*, 2021.
43. James Steinhoff, *Automation and Autonomy: Labour, Capital and Machines in the Artificial Intelligence Industry*, 2021.
44. Juan Dal Maso, *Hegemony and Class Struggle: Trotsky, Gramsci and Marxism*, 2021.

Titles Forthcoming

Gianfranco Ragona & Monica Quirico, *Frontier Socialism: Self-organisation and Anti-capitalism*

Vesa Oittinen, *Marx's Russian Moment*

Kolja Lindner, *Marx, Marxism and the Question of Eurocentrism*

Adriana Petra, *Intellectuals and Communist Culture: Itineraries, Problems and Debates in Post-War Argentina*

George C. Comninel, *The Feudal Foundations of Modern Europe*

Spencer A. Leonard, *Marx, the India Question, and the Crisis of Cosmopolitanism*

Joe Collins, *Applying Marx's Capital to the 21st century*

Levy del Aguila Marchena, *Communism, Political Power and Personal Freedom in Marx*

Jeong Seongjin, *Korean Capitalism in the 21st Century: Marxist Analysis and Alternatives*

Marcello Mustè, *Marxism and Philosophy of Praxis: An Italian Perspective from Labriola to Gramsci*

Satoshi Matsui, *Normative Theories of Liberalism and Socialism: Marxist Analysis of Values*

Shannon Brincat, *Dialectical Dialogues in Contemporary World Politics: A Meeting of Traditions in Global Comparative Philosophy*

Francesca Antonini, *Reassessing Marx's Eighteenth Brumaire: Dictatorship, State, and Revolution*

Thomas Kemple, *Capital After Classical Sociology: The Faustian Lives of Social Theory*

V. Geetha, *Bhimrao Ramji Ambedkar and the Question of Socialism in India*

Xavier Vigna, *A Political History of Factories in France: The Workers' Insubordination of 1968*
Attila Melegh, *Anti-Migrant Populism in Eastern Europe and Hungary: A Marxist Analysis*
Marie-Cecile Bouju, *A Political History of the Publishing Houses of the French Communist Party*
Gustavo Moura de Cavalcanti Mello & Henrique Pereira Braga (Eds.), *Wealth and Poverty in Contemporary Brazilian Capitalism*
Peter McMylor, Graeme Kirkpatrick & Simin Fadaee (Eds.), *Marxism, Religion, and Emancipatory Politics*
Mauro Buccheri, *Radical Humanism for the Left: The Quest for Meaning in Late Capitalism*
Rémy Herrera, *Confronting Mainstream Economics to Overcome Capitalism*
Tamás Krausz, Eszter Bartha (Eds.), *Socialist Experiences in Eastern Europe: A Hungarian Perspective*
Martin Cortés, *Marxism, Time and Politics: On the Autonomy of the Political*
João Antonio de Paula, Huga da Gama Cerqueira, Eduardo da Motta e Albuquer & Leonardo de Deus, *Marxian Economics for the 21st Century: Revaluating Marx's Critique of Political Economy*
Zhi Li, *The Concept of the Individual in the Thought of Karl Marx*
Lelio Demichelis, *Marx, Alienation and Techno-capitalism*
Dong-Min Rieu, *A Mathematical Approach to Marxian Value Theory: Time, Money, and Labor Productivity*
Salvatore Prinzi, *Representation, Expression, and Institution: The Philosophy of Merleau-Ponty and Castoriadis*
Agon Hamza, *Slavoj Žižek and the Reconstruction of Marxism*
Kei Ehara (Ed.), *Japanese Discourse on the Marxian Theory of Finance*
Éric Aunoble, *French Views on the Russian Revolution*
Paolo Favilli, *Historiography and Marxism: Innovations in Mid-Century Italy*
Terrell Carver, Smail Rapic (Eds.), *Friedrich Engels for the 21st Century: Perspectives and Problems*
Patrizia Dogliani, *A Political History of the International Union of Socialist Youth*
Alexandros Chrysis, *The Marx of Communism: Setting Limits in the Realm of Communism*
Stephen Maher, *Corporate Capitalism and the Integral State: General Electric and a Century of American Power*
Paul Raekstad, *Karl Marx's Realist Critique of Capitalism: Freedom, Alienation, and Socialism*
Alexis Cukier, *Democratic Work: Radical Democracy and the Future of Labour*
Christoph Henning, *Theories of Alienation: From Rousseau to the Present*
Daniel Egan, *Capitalism, War, and Revolution: A Marxist Analysis*

Genevieve Ritchie, Sara Carpenter & Shahrzad Mojab (Eds.), *Marxism and Migration*
Emanuela Conversano, *Capital from Afar: Anthropology and Critique of Political Economy in the Late Marx*
Marcello Musto, *Rethinking Alternatives with Marx*
Vincenzo Mele, *City and Modernity in George Simmel and Walter Benjamin: Fragments of Metropolis*
David Norman Smith, *Self-Emancipation: Marx's Unfinished Theory of the Working Class*
José Ricardo Villanueva Lira, *Marxism and the Origins of International Relations*
Bertel Nygaard, *Marxism, Labor Movements, and Historiography*
Fabio Perocco (Ed.), *Racism in and for the Welfare State*
Marcos Del Roio, *Gramsci and the Emancipation of the Subaltern Classes*
Marcelo Badaró, *The Working Class from Marx to Our Times*
Tomonaga Tairako, *A New Perspective on Marx's Philosophy and Political Economy*

Acknowledgments

This book is a full translation by the author himself of the Rōdō shōken ron no rekishiteki isō [*Historical Phases of the Theory of Labor Note: Visions of Money and Market*], a book that was awarded the Fifth Japanese Society of Political Economy's Encouragement Award. Despite having received considerable appreciation in Japan, it was previously inaccessible to English-speaking readers. However, descriptions that may not necessary for English-speaking readers have been corrected accordingly. I would like to thank Kohei Saito, Marcello Musto, and anonymous referees for accepting this book for the Marx, Engels, and Marxisms series. In addition, without the collaboration of Yuri Shiomi, Joel Rasbash, and Michael Schauerte, this book could not have been written so smoothly. Some of the Warren materials used in this document were provided by Gregory Claeys. This study was supported by JSPS KAKENHI Grant Number JP18K01529, ISHII Memorial Securities Research Promotion Foundation Research Fund, and The Economics Society of Saitama University. I want to thank everyone for their help and support.

In the process of conducting this research, I received the grant from JSPS KAKENHI Grant Number JP23730204 in 2011–2013, JP245164 in 2012, and Saitama University's Project Research Fund (Project Number A11-09) in 2011, for which I would like to express my appreciation.

Finally, I would like to present this book with all my heart to Chie, Chifuyu, Shifumi, and Kazuha who have supported me when I did not have the means to make a living.

Contents

CHAPTER 1

Issues, Methods, and Scopes

1.1 Introduction to the English Edition

Revisiting the Theory of Labor Money

For us, living in the post-Marxist era, the labor note and labor money theories referred to in the title may seem to belong in the prehistory of community currencies, instead of being heterodoxic-socialist or monetary-reform theories. For pre-Marxist socialist factions, however, "socialism" meant market socialism and monetary or credit-reform theory. Marx used the theory of labor money to absorb the monetary and credit-system reform theories of utopian socialism, Ricardian socialism, and anarchism. His criticism of socialist monetary and credit-system reforms was elaborate and thorough. Given that socialists have never developed effective counter-criticisms, with their arguments generally seen as either unscientific utopian views or petit-bourgeois deceptions, Marx can be said to have won the theoretical debate over labor money theory. However, while we may admire the strength of Marx's intellect, the state of global capitalism since the collapse of the Soviet Union makes it necessary to revisit the historical debate over heterodoxic monetary and credit-system reforms.

Given the history of this debate, it is important to proceed in two stages: first, to accurately understand the implications of Marx's criticism; and second, to inherently understand each theorist's doctrine, as

© The Author(s), under exclusive license to Springer Nature Switzerland AG 2021

T. Yuki, *Socialism, Markets, and the Critique of Money*, Marx, Engels, and Marxisms,
https://doi.org/10.1007/978-3-030-80408-4_1

construed through the concept of labor money theory. The first issue is explained below.

Marx's conceptualization of labor money is a socialist monetary and credit-system reform theory, which claims that equal labor exchange can be realized by issuing paper money as a representative for the value of bestowed labor time. In his summary of the theory of labor money, the first point Marx makes is that prices, determined by subjective consumer values and the supply–demand relationship, do not represent a true social relationship because they fluctuate in arbitrary ways. If monetary prices are eliminated, objective value must be defined by the amount of labor bestowed (determined technically and externally). Producers exchange products using paper money, the face value of which represents hours of labor (labor money). In this way, equal labor exchange is realized naturally, eliminating exploitation from the circulation process. The theory of labor money is based on this idea of fair exchange. The second point in the theory of labor money is a philosophical critique of metallic currency, which argues that money can be eliminated, as an obstacle to circulation, if it is converted into purely intermediary bills (labor money), through the demonetarization of gold; this critique recognizes that gold is considered the fundamental form of money, thus depriving commodities of exchangeability.

The first point in equal labor exchange theory has been criticized from the standpoint of Marx's theory of measure of value, while the intermediary (means of exchange) theory discussed in the second point has been criticized using value form theory. The "transformation of money into capital" theory, which proves that production processes can be exploited, even when circulation processes are not, delivers the final blow.

In other words, when bestowed labor time is used to measure value in a commodity economy with supply-and-demand discrepancies and production-technology changes and heterogeneity, it is impossible to make reasonable economic calculations that can minimize costs. It is clear that individual labor time cannot be used to measure disparities in supply, demand, or technology as long as the capitalistic mode of production requires money prices. The logic of the value form thus proposes the monetary nature of commodities, in which any commodity can take the position of the money form. As researchers have pointed out, the money form cannot be abolished simply by demonetarizing gold. Finally, even if social control of the marketplace limits it to a simple circulation of commodities as C–M–C, merchants can revive capitalism by reselling commodities and exploiting the production process.

These criticisms present the fundamental proposition that socialist monetary and credit-system reforms cannot be undertaken under the capitalist mode of production. However, beyond this argument is a world of logical inferences and realistic challenges, which sometimes require acrobatics. In other words, in this context, Marx is saying only that we cannot change the circulation process; he is not necessarily saying that the production process can be changed in its place. He does not say what type of economic system can be built after the production style is changed through the abolition of commodities, money, and capital. Questions involving the domain of freedom have also been developed.

Critical arguments, however, should take into account the fact that social reproduction is premised on having a society that is comprehensively organized through the commodity economy, capitalistic profit-seeking subjects, and a single pricing system. Under these conditions, Marx can be praised for having challenged socialist theories of monetary and credit-system reform.

This book presents the following argument. If the social division of labor is implemented in society after markets are abolished, with social resources allocated via some kind of economic measure or unit, then economic calculations by labor time can be included in the choice, after the theoretical conditions presented in the debate have been examined. In this case, there may be a market socialist allocation using labor money, as well as a socialist allocation of labor through the planned economy.

Furthermore, under the conditions of partiality of capitalism, cooperative actors, and multi-value systems, equal labor exchange can be understood, not as a philosophy of equivalent exchange, but as an exchange of natural time with the acceptance of inequivalence. It should thus be reinterpreted in conjunction with the realistic possibility of community currencies, in line with the theory of labor money, which seeks a valuation that differs from the market assessment of labor.

Although Marx argued persuasively that labor money could not be money, labor money was originally a theory of monetary and credit-system reform, which was oriented toward socialist money (= non-money); for this reason, it should not be treated as equivalent to capitalist money. Under market socialism and cooperative social relations, the present study refers to non-monetary labor money (in which monetary function is restricted or recombined) as "labor notes." This is the first step in the reassessment, returning to the second issue cited above.

The relative independence of the forms of circulation clarifies which subject is responsible for producing and providing commodities for the market. Capitalistic liberty and efficiency involve sacrifices, achieved by exploiting and repressing the working class. The goal of achieving freedom and efficiency by eradicating exploitation and reducing repression is embraced by workers' cooperatives and self-managed enterprises, under the autonomous control of their workers.

If we examine socialist theory today, it seems clear that researchers have fundamental reservations about the feasibility of combining social ownership of the means of production with a centrally planned economy. First, socialist philosophy must be functionally broken down and pursued at each level through workers' cooperatives, via a production and circulation approach that involves labor notes.

How Is Money Socialized?

Deciding where to begin is a significant problem for researchers attempting to overcome the contradictions of capitalism. Community-currency movements that aimed to socialize money began in fields where labor was difficult and uneconomical to market, due to intensive social issues; these fields included domestic and care labor and shared labor in communities responsible for local material cycles. Transforming the things (money) that connect people has continually been described as a bad move, from the perspective of things. Although the updated theory of modern social reform does consider the role played by relations and networks of private labor, it aggressively supports the reform of reified social relations and abandons the economic reductionism. Although beyond the scope of this book, the Uno school's welfare-state theory, which the author has systematically studied, foresaw a "new welfare state" (Okamoto 2007), as the basis for accepting the vitality of the new social movement. The theory of monetary reform can be positioned within this movement. It is important to ask, however, why monetary reform is such a bad move in the first place.

Theories of socialist monetary and credit-system reform, such as anarchism and Ricardian socialism, do not have a monopoly on the idea of detaching society from money to resolve the intense contradictions of capitalism. Various social-reform theories, including Christian socialism, social credit, 100% reserve banks, community currencies, and anti-austerity, have been drawn to this idea. Although they differ in their details, all of these theories transform private money into social money, regulate capital movements, and socialize or democratize money. In doing so, they encounter some difficulties. First, money reflects social relations under the capitalist mode of production; for this reason, no attempt to improve the circulation process or the money within it can succeed without also reforming the production process. It is equally impossible to do away with capitalistic production, in which labor is expended privately while money is changed, with money qua thing; this is a false problem. Even the Uno school, which does not adopt reification theory, argues that community currencies or commodities will inevitably be converted into money if free-trade activities are accepted within the circulation process.

In short, under capitalistic markets, conflicts between private and social labor are mediated through the separation of value and price. The theory of labor money, a typical socialist monetary and credit-system reform theory, argues that equal labor exchange, in terms of the amount of living labor, can be achieved by issuing denominated bills in proportion to the labor time or labor value needed to produce a product. According to Marx, who singled it out for criticism, this approach confuses value with price and makes the mistake of treating private labor as social labor. The issues raised by Marx span the following six theoretical fields: (1) There is no way to equalize the quantity of private labor objectified as the product with the quantity of social labor (theory of measure of value); (2) the possibility cannot be excluded that, even if gold money is replaced with paper money, another product will become money (theory of value form); (3) the correlation between the amount of value of products and the face value of labor money does not guarantee that individual transactions will be concluded (exchange-process theory, value-realization theory); (4) the transformation of labor money to capital cannot be prevented (money-hoarding theory); (5) products are at risk of being resold via merchant capital whenever a labor money economy and a money economy coexist; and (6) it is not necessary to exploit the production process, even if an equal labor exchange is achieved (transformation of money into capital, exploitation theory). The socialization theory of money must overcome these hurdles. When there is capitalist production, however, it is almost impossible to overcome all of these hurdles at once. It can therefore be said that one way of socializing money has been closed off.

Although Marx's criticism of labor money theory was exhaustive and did not overlook any avenue, modern capitalism still retains three aspects of socialization of money.

The first is a managed currency system, which regulates the free movement of money through the power of the state and sends it in directions that help to develop the national economy. Most economists, not just anti-austerity groups, have adopted this approach, even though it preserves the power of the state. As it cannot effectively restrain capitalist production, it cannot eliminate the repression and exploitation of labor and production processes. In addition, policy decisions depend on political processes. The best we can expect from a welfare state with a full-employment policy is a temporary condition that facilitates the sale of the labor power and does not sublate its commodification.

Second, as Itoh (2012) has pointed out, there are three types of socialist money. Soviet-style socialism's failure to attempt labor-volume calculations is problematic; Itoh categorizes the ways in which socialist money ("s-money") is used to recognize the social nature of labor into three approaches. The first—perhaps the most desirable—is the labor note, which pushes markets out of society and represents the hours spent in social labor. The second is s-money that incorporates outside markets into society and represents face values in direct proportion to hours of living labor; the third is s-money that is not directly linked to labor time (e.g., rubles). If currencies in socialist countries have similar properties to managed currencies, while socialist money that appears after the "original transition period" (Otani 2011: 32) has essentially non-monetary properties, the actual problem becomes money in market socialism. Given this, nominal amounts in direct proportion to the quantity of labor or the direct use of labor time can help to reveal the social nature of labor and determine the distribution and allocation of social labor and social-investment decisions.

The third approach involves community currency, used as a medium of exchange for labor in non-capitalistic areas of activity, which in theory, exist outside capitalism, despite occurring within a social system based on capitalist production. Traditionally, local currencies have been thought to have only negative implications, in accordance with Marx's criticism of the labor money theory. They have been seen as replacing capitalistic social systems or complementing capitalism, while, in fact, they are parasitic. If community currencies are judged by their ability to mediate the transformation of private labor into social labor, they do not seem significant. The true significance of community currencies, however, is the fact that they are not subject to commodity-economic valuation. In terms of the socialization of money, community currencies aim to partially and progressively achieve the real internal goals of market socialism in the "here and now." In other words, community currencies offer a direct exchange for living labor. Socialism and Marxism replace prices with labor time to measure community-currency movements, which are supposed to evolve with no clear relationship. Such ideas are unconvincing in the same way as labor money treats private labor directly as social labor. This is certainly the case when we envisage community currencies within social systems designed to replace capitalism. However, there are theoretical spaces and conditions in which it can be useful to reconsider community currencies.

For example, Otani (2011) makes the following comment:

> First of all, we can imagine something like a place in which a product is received in exchange for some kind of writing, when obtained from the gross product of society, and referring to this place as a "market" and then thinking that there is no way to get rid of this market because no society could exist without such a mechanism is out of the question. Furthermore, something like the local exchange or "sale" of "commodities," which may remain outside the basic mechanism of social production, is not the "market" in question. Commodity circulation, which must remain long-term during the transition to association (transitional period), is a separate issue that should be discussed independently. (Otani 2011: 316)

In other words, Marx's criticism of labor money theory and the criticism of community currencies, which invokes the same reasoning, consider whether money functions correctly in the "market," as referred to by Otani. However, community currencies actually circulate through the circulation of commodities that remain during the transition period; this is considered to be "something like the local exchange or 'sale' of 'commodities' that may remain outside of the basic mechanism of social production" and "a separate issue that should be discussed independently." Similar theoretical spaces are found in Sasaki's explanation below:

> If, for example, one person exchanges a comic book he is tired of reading with his best friend and obtains another, they have certainly made an exchange to satisfy their desires, but that does not mean that the comic

> book is a commodity. Further, no one will call the place where this exchange occurs a market.
>
> In the previous example of a comic book, items were not exchanged through a negotiating of price. The two participants were best friends from the beginning, not in a relationship in which each tried to profit from the other. Moreover, what they exchanged was a comic book that one had already read and grown tired of, and the proportion in which they were able to exchange them did not affect their lives. Therefore, they certainly profited from the exchange, but the way they exchanged was very inexact and they did not negotiate on price at each step. (Sasaki 2019: 175–176)

This passage precisely describes the world of community currencies. There is no market between close friends. Therefore, things do not command such exchanges. What is important in this example is that not all exchanges create a market; here, the involvement of the parties involved in the exchange is the issue. The example above shows that it is possible to conceive of relationships that are completely separate from capitalism. To escape the command by things, the only option is to have more close friends. However, best friends do not grow by themselves; nor do they grow easily, even when people put in a lot of effort. This book aims to enable the spread of relationships between close friends within capitalism and in the context of capitalism. In other words, human societies need schemes through which people can relate to each other like best friends, even if they are not friends. What is likely to be achieved between markets and non-markets is a relationship in which participants profit from the exchange, while adopting a gentle approach and avoiding the need to negotiate prices at every step. Community currencies are positioned in just such a narrow theoretical space.

The key to socializing money through community currencies lies in aggregating the quantity of private labor or non-market labor and the direct management of money by individuals. According to Yuki, "labor notes can be a mechanism for securing the sovereignty of individuals in labor self-assessment and production decision-making;" the modern application of labor notes is also sketched out (Yuki 2009: 232). Labor notes can be structured in two different ways: The first is conscious of the bottom-up formation of society and assumes single transactions, while the second aggregates the history of labor from the viewpoint of recognizing the social basis or organization of labor.

However, the reason why labor aggregation is useful in community currencies lies within capitalism because people who are completely separated from the market have no reasonable basis for calculating the value of labor within their communities. Under capitalism, all work is essentially disciplined; the quantity of most productive labor and some consumption-related labor is technically determined. It is easier to recognize the interdependence of labor when the social division of labor is highly developed; the compatibility and abstract quality of human labor relate to the spread of national education and the unpredictability of employment. Without market attention, labor in the workplace and labor at home are equally necessary. Community currencies play a role in visualizing the types and quantities of work needed by communities, even if they are not valued in capitalistic markets.

Although the total amount of social labor time spent on social products remains invisible, individual capital contains the aggregated demand for investment and production planning. Although the aggregated labor time spent on labor management and the workload objectified in individual products can be aggregated, they are hidden behind the commodity price. Despite being weak, the market penetration of community currencies indicates this. Even when hours are spent on private labor, they technically constitute objective time (e.g., "a smartphone for 80,000 yen or 20 hours"). Thus, it is better to aggregate private labor time because it can reveal how many "bullshit jobs" have been absorbed. Such jobs can be referred to as "labor mileage" or the "labor footprint," following the examples of food mileage and the ecological footprint. The history of labor reveals various factors, including the relationship between different types of labor, the amount of labor commanded through prices, and the actual state of technical selections that waste human beings. The importance of recognizing who worked—not just upstream in production, but downstream in consumption—has not been recognized, either in the welfare states that support labor associations or in the sublated commodification of labor power.

It is worth noting that although cryptocurrencies such as bitcoin also form bottom-up societies, there is no real object corresponding to a coin, and subjects have little reason to cooperate. Despite presenting technical possibilities that link individuals directly, the system provides no reason to associate. The socialization of money through nations lacks a channel that individuals can use to manage money directly. Supply and demand adjustments, transactions linking individuals, and the tools to manage them are increasingly used on a daily basis. Labor alone is not recognized, despite being originally connected. As Itoh says, "The failure of the Soviet-type society occurred when sophisticated computerization could not be incorporated into its economic planning or its economic life; socialism using advanced information technology belongs to a future possibility of history that has not yet been attempted" (Itoh 2010: 131). In this way, Itoh raises awareness that links between labor may still emerge from unexpected places.

This introduction corrects Section 4 "Kahei no shakaika" [Socialization of Money] in "Posuto Kyapitarizumu ron no Shosō: Kahei no Shakaika he no Shatei" [Looking Back on the Theories of Post-Capitalism: Range to the Socialization of Money] published in the special issue, Towards Post-Capitalism, *Political Economy Quarterly*, Vol. 57, No. 2, 2020, edited by Sasaki, R., and "Rōdō kahei ron kara Rōdō shōken ron he: Itan no Kahei, Shin'yō seido kaikaku ron shi" [From the Theory of Labor Money to the Theory of Labor Notes: The History of Heterodoxic Theories of Monetary and Credit-System Reform], *Henkaku no Asoshie* [Associate to Transformation], No. 9, 2012.

This book is a full translation by the author himself of the *Rōdō shōken ron no rekishiteki isō* [Historical Phases of the Theory of Labor Note: Visions of Money and Market], a book that was awarded the Fifth Japanese Society of Political Economy's Encouragement Award. Despite having received considerable appreciation in Japan, it was previously inaccessible to English-speaking readers. However, descriptions that may not necessary for English-speaking readers have been corrected accordingly. I would like to thank Kohei Saito, Marcello Musto, and anonymous referees for accepting this book for the Marx, Engels, and Marxisms series. In addition, without the collaboration of Yuri Shiomi, Joel Rasbash, and Michael Schauerte, this book could not have been written so smoothly. Some of the Warren materials used in this document were provided by Gregory Claeys. This study was supported by JSPS KAKENHI Grant Number JP18K01529, ISHII Memorial Securities Research Promotion Foundation Research Fund, and The Economics Society of Saitama University. I want to thank everyone for their help and support.

1.2 Issues and Methods: The Invisibility of "Labor Notes"

Regarding Terminology

The term "labor note theory" is used in the title of this book. As terms go it is unlikely to be familiar even to more experienced researchers in the field. Where it is familiar, the term is usually assigned a minor role within research on theories of labor money advocated by various schools of socialists during the nineteenth century. In academic literature and university textbooks, the subject has rarely been mentioned under this name.[1] However, when the subject is referred to as "labor money theory," it evokes an atmosphere of classical debates that have long been settled.[2] Nowhere is this more evident than in the context of Marxian political economy. In this book, the term "labor note theory" refers to the same subject as the ideology that has been circulating under

[1] In "Chapter 4: Shaking of Classical Political Economy" (Makoto Noguchi) of *History of Political Economy*, edited by Makoto Itoh, the section titled "Cooperative society and labor money: Thompson, Gray and Bray" is devoted to commentary on labor money theory (Noguchi 1996: 101–105).

[2] This is related to the understanding of money functions (in particular, measure of value and means of hoarding). In many discussions, labor money theory has been criticized from the angle of money theory. For example, see Obata (2009: 64, 296) "Question 40" and its "Answer."

The following is the outline of the Marxian school's criticism of labor money theory. There are three points: (1) measure of value, (2) means of hoarding, and (3) the system of commodity economy (private ownership). In this book, "labor money" is defined first as labor time notes used in the commodity economy. We observe the purpose of labor money being to eliminate exploitation in the circulation process (the unequal exchange of capital and labor, and that of commodities and money), and the crisis of under-consumption by facilitating circulation. By using labor money, the function and nature of money are changed; the function of money is purified into the means of circulation, and a market economy free of price and capital is thus created. Labor money theory is composed of the purpose, which is the equivalent (= equal quantities of labor) exchange, as well as the means to achieve it.

However, the Marxian school's findings point out that the means and purpose are wrong on two counts. Labor money that does not function as a measure of value has a disadvantage whereby markets without prices accumulate excesses and shortages of production. Also, it cannot be ruled out that hoarded labor money can be a source of capital, because the market's supply–demand adjustment function based on money prices is lost. Moreover, labor money can be converted into capital. This is why there is such a negative evaluation, concluding that the attempt simply to reform the circulation process in a commodity economy is useless.

the label of "labor money theory," but I also want to emphasize that in reality there are certain practical differences between the two. This book is probably the first to attempt systematically to organize the principles of labor money and labor notes. At the same time, the term "labor note theory" was chosen over alternative terms in order to clarify the significance of the history of political economy and to maintain its strategic and practical value, while treating the various versions of labor notes as a single subject. While there is a rationale for using the term "labor note theory" to denote the entire field, there is a dual problem that needs to be confronted. First, there is a risk of dwarfing the theoretical implications of labor money theory (especially as it has been explained in the history of the existing canon), and second, the novelty of the phrase "labor note theory" used in this book might cause the subject under study to seem ambiguous. In addition, there will be an obligation to respond to doubts that this is simply a masquerade to replace the term labor money with labor notes. Hence, it will first have to be understood that it is necessary to rid ourselves of preconceived ideas attached to labor money theory if we are to hope to develop new knowledge of the subject.

Most strikingly, a review of contemporary terminology reveals that the term "labor note theory" accords better with contemporary usage, even though the term "labor money theory" has come to be most closely associated with Marx's writings on the topic.[3] It is important to note that the term "labour money" [*Arbeitsgeld*] (Marx 1986/1857–1858: 61)[4] was used and defined by Karl Marx (1818–1883), but it differs from the terms used by Robert Owen (1771–1858) and others who are known as advocates of labor money.[5] For example, Owen called it "a paper

[3] With regard to Marx's conceptualization of labor money, while the money and credit reform theory of Proudhon and Gray has a socialist bent toward abolishing money, by shelving the transformation of production relations, the content remains such that the theory is based on reform, which preserves the nature of money. In general, these monetary reform concepts tend to be understood as labor money theory, but in other parts of *Economic Manuscripts of 1857–58* [*Grundrisse*], Marx also described it as a "money representing x labour time," an "labour-time tickets" [*Stundenzettel*] (Marx 1986/1857–1858: 90), "**tickets**" (ibid.), or "a draft" [*Anweisung*] (ibid., 91).

[4] "Labour money" is used in English-speaking countries. See Saad-Filho (1993, 2002: Sec. 8) and Lapavitsas (2003: Sec. 7).

[5] The idea of using money as a representative of labor existed before Owen. John Bellers (1654–1725), who can be considered a Quaker and a Christian socialist, said, "This colledge-fellowship will make labour, and not money, the standard to value all

representative [of] the value of labour" (1993a/1821b: 96, 326), "notes or vouchers" (Owen 1968/1821a: 102, 210), and "notes or community bank paper" (Owen 1993b/1826–1827: 72, 240) and did not use "labor money." Furthermore, phrases such as "labour note" and "time notes" are found in the journal *Crisis*, which belonged to the Owenites (*Crisis*, Vol. 1, Nos. 15 & 16, June 30, 1832, pp. 59, 61). Also, Pierre-Joseph Proudhon (1809–1865) used "exchange ticket" (*bons d'échange*) (Proudhon 1868/1848: 188) and "circulation ticket" (*bon de circulation*) (Proudhon 1849), and John Gray (1799–1883) used "receipt" (Gray 1873/1831: 63). It should be noted that the term "money" was carefully avoided by the authors cited above.[6] To their distress it was apparent that labor notes partially performed functions similar to those of money, but

necessaries by; and though money hath its conveniences, in the common way of living, it being a pledge among men for want of credit; yet not without its mischiefs; and called by our Saviour, *The Mammon of Unrighteousness*; most cheats and robberies would go but slowly on, if it were not for money: And when people have their whole dependance of trading by money, if that fails, or is corrupted, they are next door to ruine; and the poor stand still, because the rich have no money to employ them, though they have the same land and hands to provide victuals and clothes, as ever they had; which is the true riches of a nation, and not the money in it… / Money in the body politic, is what a crutch is to the natural body, crippled; but when the body is sound, the crutch is but troublesome: So when the particular interest is made a publick interest, in such a colledge money will be of little use there" (Bellers 1858/1696: 155–181); he expressed the notion of making labor the standard of value. Owen found a commonality with Bellers's argument and reprinted 1,000 copies in 1818, then recorded it again in the second edition of *The Life of Robert Owen* (1857–58). This citation refers to the second edition. The first edition was issued in 1695.

[6] Strictly speaking, Owen did not actively use the term "labour notes." Rather, this is only found in Owenite journals. The term was likely used among the Owenites of the time and practitioners' groups with socialist tendencies. Looking at Japanese translations from previous studies, Shirai and Hijikata translated labor note as "*rōdōken*" (labor ticket) (Shirai 1991: 95; Hijikata 2003: 89), Kamata used "*rōdōshiken*" (labor paper) (Kamata 2000: 12), and Maruyama used "*rōdōshōken*" (labor note) (Maruyama 1999: 62–64). If translated literally, it must be one such translation, but the positive implication of labor money is not explicit. Marx's criticism would have been a passive judgment that no matter what term is chosen, it was merely money. Although criticism by the classical school is also observed, its impact on the literature is relatively small. For example, see Torrens (1819).

Conversely, in his paper "John Gray's Theory of National Banks and Labour Money" (1980), Ebihara gave certain consideration to the term used by Gray himself, and while taking the expression "'money' as a 'receipt'" (Ebihara 1980: 71, 81), he referred to "Owen's 'labour money' (labour-note)" (ibid., 84) in the title and Note 18, in accordance with Marx's conceptualization. Yet in any sense, it is not always pursued whether "'money' as a 'receipt'" has a monetary substance. Also, according to Kishi, "for both Gray and their intention was that they should not be used like money. The position of the Marxian school has been to expose the contradiction of attempting to partially perform the functions of money without having the role of money. Yet, for labor note advocates, finds a way to live in gray economic areas, where the inconsistency can be seen to be operating according to its own particular logic.

Even if Marx thought labor notes were the equivalent of "money" in reality, it should be noted that the label assigned reflects a high degree of subjective judgment on the part of the theorist. In any case, it should be clear that the matter at hand basically refers to a non-monetary form of security (a note, paper, or voucher). Ultimately, it is necessary to question whether the name corresponds with the reality.

Adjacent Categories

Labor note theory is embedded in a series of non-Marxian socialist theories, ideas, and practices, such as petit-bourgeois socialism, anarchism, Ricardian socialism, and utopian socialism. Hence, not only has there been no explicit consideration of labor note theory, but the many labels attached to it have acted as an inherent obstacle. Therefore, we must start by carefully peeling off each of these labels and exploring labor note theory based on the various socialist political traditions that espoused some variant of a labor note theory.

The various conceptualizations regarding socialist theory suggest that the history of socialism has so far constituted a large part of the history

Bray, money was equally a 'voucher'" (Kishi 1978: 69). Kishi deemed this "time ticket theory" (ibid., 72).

Although previous studies had salvaged some of the ideas of Owen and utopian socialism, such as co-operative thought and gradual approaches to social change, "the idea was developed that the Ricardian socialist Gray, under the influence of Owen, had sought to solve social problems through labor money in particular" (Shirai 1991: 101). In other words, even those studies that recognized the legitimacy of utopian socialism vis-à-vis scientific socialism have paid little attention to labor note theory, which is treated merely as a minor detail. First, the trunk is more important than the foliage, and of course, this book is developed based on a detailed re-assessment. Thus, regarding the results that have been derived so far, I would like to express my sincere appreciation that the academic environment that allows labor note theory to be discussed in such detail. In the literature, it seems that labor note theory has begun to be recognized as an independent subject of study, in line with the real impact of local currencies.

of political economy. As described below, those who have conceptualized these terms have assigned critical meanings to each appellation, and there is a wealth of research that has come from each perspective. However, the challenge of researching labor notes relates to the abundance of conceptualizations surrounding socialist theory, which makes it easy to become lost in the labyrinth of early socialism and its multiple variants. For example, it is difficult to assign the category of labor notes to any single political tendency or tradition. Variants on the theme can be found among petit-bourgeois socialists, anarchists, Ricardian socialists, and utopian socialists. This means that any attempt at theorizing labor note theory must contend with multiple paths traversing different political tendencies, while acknowledging that the concept has failed to occupy an established position within the main axis of research into the history of socialism. This leaves us with no option but to extract the specific topic of labor notes in order to place it more securely within the rich history of socialism. This is a task that will require us to revise our received analytical framework.

When it comes to the question of revising our received analytical framework for theorizing socialism, it quickly becomes apparent how dependent we are on the way in which Marx and Friedrich Engels (1820–1895) structured and conceptualized many of the categories we use to conceptualize political tendencies operating at the time. When it comes to our conceptualizations of petit-bourgeois socialism, anarchism, Ricardian socialism, and utopian socialism, two were conceptualized by Marx, one was conceptualized by Foxwell (1899) (albeit through his association with Marx in reality), while the other was based on the research of Engels. This means that almost all the basic socialist concepts that inform our discussion come from Marx and Engels—reflecting their own position as political actors within the field.

For Marx and Engels, the critique of preceding socialists played a key role in helping them develop their own positions. One legacy of their success in so doing has been to flatten the range of disputes that informed the development of socialism as an ideology, creating the impression of socialist history as a convergence toward a uniform type of socialist philosophy. We can see this speculative process at work most strongly in Marx's *Theories of Surplus Value* (1861–63) and Engels' pamphlet *Socialism: Utopian and Scientific* (1880). In these works, we see how the discourse of various socialist writers was appraised positively or negatively to the extent to which they contributed to Marx's and Engels' own theoretical evolution. But the moment at which these various strands of pre-Marxian socialism had been assimilated and overcome, their proper name came to be abandoned.

Meanwhile, labor note advocates had to confront inherent difficulties and limitations that they struggled to resolve. This made them into an easy target for scientific socialism and theories based on Marx's concept of surplus value while preventing them from mounting an effective counter-offensive. Furthermore, many of the theorists critiqued were from a previous generation, making it easier for Marx and Engels to create a space for their own form of a critique of political economy. The extent of Marx's hegemony can be seen stretching into the twentieth century when Silvio Gesell (1862–1930) took up the debate between Marx and Proudhon, by attempting to stage a defense of Proudhon, but it did nothing to alter the trend.

In order to position labor note theory, we have to reconstruct the dialectical process of its development which follows a pattern of criticism, evaluation, and succession-criticism. This is set out in the following Fig. 1.1.

As seen in the Fig. 1.1 on the disputes regarding labor note theory, labor note theorists merely shared an agenda on labor notes (or the goal of reforming money and the credit system), without any clear consensus among them, rather than forming a common school. One intrinsic limit that weakened the camp of labor note theory may be that the theoretical, ideological, and practical groups that had labor notes as their central axis could not deepen their discussions through mutual criticism.

A brief look at the history of socialist theory in relation to labor notes reveals the enormous impact of the critical view of utopian socialism provided first and foremost by Marx and Engels. Representative works by them relevant to the conceptualization of utopian socialism include Marx and Engels (1976/1848) and Engels (1987). In this literature, utopian socialists, including advocates of labor notes, were defined on the basis of juxtaposing utopian to scientific socialism. The expression "utopian" may be perceived as positive in some respects (in the sense of a utopia), but in this case, it carried a negative connotation with overtones of an "unscientific," "visionary," or even "mystical" approach. Socialists deemed to be utopian were subjected by Marx and Engels to a dialectical criticism, in which their own concerns were turned against them to the point where the concept of utopian socialism comes to mean the opposite of what it intended due to the pressure of its own internal contradictions. Yet

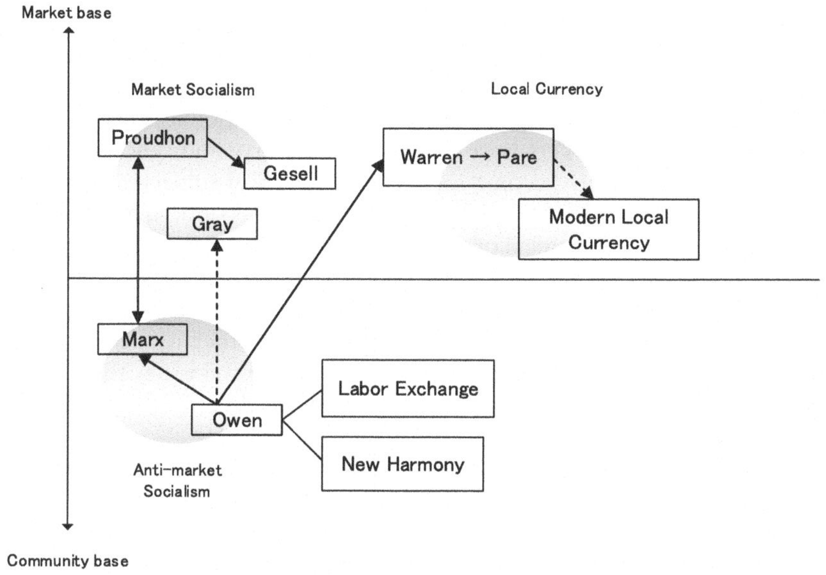

Fig. 1.1 Proudhon-Marx (criticism), Owen-Marx (evaluation), Owen-Warren (criticism), Warren-Pare (evaluation and succession), Owen-Gray (criticism), Proudhon-Gesell (evaluation and succession), and Marx-Gesell (criticism)

whatever the merits of dialectical exposition, the practical outcome of the method of Marx and Engels was to reshape the field using the categories of scientific and utopian socialism, while placing ideas such as labor notes on the utopian side of the ledger.

Engels stressed that socialism must be grounded in science and sought to develop a foundation for economics that recognized the objective laws of economic phenomena. He concluded that a non-scientific utopia was a oughtness doctrine that was not based on economic analysis. In other words, his main criticism was that utopian socialism (which does not rely on objective perceptions) makes the methodological error of imposing an exaggerated plan on the masses of workers (who in turn have been abstracted from the realities of society). In a remarkable dialectical move, Engels realized that this mistake had its roots in enlightenment rationality, which had encouraged a strain of constructivist thinking that ignored the material realities of history, political conjunctures, and political economy;

transplanted from the Enlightenment, it came to denote a method of salvation, namely, socialism reduced to a philanthropic endeavor, by which socialism is delivered from above to the masses below (Engels 1989/1880). Undeniably, utopian socialists were economically naive, and many felt that the workers were so mired in poverty and ignorance that they could not possibly become independent political subjects. Nonetheless, Engels' claim that the scientific perception of economic laws allows workers to become the rulers of such laws is not as solid in retrospect as it may have appeared at the time (Engels 1976/1847: 347–348, 352–354; 1989/1880: 310–312, 319–320). One of the most troubling questions to come down from the nineteenth century is whether its belief in the historical agency of the working class can withstand the issues thrown up by the historical failure of planned economic socialism in the twentieth century.

Petit-bourgeois socialism and Ricardian socialism overlapped in several respects, though it is still possible and relevant to distinguish them.[7] What both lacked was a clear-sighted critique of capitalism, whereas Marx boldly conceptualized the evolving society as a capitalist one, whose central fault-line was the class division between workers and capitalists. In view of the conflict between these two classes, the petit-bourgeoisie (so-called independent small producers), who owned the means of production on a small scale and made a living through self-employment, lost their social significance in the face of a growing body of wage laborers. Whereas petit-bourgeois socialism was clearly impacted by the expansion of wage labor, the case was less clear among Ricardian socialists. Foxwell (1899: lxxxi) conceptualized the school based on Ricardo's labor theory of value. Here the value of a commodity was commensurate with the total labor time bestowed on its production. For Ricardo only the petit-bourgeois could claim an unambiguous right to the whole produce of their labor, because, as independent, self-employed producers, they owned the means of production and could, therefore, attribute all the proceeds of production to themselves. This is ironic given the common perception that

[7] Such distinctions apply even within the category of petit-bourgeois socialism S. de. Sismondi (1773–1842) stressed the role of the petit-bourgeois as a social subject, thus connecting him strongly to petit-bourgeois socialism, while for Marx, Proudhon's stronger adherence to bourgeois society made him a "bourgeois socialist." The fact that both could not think beyond the horizon of bourgeois society was decisive in the characterization of their mode of socialism (Marx & Engels 1976/1848: 509–510, 513–514).

Marx's claims about the working class having the right to claim the entire product of their labor were based on his adherence to Ricardo's labor theory of value.

Given the aim of this book, I will not delve into a detailed analysis of Ricardian socialism (Kamata 2000). Rather, I will simply note that the prefix "Ricardian" has come to denote a group of individuals who have adhered to the labor theory of value, without necessarily being followers of David Ricardo (1772–1823), thus raising the questions of whether they indeed constituted a school. Certainly, when it comes to individuals associated with Ricardian socialism, none were strict followers of Ricardo. Thomas Hodgskin (1787–1869) adhered perhaps the closest to Ricardo, and there were others whose thinking closely resembled Ricardo's,[8] but in many instances their analysis of the labor theory of value owed as much to Adam Smith (1723–1790) and to John Locke (1632–1704) and his labor theory of property. Yet Locke's theory, which was based on ownership of products rather than the production of commodities, does not qualify as a labor theory of value. Yet without doubt, the series of ideas connecting labor, value, and ownership in some way inspired Ricardian socialists to put forward various theories of the right to the whole produce of labor. If labor notes were proposed as a means to realize this right, then the Ricardian school and labor note theory do overlap (Kamata 2000). This still leaves open the question of the degree to which each theorist supported the system of private property ownership, which has subsequently been used a criterion to determine whether they belonged to the school of petit-bourgeois socialism.

In Foxwell's work, we find the first attempt to synthesize a range of thinkers under the rubric of Ricardian socialism. His work continues

[8] Who exactly were the Ricardian socialists? As mentioned earlier, Foxwell (1899) basically listed them as "Godwin, Hall, Thompson, Gray, Hodgskin and Bray" (xxvii), but in *The Poverty of Philosophy*, Marx mentions Hodgskin, Thompson, Gray, Bray, T. R. Edmonds (1803–1889), and others. Could T. Hopkins be added in the sense of being a socialist who could point out the Ricardian system's effects? In *Dictionary of the History of Economic Thought*, "Ricardian socialism" includes "Ravenstone, Thompson, Hodgskin, Gray, Bray, and others who argued about the 'right of labor' to acquire the whole product during the 1820s and 1840s, and they are generally called Ricardian socialists" (Ebihara 2000: 430). Ultimately, there are no strict criteria, so the only approach is to note the Ricardian tendencies in the texts of each scholar. For example, it may be an overinterpretation to claim that "the base of Owen's views lies [in] Ricardo's labour theory of value: labour is the creator and measure of value; the exchange of commodities should take place according to labour" (Anikin 1979: 551).

to provide as a *locus classicus*, in that it conforms most closely to the precepts developed by Ricardo in his book *On the Principles of Political Economy and Taxation* (1817). His analysis stems from the precept that "with a single claim or first principle of socialists, the asserted right of the labourer to the whole product of industry"; in other words, "the denial of a right to 'unearned' income" (Foxwell 1899: vi). Foxwell states that it "was Ricardo, not Owen, who gave the really effective inspiration to English socialism" (ibid., lxxxiii). Unjustifiably, this promoted Ricardo's position in the history of British socialist thought. Foxwell then mentions the names of "Godwin, Hall, Thompson, Gray, Hodgskin, and Bray" (ibid., xxvii) and points to Thompson's *An Inquiry into the rinciples of the Distribution of Wealth most conducive to Human H appiness* (1824), Gray's *A Lecture on Human Happiness* (1825), Hodgskin's *Labour Defended against the Claims of Capital* (1825) as "the three most notable works of the Ricardian socialists" (ibid., lxxxi). A typical explanation offered by Anton Menger (1841–1906) is that this definitely proves that "all the fundamental ideas of modern revolutionary socialism, and especially of the Marxian socialism, can be definitely traced to English sources" (ibid., xxvi–xxvii), and that Marxian socialist ideas are positioned on an extension of the Ricardian school (although this is not necessarily exceptional in the analysis of British economic thought). Foxwell's work almost single-handedly has been responsible for the subsequent view that closely associated Marx's critique of political economy with Ricardian socialism.

Anarchism. When it comes to anarchism the first point worth making is that in the eyes of many anarchists, Marx was the first to give the term "anarchism" the negative slant that many now associate with it. Anarchists such as Proudhon and Bakunin reinterpreted the term "anarchy" (which was lexically a synonym for "a state of disorder") to denote a state in which there is no authority (e.g., a god or state) imposing order. Thus, anarchy is not to be understood as disorder, but rather as non-control. The condition whereby the principle of non-control reigns is the natural order. This is a social vision in which an ecological and physical order of nature exists even in a world without authorities; dynamic stability is maintained, despite a state of non-control. However, Proudhon included the market within his state of non-control, which acted as a prompt for Marx to launch a vigorous critique. As I shall demonstrate in this chapter and Chapter 2, Marx's careful presentation in *Capital* owed much to his critique of Proudhon's anarchism. In Part

8 of Volume 1, "The So-called Primitive Accumulation" Marx showed that Proudhon's vision of the market (as having a natural order) did not encompass the natural-historical developmental course through which the capitalist market economy evolved. Marx also proved that Proudhon's perception of non-equivalent exchange in the market (exploitation in the circulation process) could allow for exploitation within the production process, even if an equivalent exchange in the market were to be maintained. In addition, he demonstrated that two intrinsic factors—the anarchy of production and the market's undisciplined nature (uncertainty of circulation process)—betrayed the market's so-called natural order. Marx replaced the concept of "anarchy" used by Proudhon (in the sense of something "self-regulatory" and "spontaneous") with a concept in terms of the disorder of commodity production.[9] In the early twentieth century, Gesell clearly recognized that these three issues entailed criticism of the kind of anarchism that believes in market order, as well as the counter-arguments employed by anarchists to back up their arguments.

As we start to gain a clearer idea of the range of ideas among the various advocates of labor notes, it becomes clear, that they fall into all the categories of socialism discussed above—thus demonstrating their overlapping nature during this period. The advocates fell within Engels' conceptualization of utopian socialism to the extent that they viewed labor notes as a system that could be foisted upon the masses of workers; they fell within Ricardian socialism to the extent that they hoped the use of labor notes would provide legitimate rewards for self-employment; they fell within the category of petit-bourgeois socialists to the extent that they treated independent small producers as economic subjects; and they fell within the category of anarchism to the extent that they believed in a Proudhonian market order. To this extent, proponents of labor note theory can be made to fit within each of the variants of socialism discussed above, even though it makes sense analytically to retain and clarify the distinctions that have been handed down to us from the period.

[9] Unlike Proudhon and Gesell, who found a natural order in the market, there has not been much criticism of M. A. Bakunin (1814–1876) and P. A. K. Kropotkin (1842–1921), who supported Marx's *Capital* and advocated for anarchist communism. This may have resulted in a revolutionary, strategic debate on whether the working class should tolerate transitional dictatorships.

Concerning the Different Phases

When looking at the history of labor note theory, it gradually becomes clear that it cannot be plotted along a single line that culminates in a fully formed notion of labor notes. Along with economic changes over time, the trajectory of labor note theory is marked by discontinuity and phases of development followed by stasis. In this sense, this book's subject comprises the "historical phases of labor note theory." Just as different theories of labor notes appear and disappear over time, so the ideology surrounding labor notes has had an intermittent character and cannot be reduced to simple notions of growth and progress.

Labor note theory is like a polyhedron, in that it consists of multiple ideas and captures the passions of the supporters espousing it, to such an extent that it can be discerned as a type of practice as well as bearing the traces of a social movement. The theory was manifested in various ways, yet throughout it is possible to discern a set of underlying principles and a fundamental commonality, which enables us to speak categorically of "labor note theory." However, in this book, while seeking to preserve the underlying unity between labor note theorists, I have also sought to trace the divergent ways in which they developed their ideas, and the tensions and contradictions within the field of labor note theory and also with those who critiqued labor notes theory.

Just as there is no steady pattern of development, the phases of labor note theory can emerge very suddenly and often in response to specific historical circumstances. We also find that different facets of labor note theory come to the fore at different points in time. Sometimes these features appear on the surface and look positive, but at other times, they only seem negative. Even though they are encompassed in the same version of labor note theory, the researcher's task is to judge them on their own terms. Of course, highlighting the multifaceted elements of labor note theory risks blurring the focus of the overall doctrine. In other words, our task in tracing labor notes theory through its phases is to be able to retain the sense of a core notion of labor notes that remains throughout its various manifestations. If we shed light on the main axis of labor note theory, it can be reduced to two key categories: money and production. The first links "labor to production theory" and the second "money to note (security) theory." All proponents of labor note theory start by stressing its relation to the theory of money. From this premise their thinking goes from monetary analysis to the consideration of labor and questions of production. This book aims to deepen the understanding of money and labor (and eventually the market society as a whole) by analyzing the role they play in the various forms of labor note theory. Also, depending on each theorist's approach to money and markets, labor note theory is seen as a policy proposal—or even a practical guide—to achieve social reforms grounded in monetary reform. The approach to changing society based on money also resonates with modern initiatives and can be construed as a systematic theory that historically anticipates contemporary discussions of local currencies. While the influence of labor note theory is undeniable, the systematic status of the theory in terms of questions concerning its applicability to total social reproduction remains unexplored. In other words, this ideology which was originally intended to provide a systematic basis for an emerging socialist politics has in practice been canalized into more narrow debates on local currencies.

Gesell represents a later phase spanning the turn of the twentieth century. His arguments are discussed in Chapter 8, and although they do not refer explicitly to labor notes, it would appear, at first glance, that they would have no place in an investigation into the category of labor note theory. Yet when examining the components of his theories one by one, it becomes clear that there are unexpectedly many points in common between his ideas and labor note theory. In the standard narratives concerning labor notes in the context of money substitutes, there is a disconnect that prevents researchers from seeing Gesell's relation to the topic. His interest in the link between labor, socialist monetary reform, and the notion of laborers retaining the right to their whole produce of labor sits within the discourse of labor notes theory.

From this preliminary outline, we can assert that the assorted elements of labor note theory are connected by a baseline notion of the labor note that never fluctuates regardless of local, historical, and regional variations, and different phases in which labor note theory had flourished. The basic premise that underpins the discrepant theories of labor notes lies in their attempts to explain the relationship between money and the functioning of markets. When reviewing this history, it becomes clear that each theorist who advocated a form of labor notes theory furnished arguments based on their theory of money, along with theories to explain the functioning of markets, and in varying degrees, a theory of capitalist market societies. Each of the theorists developed their own hypothesis, as we shall explore.

Structure of This Book

The basic conflict over the vision of money and the market is outlined in Chapter 2, "Free Credit versus Value Form Theory: On the relation between Proudhon's Market Socialism and Marx's Market Realism." Although Robert Owen had already presented a version of labor notes as early as 1821, the key problems involved in labor note theory only really came to fruition in the discourse of the late 1840s. This was exactly the crossroads at which the "visions of money and the market" were being questioned most acutely and when labor notes took its place at the center of such debates. In this sense, Chapter 2 plays a role in determining the form that questions take throughout the book.

In Chapter 2, the vision of labor note theory is organized around the notions of idealism and realism. These notions were used to explore the impact of one person in a market exchange holding money in terms of the overall state of market and the world it has constituted. Proudhon believed that market exchange (which is supposed to be equal) had been distorted by money into an asymmetric power relationship. With no money, the power relationship between seller and buyer is equalized, and the market's ideal is realized. This can be viewed as the immediate realization of the principle of equivalence that is said to be the defining feature of market exchanges. The argumentative or logical tactic deployed by Proudhon was to deny the existence of real money, while positing the notion of an idealized currency in the form of a labor note. If Proudhon was a leading figure for denial of money's real status, Marx's strategy stressed the realism of money. Marx was far more interested in the way that money mediated social relations, and thus stressed its realist status. In his realist view, a world appears in which the asymmetry of buying and selling through money is especially emphasized, and the market's undisciplined nature (that prevails when equivalence is denied in reality) is explained. Despite both thinkers stressing the fact of asymmetry in market exchanges, their conflicting interpretations concerning the role of money was played out in the role that labor notes played in their respective discourses.

As briefly reviewed at the beginning of "Issues and Methods: The Invisibility of 'Labor Notes'," labor note theory is often indiscriminately regarded as an unfounded ideology that focused solely on monetary reform. However, the debate between Proudhon and Marx demonstrates that there is a lot more at stake, namely: What shapes do the money and market take on, and how should they be understood? By reducing this question to a debate on monetary policy without realizing that questions about labor note theory also concern social forms, we run the risk of underappreciating the whole purpose of the debate; particularly since it becomes clear that we can trace subsequent thinkers linked to labor note theory in terms of the degree to which they adhere to Proudhon's idealist view of money or Marx's realist view. Even in cases that preceded the Proudhon-Marx controversy, the lines of their debate can cast retrospective light on the issue that was at stake from the earliest discussions. That said, it is important to realize that the terms of debate were not as clear-cut in many of scholars' minds as it was for Proudhon and certainly for Marx. Many theorists had polemical or visionary attachments to their theories of labor notes, and we will have recourse to examining their notions, sometimes to the extent they conform to the terms laid down by the Proudhon-Marx dispute and sometimes on their own terms. If we use the Proudhon-Marx dispute to chop back the independent contributions of each theorist, we will be left with a much reduced and limited picture of labor note theory. Hence, while piecing together the debated history of labor note theory based on the "visions of money and the market," it is necessary to examine issues that have not been thoroughly explored along the Proudhon-Marx axis.

In Chapter 3, we return to Owen's theory, its place within labor note theory, and the importance of making links between his positions and Marx's. In Chapter 2, we explained that Marx pointed out that Proudhon's vision for the market was contradicted by reality. Marx countered Proudhon's vision, by pointing to the undisciplined nature of markets and noting that it is not possible to develop a socially rational organization of labor by eliminating the market. In Chapter 3, we examine Marx's assessment of Owen's social vision of a market-less, money-less economic society, and how, when combined with his critique of Proudhon's market idealism, this opened the way for him to focus on the anarchy of production. Yet this raises questions around the way we grasp how Marx's theoretical solutions to the question of the realities of money and markets—and in what ways they go beyond an Owenite position on the economy and society.[10] In the context of Chapter 2, Marx indicates that labor time can serve as a dual measure for the allocation of labor and its distribution, but under an economic system in which the economic foundation is commodified, it leads to undisciplined markets. It was against this that he viewed Owen's vision of a society in which the significance of the scale and unit of labor time is at the center. This raised a major question concerning whether it would be possible to step beyond a system based on equality in terms of labor being exchanged for its equivalent, through labor time, to one in which a more substantive notion of equal human relationships beyond commodification, could be achieved. Marx claimed that the time-dollar, a modern local currency, was a partially realistic method of monetary reform. Here, he sensed the possibility of overcoming a chaotic market and the possibility of taking this in a socialist direction, though it also marked out a path that led toward local currencies, and a new dependence on the undisciplined nature of the market.

We will take up this question of undisciplined markets more fully in Chapters 4 and 5 when we examine the relationship between the writings of Owen, Warren, and Pare.

Scrutinizing Owen's labor note theory, and especially when doing so through the appraising eye of Marx, offers insights into some of the more disputed areas concerning labor notes and their relation to the problem of money. Owen declared that labor notes would be a medium of equal quantities of labor exchange in a cooperative community with a balanced labor composition, but this involved addressing a two-fold difficulty. As Chapter 5 clarifies, the first difficulty was that labor notes were assumed to be used in idealized markets. Second, to maintain the cost of preserving social balance in the labor composition, community management had to be oppressive. On the other hand, Warren argued that individual independence was suppressed in Owen's New Harmony community, suggesting that it was necessary to move away from an idealized market vision in order to create independence.

In Chapter 5, we will return to the case of the UK and through a close inspection of the Owenite journals, will reveal the extent to which Owen's market vision remained idealistic. Following this, we shall see how Pare

[10] For the time being, Engels' interpretation may serve as a hint. Engels views Owen's significance for Marx from the angle of a planned economy, but yet it is debatable whether Engels' vision falls into an idealistic vision (Yuki 2009: 228–231).

sharpened Warren's vision and developed a perspective on labor notes that had the real workings of the market in mind. Discussions are not necessarily developed along the same lines as the modern local currency and labor note theories, which emphasize a strategy of starting from inside the commodity economy and branching outward to open new market areas outside it. This is the moment when the two sides are closest, as they approach the real vision of the market.

In Chapter 6, we compare the Owen-type labor note with modern local currencies and provide a summary of the characteristics of each note and currency. By doing this we can better highlight the limitations of Owen's labor note theory, and it will be easier to understand how close the Warren-Pare type of labor notes are to local currencies. A series of binary oppositions are used to provide a framework for setting out a typology of labor notes: full and partial, inside and outside the market, concentration and dispersion, tangible and intangible.

Conversely, Chapters 7 and 8 trace the lineage of labor note theory, by looking at those lines of development that deviated from the concept of local currency. Owen's labor note theory, proposed in 1821, was organized by Warren and Pare into a form close to local currency. On the other hand, Gray critically inherited Owen's ideas, but expanded the scope by developing a version labor note theory suitable for nationwide implementation. The local monetary development of Owen's labor note theory was an unforeseen consequence of having to realistically respond to the failure to implement labor notes on a national scale. Hence, if we take Owen's opinion honestly, it is not surprising that it evolved into a socialist ideology that sought to reach a balance between supply and demand, as well as equality in distribution. Moreover, in contrast to Owen's labor note theory (which always considered the static distribution problem without the concept of a period), Gray was clearly aware of the significance of the labor commanded theory of value (which was lurking in Smith's value theory) and took on a new domain regarding how to achieve equity in distribution, with a long-term view of the growing economy. The limitations of the type of labor note theory developed Owen, Warren, and Pare type are striking because the matter of inter-temporal distribution is never addressed.

In Chapter 8, Proudhon's vision of money and the market (which is refuted in Chapter 2) is taken up again through the works of Gesell. Gesell observed that Marx defined money as a means of exchange in Volume 1 of

Capital. Gesell attempted to counter Marx's critique, stating that Marx—not Proudhon—maintained an idealized vision of money and markets, and developed a static theory. In order to understand the more realistic dynamic of the market, he argued that we should not perceive capital as the real capital of goods (as Marx did), but rather, capital should be viewed in terms of money capital. This was a twisted criticism that Marx (who defined money as a mere intermediary, and excluded money capital from the notion of capital) could not grasp the market's true shape, because the interest-bearing money capital creates market dynamics. Through such a critique, Gesell demonstrated that the Proudhon-Gesell understanding of money and markets had a more realistic nature, and by so doing, aimed to win ground lost to Marx. However, in a concession to Marx, Gesell acknowledged that money capital disrupts real money and markets. Also, compared to Proudhon, he presented a more idealized market vision with a solution, whereby the quantity theory of money was established by issuing a national currency. Gesell's perspective is a more vigorous representation of Proudhon's desire to have a static, stable market as a principle. Also, although he did not support the labor theory of value like Gray did, Gesell still relied on the historical context of labor note theory. For example, Gesell expanded upon the concept of the right to the whole produce of labor (which was previously considered an individual principle). Moreover, Gray and Gesell were trying to realize the right to the whole produce of labor by increasing overall working-class income. Depending on one's perspective, Gesell further promoted Gray's individualist tendency and tried to achieve fairness in distribution by modifying the distribution ratio between classes. He encouraged individual responsibility and independence, as Warren pointed out, and his anarchist character is demonstrated in that he depicts a worker's vision as being full of pride. Based on the nationalization of land, the point of attempting to convert rent from the national treasury into basic income for women and children is an issue that is difficult to handle through the individualistic, Warren-Pare type of labor note theory, and the problem of considering labor note theory in the context of socialist theory remains.

Finally, in Chapter 9, the historical aspects of labor note theory will be explained. The possibilities of labor note theory will be mentioned based on the knowledge obtained through this book.

Explanatory Note In the case of literature already translated into English, existing translations were quoted directly. Sources without English translations were translated from German, Japanese, and other languages, as appropriate.

Bibliography

Anikin, A. V. (1979). *A science in its youth: Pre-Marxian political economy*. International Publishers.

Bellers, J. (1858/1696). Proposals for raising a colledge of industry of all useful trades and husbandry, with profit for the rich, a plentiful living for the poor, and a good education for youth. Which will be advantage to the government by the increase of the people, and their riches, 2nd ed. T. Sowle. In *A supplementary appendix to the first volume of the life of Robert Owen* (pp. 155–181). Effingham Wilson.

Ebihara, R. (1980). Jon Gurei no Kokumin Ginkōron to Rōdōkahei ni tsuite [John Gray on the National Bank and labour-note]. *The Journal of Economics, Niigata University, 28*, 61–85.

Ebihara, R. (2000). Ricādoha Shakaishugi [Ricardian socialism]. The Japanese Society for the History of Economic Thought (ed.). In *Keizai Shisōshi Jiten* [Dictionary of the history of economic thought] (pp. 430–431). Tokyo: Maruzen.

Engels, F. (1976/1847). Principles of communism. In *Marx & Engels collected works* (Vol. 6). Lawrence & Wishart.

Engels, F. (1987/1878). Anti-Dühring. In *Marx & Engels collected works* (Vol. 25). Lawrence & Wishart.

Engels, F. (1989/1880). Socialism: Utopian and scientific. In *Marx & Engels collected works* (Vol. 24). Lawrence & Wishart.

Foxwell, H. S. (1899). Introduction. In A. Menger (Ed.), *The right to the whole produce of labour*. Macmillan.

Gray, J. (1873/1831). *The social system*. Augustus M. Kelley.

Gray, J. (1997/1825). A lecture on human happiness. In *The Ricardian socialists* (Vol. 2). Routledge/Thoemmes Press.

Hijikata, N. (2003). *Robāto Ōen* [Robert Owen]. Kenkyusha.

Hodgskin, T. (1997/1825). Labour defended against the claims of capital. In *The Ricardian socialists* (Vol. 3). Routledge/Thoemmes Press.

Itoh, M. (2010). Gyakuryūsuru Shihonshugi [Reverse capitalism]. In *Collected works of Makoto Itoh* (Vol. 4). Shakaihyoronsha.

Itoh, M. (2012). Shijōkeizai to Shakaishugi [Market economy and socialism]. In *Collected works of Makoto Itoh* (Vol. 6). Shakaihyoronsha.

Kamata, T. (2000). *Shijōkeizai to Kyōdōshakaishisō: Igirisu Shihonshugi-hihan no Shisōtekigenryū* [Market economy and cooperative social though: The ideological origins of the critique of British capitalism]. Mirai-sha Publishers.
Kishi, T. (1978). Jon Gurei no Kōkan Ginkōron [On the John Gray's Exchange Bank]. *Keizai-ronsō* [The Economic Review], *122*(3–4), 175–194.
Lapavitsas, C. (2003). *Social foundations of markets, money and credit*. Routledge.
Maruyama, T. (1999). *Ōenno Yūtopia to Kyōseishakai* [Owen's Utopia and Symbiotic Society]. Minervashobo.
Marx, K. (1986/1857–1858). Economic manuscripts of 1857–58. In *Marx & Engels collected works* (Vol. 28). Lawrence & Wishart.
Marx, K. (1989a, 1989b, 1991/1861–1863). *Theories of surplus value. Marx & Engels collected works* (Vols. 31–33). Lawrence & Wishart.
Marx, K., & Engels, F. (1976/1848). Manifesto of the Communist Party. In *Marx & Engels collected works* (Vol. 6). Lawrence & Wishart.
Noguchi, M. (1996). Kotenha keizaigaku no Dōyō [Shaking of classical political economy]. In M. Itoh (Ed.), *Keizaigakushi* [History of political economy]. Yuhikaku.
Obata, M. (2009). *Keizaigenron: Kiso to Enshū* [The principles of political economy: Basics and exercises]. University of Tokyo Press.
Okamoto, H. (2007). *Fukushikokka no Kanōsei* [Possibility of welfare states]. University of Tokyo Press.
Owen, R. (1968/1821a). An explanation of the cause of the distress. *Economist, 2*(32), 92–104. Greenwood Reprint.
Owen, R. (1993a/1821b). Report to the county of Lanark. In *Selected works of Robert Owen* (Vol. 1). William Pickering.
Owen, R. (1993b/1826–1827). The social system. In *Selected works of Robert Owen* (Vol. 2). William Pickering; *The New-Harmony Gazette*, Vol. 2. No. 8, 14, 15, 17, 18, 19, 20, 21, 22, 23, 24.
Owen, R. (1993c/1857–1858). The life of Robert Owen. In *Selected works of Robert Owen* (Vol. 4). William Pickering.
Otani, T. (2011). *Marx no Asoshiēshionron: Mirai Shakai wa Shihonshugi no Naka ni mieteiru* [Marx's associations: The future society is seen in capitalism]. Sakurai-shoten.
Proudhon, P. J. (1849). *Banque du Peuple: Déclaration* [People's Bank: Declaration].
Proudhon, P. J. (1868/1848). Banque d' échange [Bank of exchange]. *Oeuvres Complètes de P.-J. Proudhon* (T. 6). Librairie Internationale.
Ricardo, D. (1951/1817). On the principles of political economy, and taxation. In *The works and correspondence of David Ricardo* (Vol. 1). Cambridge University Press.

Saad-Filho, A. (1993). Labour, money and "labour-money": A view of Marx's critique of John Gray's monetary analysis. *History of Political Economy, 25*(1), 65–84.

Saad-Filho, A. (2002). *The value of Marx: Political economy for contemporary capitalism*. Routledge.

Sasaki, R. (2019). Bēshikku Inkamu to Shihonshugi Shisutemu [Basic income and capitalism system]. In R. Sasaki & N. Shiga (Eds.), *Bēshikku Inkamu wo toinaosu: Sono Genjitsu to Kanōsei* [Re-examining basic income: Its reality and potential]. Horitsu Bunka Sha.

Shirai, A. (1991). *Kyōdōkumiai ronshū* [Studies on co-operatives]. Keio Tsushin.

Thompson, W. (1963/1824). *An inquiry into the principles of the distribution of wealth most conducive to human happiness*. A. M. Kelley.

Torrens, R. (1819). Mr. Owen's plan for relieving the national distress. *Edinburgh Review, 32*, 453–477.

Yuki, T. (2009). Motto Jiyū de, Motto Byōdō na: Yūtopia Shakaishugi nyūmon [More free and more equal: Introduction to Utopian socialism]. *Gendai Shisō* [*Revue de la pensée d'aujourd'hui*], *37*(10), 224–237.

Newspapers, Magazines, Etc.

The Crisis, and National Co-operative Trades' Union Gazette (Vols. 1–4). New York: Greenwood Reprint, 1968/1832–1834.

CHAPTER 2

Free Credit Versus Value Form Theory: *On the Relation Between Proudhon's Market Socialism and Marx's Market Realism*

2.1 Background

During the neoliberal period, there has been a noticeable increase in interest in certain strains of anarchism. This has been largely aided by combined impact of failure of confidence in Keynesian economic policies and the collapse of the Soviet bloc. These tendencies, sometimes referred to as the "new anarchists" (Graeber 2002),[1] took shape during the World Trade Organization (WTO) protests in Seattle in 1999 and Genoa in 2001. Some of these movements have goals close to the ideals that Proudhon once described in terms of a fair market society, and not least of these ideas have ushered in a renewed interest in local currencies. To understand the contemporary renewal of interest in anarchism, it is necessary to consider the controversy surrounding Proudhon's theories and influence.

The theory and concepts of socialism based on a fair market, also known as anarchism, are represented by Proudhon's theories of money

[1] Grubacic and Graeber (2004) declared that "there are some obvious reasons for the appeal of anarchist ideas at the beginning of the twenty-first century." They note as one of the reasons, "the failures and catastrophes resulting from so many efforts to overcome Capitalism by seizing control of the apparatus of government in the twentieth century."

© The Author(s), under exclusive license to Springer Nature Switzerland AG 2021

T. Yuki, *Socialism, Markets, and the Critique of Money*, Marx, Engels, and Marxisms,
https://doi.org/10.1007/978-3-030-80408-4_2

and credit reform, or "the theory of free credit."[2] Despite the impact of Marx's critique both theoretically and ideologically, in which Proudhon's theories were described in terms of labor money, its influence has lived on.[3] First, Marx's criticism of labor money theory begins with the stances outlined in *The Poverty of Philosophy* (1976/1847), followed by *Economic Manuscripts of 1857–58* [*Grundrisse*] (1986), *A Contribution to the Critique of Political Economy* (1987/1859) and *Capital* (1996/1867). Since various works that directly consider labor money theory were studied by Marx in relation to Proudhon, the theoretical development of *Capital* cannot be fully understood without a prior consideration of his criticism of the labor money theory. In particular, it is easy to overlook the fact that Marx's treatment of the transition from value form theory to exchange process theory was meant to contain a critique of "Proudhon's socialism" (Marx 1996/1867: 79).[4] Second, although the concept of the labor money theory given by Marx has become popular, the question remains whether it stands as a definitive critique.[5] Therefore, it is necessary to review Proudhon's claims concerning the free credit theory, while temporarily putting to one side Marx's critique, in order to bring features Proudhon's theory into focus. Third, I would like to examine the extent to which Marx's knowledge is appropriate as a criticism of Proudhon, and whether this can provide a rationale for the resurgence of Proudhon-style socialism, that is, anarchism in its modern guise.

2.2 Proudhon's Theory of Free Credit

The Bank of Exchange, later the Bank of People (hereafter referred to as the Bank of Exchange), was the embodiment of Proudhon's free credit theory. Conceived against the background of the French Revolution of February 1848,[6] the Bank of Exchange arose, according to

[2] Proudhon calls himself an "free credit theorist" (Proudhon 1849: 69).

[3] In this book, we use the term "labor money theory" to refer specifically to Marx.

[4] For example, see Oishi (1989), Yamanobe (1974), and Yamamoto (1989).

[5] Sato (1977) stated that "if there was something in common between Owen and Proudhon, it was a claim of the abolition of money rather than the labor money system" (319), meaning that Proudhon could not be regarded as a labor money theorist.

[6] When examining the timeline of Proudhon's transition plan, articles of the incorporation of the "Exchange Bank" were published in 1848 in "*People's Representative* [*Les représentants du people*]." Subsequently, the name of the Bank was changed to "People's

Proudhon, in the midst of a crisis as a "cry of distress" in which the proletariat demanded the elimination of the "Lack of work" that was driving them into poverty (Proudhon 2007/1851: 19).[7] Despite gaining political freedom through the abolition of feudal privileges and the reform of agriculture in the 1789 revolution, French citizens still lacked economic freedom and independence. In other words, the French Revolutionary slogan "Liberty, Equality, and Fraternity" had been realized in the political field but not in the economic field, so one could say the revolution was incomplete (ibid., 43).

The economic crisis that spread throughout Europe in 1847 set the scene for the poverty of the working class and the mass unemployment that ensued. In general, the causes of the depression in France can be summarized into the following three points. First, the failure of French agriculture in 1846 caused a surge in wheat imports and an outflow of cash.[8] Second, the induction of the railways provided an outlet for speculation by a privileged "financial aristocracy" and its failure contributed to

Bank." In September of the next year, through April 1850, with the exile of Proudhon, the bank was forced to liquidate. He proposed a "Permanent Exposition" during the Paris Expo of 1855, a showcase for production at the Palace of Industry. From the above, it can be surmised that Proudhon's plan was twofold, including the Exchange and People's Banks, and Permanent Exposition (Sato 1977: 323–325). Also, in *General Idea of the Revolution in the Nineteenth Century* (2007/1851), Proudhon uses the term "National Bank." This was probably due to it being used as a revolutionary model for the National Discount Bank, established by the February Revolution's provisional government.

[7] In fact, poverty at that time was serious. Mendelson points out that French workers were half-starved before the depression, and that the depression led to an increase in unemployment, lower wage rates, and higher grain prices, causing further poverty and higher mortality rates. (Mendelson 1960/1959: 343–346).

[8] One of Proudhon's followers, Alfredo Darimon (1819–1902), explained that the "characteristics of the crisis" was determined by the "stopping of circulation" and the "monetary crisis is triggered directly by the metal outflow associated with a bad harvest. Along with the outflow of precious metals, as the bank's metal holdings decrease and the guarantees on banknotes weaken, banks will tighten credit by "raising bill discount rates, refusing to pay in specie, shortening bill periods, etc." Darimon originally criticized the bank's actions to tighten credit during the crisis, that most people needed access to bank credit and argued that the bank's issuing business needed to be released from precious metals that were only "an illusory guarantee." As such, he viewed products as the best way to guarantee banknotes, which with free credit would eliminate the requirement for metal money, which only serves to divide exchange into selling and buying and makes the 'products exchange for products' uncertain. As a result, the original form of exchange must be restored (Motoike 1979: 41–42).

a drying up of capital.[9] And, third, there was the expansion of national treasury expenditures coupled with an increase in the tax burden.[10]

However, for Proudhon, these factors are only external. This is because factors that can turn into a crisis, such as those mentioned above, can take various forms, but what really transforms the various shocks that occur outside the market into a crisis is nothing but a flaw in the credit system. At the very moment when various economic conditions worsen and producers need credit, banks and financiers fall into crisis by tightening lending conditions and raising the discount rates on bills. Such a crisis is the result of limitations on purchasing power that originate from tightening credit and the reductions in sales that accompany them. Therefore, "of all economic forces, the most vital, in a society reconstructed for industry by revolution, is *credit*" (ibid., 51).

For Proudhon, the credit system was of the highest significance, and his proposals for reform were based on his identification of two internal deficiencies in the credit system. First was the precious metal reserve system that demanded banks keep precious metals to guarantee banknotes, thus making the general exchangeability of banknotes dependent on the metal held in reserve. Consequently, banknotes were issued to maintain a certain circulation rate that accorded with the Bank of France's reserves. This resulted in an external outflow of specie because poor harvests forced a tightening of various monetary policies. The basis for Proudhon's theory of free credit lay in his critique of a metal-based currency, that is, precious metals used as guarantees and hard currency. He believed that such metals were an impediment to the exchange of products due to the special position metals were given in monopolizing general exchangeability. Based on the materials of the Bank of Exchange (Cohen 1927; Morino 1998b), metal monopolized the exchangeability of gold and became the basis for the feudal authority to collect interest on exchanges. In other words, precious metals deprived products of their exchangeability and, in addition, caused the authority to collect interest from those not holding precious metals but who were forced to exchange products in them. A solution to the first deficiency would be simply a freeing up of the need

[9] For more details on railway stock speculation, see Koga (1964: Chapter 2) and Tsugita (1972, 1973).

[10] In addition to military spending, "the expansion of miscellaneous expenses, including public works expenses, and the accumulation of public debts… led to an increase in taxes" (Mori 1967: 112).

for exchange transactions based on precious metals, so currencies would cease to obstruct the exchange of products.

The second intrinsic flaw lay in the private character of the Bank of France and the high rate of interest based on it, or the very existence of interest. The Bank of France had been granted by the government, free of charge, "the privilege of issuing bank notes and of gradually displacing coin by paper in circulation" (Proudhon 2007/1851: 176). And, since the French bank was established as a corporation, banks must pursue private profits. This enabled the "financial aristocracy" who were shareholders of the Bank of France to earn more than could be generated by their capital, while enabling bankers and lenders to garner huge profits by arbitrarily setting the rate of interest—usually at a high rate (ibid., 99).[11] This second deficiency, inherent in the credit system of a private bank that exclusively enjoys precious metal privileges, is the consequence of interest. According to Proudhon, interest was nothing but an appropriation of profits generated in the productive economy, which was based solely on the privileges granted by the state to the "financial aristocracy" concerning the control over metal specie, and the creation of a private banking monopoly. In other words, the way the bank was constituted had led to exchange being hampered by the charging of interest based on its monopoly of precious metals. In addition, to avoid stagnating circulation, Proudhon believed it would be best to release the bank from the metal reserve system, make the private character of the bank public, and transform interest-bearing bill discounts and loans into interest-free credit. In short, banks must be transformed from being a barrier to circulation to becoming a driver of circulation.

While he saw these as issues inherent in the way the banking system had been constituted, Proudhon did not neglect the role played by wider or conjunctural factors, especially those unique to France at the time. At

[11] "It was not the French bourgeoisie that ruled France under Louis Philippe, but one faction of it: bankers, stock-exchange kings, railway kings, owners of coal and iron mines and forests, and part of the land proprietors associated with them – the so-called financial aristocracy. It sat on the throne, it dictated laws in the Chambers, it distributed public offices, from cabinet portfolios to tobacco bureau posts" (Marx 1978/1850: 48). In this way, Marx points out that financial aristocrats made huge amounts of money by exploiting fraudulent market manipulation, speculation on government bonds, and railway facilities. According to Tsugita (1972), financial aristocrats "reigned over the foundation of underdeveloped and unevenly distributed financial markets and monopolized money with speculation and high interest rates" (60).

this level of analysis, he highlighted two key points. The first point was that due to its monopolistic position the "financial aristocracy," had made France vulnerable to wider shocks, most especially because they were likely to play out in terms of a squeeze in the credit system. This meant that shocks inevitably turned into depressions, so that their manipulative operations, most notably through speculation and high interest rates, had resulted in "economic chaos" (ibid., 50). As to his second point, Proudhon criticized the state as a hotbed for the interests of the "financial aristocracy" and all those living off interest. Social programs such as national retirement pay, national bonds, and pensions were "taken away by parasites" (ibid., 54). To achieve the principles of the revolution, it would be necessary socially to liquidate the economic hierarchy based on the vested rights and privileges whose fulcrum was the state. By achieving this, it would be possible to base society on the principles of individual economic freedom and relational equality. Therefore, the dismantling of the "financial aristocracy," whose only loyalty was to the credit system and the hotbed of the privileged hierarchy, was a necessary condition for resolving the credit crunch that had struck in 1847.[12]

Proudhon contrasted the idea of the French Revolution with the current state of the credit system, which enabled him to highlight four deficiencies that resulted from its internal workings which were exacerbated by the impact of external forces. He stated that in a free and equitable post-revolutionary society "every privilege is public property" (ibid., 176), so the French bank must become a "public institution" (ibid.). Moreover, citizens should have the right to establish banks freely, and if the Bank of France becomes a "public institution," it can stop serving certain interest groups and start to discount bills at low or no interest. As a result, the banking business would be personalized, and the financial aristocracy, which had been making vast profits unfairly and at high interest rates, would gradually be pushed out of the process of credit

[12] Proudhon's conception of the dismantling of the state was based on lessons he had learned from the experience of the French Revolution. In his "Fifth Study" of the *General Idea of the Revolution in the Nineteenth Century*, he developed a series of proposals that he described as a form of "social liquidation." "Social liquidation" refers to examples of economic subordination through the repurchase of feudal privileges at low or no interest. This followed the example of the abolition of compensation from feudal rents and the repurchasing of the rights to collect rent, implemented during the French Revolution. In other words, the dismantling of the state amounted to nothing more than remunerating various rights of the state and transferring these rights to the public.

transactions. It would be possible to shift to a mutual, exchange-based relationship between equal lenders and borrowers, away from one-sided lending of credit.

This led him to specify the functions and operations of the Bank of Exchange. The main operations of the Bank of Exchange would be to provide free discounts on commercial bills signed by bill drawers and endorsers (such as secured, interest-free loans, sales and purchases of consignments). After imposing any necessary operational fees, the bank would discount commercial bills free of charge, "the bill of exchange stripped of the circumstantial qualities of date, place, person, object, term of maturity, and reduced to its essential qualities – *exchange, acceptance, provision*" (Cohen 1927: 63–64) and replace them with generalized banknotes.[13] The "bank paper" or "the paper of the Bank of Exchange" would use the best commercial bills representing delivered (rather than unsold) products as collateral (ibid., 62–63, 67); thus, banknotes could be collateralized by products, instead of precious metals. Further, they could be issued only in proportion to the value of products that were seen as having realized value by virtue of their being sold for commercial bills. It is said that "circulation can never be inflated" (ibid., 70). In the case of lending, the relationship with interest-free discounts of commercial bills could be changed so that producers would deposit products in a bank, and banks use these deposited products as collateral for loans without interest. In the case of discount bills and loans, equivalent exchange is always carried out in relation to the bank and each producer, its value guaranteed and fixed in cost at the time of exchange, so value reciprocity is established.[14] In the case of loans, the relationship of free discounts on commercial bills can be changed to a relationship in which the producer deposits a product at the bank and the bank lends the deposited product as collateral without interest. In the case of discounts on bills and loans, equivalent exchange would be always carried out in

[13] The basic function of the Exchange and People's Bank is the "generalization of commercial bills" (Sato 1977: 322) or the "generalization of the bill of exchange" (Cohen 1927: 62).

[14] "*Reciprocity*...consists of the sellers and buyers guaranteeing each other, irrevocably, their products at cost price" (Proudhon 2007/1851: 91). This relationship between producers is not just the idea of equality in exchange, but is thought to include an ethical provision that, like merchants, they must not be seized from others by pursuing price differences. In other words, the product has an inherent value before being put on the market, and the value is not sensitive to market trends.

relation to the bank and each producer, its value guaranteed and fixed in cost at the time of exchange. This would facilitate "reciprocity, equity in exchange, the *organization of credit*" (ibid., 49). Further, if we assume that as commercial bills circulate among producers, or the payers of these bills, and that banknotes of equal value are circulated back to the banks from the producers, at which point all market transactions are completed, then social allocation for labor would also be completed smoothly. In doing so, the amount of labor objectified by each producer would be appropriate in terms of social standards and would maintain "proportionality of values" (Proudhon 1888/1848: 102).[15] The periodic circulation of banknotes in conjunction with the payment of bills is an argument against the possibility of excess circulation of banknotes. The market principles of "*Products exchange for products*" (Cohen 1927: 48) would be realized through the market transaction process.

Taking the above into consideration, it seems that the Bank of Exchange confronted two problems. The first point is that banknotes would be issued with good bills as collateral, but that the standard of excellence would be based on the track record of the delivery of products. However, if a product is passed forward without considering the ability to pay in the future, and the sale is realized, the discount is negligible. In order to settle bills, the recipient must, after all, eventually make a successful sale for banknotes or cash. The second point concerns the methods related to the depositing of products and issuing banknotes. Products can be deposited at the bank as collateral for loans, but the treatment of such products will have to be done in the same way as the settlement of commercial bills. In other words, just as the producer pays his or her bills with banknotes or cash after a certain period of time, it may be necessary to buy back deposited products. In either case, it only has the effect of deferring the uncertainty of sales, so the final collateral of the banknotes of the Exchange and People's Bank will depend on whether the sale by the payer of the commercial bills or the bank that keeps the deposit is successful.

[15] "Proportionality of value" means (A) "proportionality" in which each product is correctly exchanged according to "exchange value" measured by labor "time and expense" spent on its production and (B) a certain correlation between the "use value" and "exchange value" of each product—in this case, it has the double meaning of "proportionality" (Fujita 1993: 14).

While Proudhon's Bank of Exchange posed the aforementioned problems, he also proposed it could fulfill the following social roles. First, the value of products in individual transactions would be guaranteed mutually by both parties through the issuance of notes by the Bank of Exchange, which would serve to convert mutually acknowledged value. Thus, banknotes would become credit securities representing relationships of mutual guarantees and promises. In addition, the promise of payment, which is only a private relationship in commercial notes, is converted into a collective payment promise between members.[16] Therefore, in issuing banknotes, the Bank of Exchange would effectively convert private receivables and payables, in the form of commercial bills, into banknotes that represented contractual relationships acknowledged by society.

Furthermore, through a series of procedures, the monopoly of money is eliminated and equality between members is guaranteed. In doing so, it must be considered that although there remains uncertainty in the settlement of commercial bills, this scenario also creates responsibility in that the creditor must make certain transactions, to put a stop to the moral hazard of drawing bills, for example, or in terms of the fact that the credit of producers who are group members would become the origin of the issuance of banknotes, thus preventing the central bank from monopolizing monetary issuance. After all, free credit is supported by the certainty of reimbursement by the recipient. Therefore, there is a responsibility for creditors and banks to conduct strict audits even though they are involved in cooperative operations.

As discussed, Proudhon's ideal for an economic revolution lay in the realization of a market economy in which producers dealt with each other as equal parties to an exchange. According to Proudhon, this could be achieved through the removal of large-scale ownership and monopolies typified by the large feudal landowners and the high rates of interest that impeded exchanges among producers. Therefore, the ideal market envisioned by Proudhon was one in which "money, interest, and the state" had ceased to act as impediments to free exchange. In his vision, the ideal primary subjects of economic activity were the independent

[16] "The People's Bank could and should operate without capital; as it has for its *base* the essential gratuity of credit and of exchange; for its *object*, the circulation of values, not their production; for its *methods*, the reciprocal agreement of producers and consumers" (Cohen 1927: 97).

small producers who had their own means of production, made independent decisions, maintained their economic independence regarding production, and whose ownership was limited in scope such that they did not impinge upon one another's property. By presenting these concepts, Proudhon felt he was in a position to make the case for a replacement of the current model of market transactions and to show how it was being systematically distorted by "money, interest, and the state." Admittedly, Proudhon attributed various causes to these market distortions, and this has led to different interpretations that have given birth to several political movements. Nevertheless, at their core, these movements share a similar vision of the market.

2.3 Marx's Conceptualization on the Labor Money Theory

As shown in Sect. 2.2, Proudhon's theory of free credit was a concept that advocated the abolition of interest and metal money. In this section, we confirm Marx's conceptualization of the labor money theory and examine how Proudhon's theory of free credit and his plans for the Bank of Exchange are related to Marx's critique of the labor money theory.

Prior to Proudhon's publication of the free credit theory, Marx (1986/1857–1858, 1987/1859) made the following assertions regarding the attributes of Proudhon's theories in the *System of Economical Contradictions: or, the Philosophy of Poverty* (Proudhon 1888/1848). Marx questioned whether Proudhon was the first to conceive the notion of social revolution by changing humankind into direct laborers who made exchanges with each other for equal amounts of labor. Marx responded to his own question by stating that anyone conversant with economics "should know that socialists in England advocated almost everything about the egalitarian application of Ricardo's theory in various ages." For Marx, therefore, Proudhon was simply a "Ricardian socialist."[17] From this dialogue we see that Marx sought Proudhon's

[17] In the Preface to the first German edition (1885) of *The Philosophy of Poverty*, Engels commented on "the utopia of labour money" [die Utopie des Arbeitsgelds] (Engels 1999/1885), saying "And the petty bourgeois especially, whose honest labour – even if it is only that of his workmen and apprentices – is daily more and more depreciated in value by the competition of large-scale production and machinery, this small-scale producer especially must long for a society in which the exchange of products according to their

"regenerating formula of the future" in "the determination of value by labour time," and defined this formula as an idea for exchanging equivalent amounts of labor based on small producers (Marx 1976/1847: 138). McKay confirms this point by stating that "We must destroy the royalty of gold; we must republicanise specie, by making every product of labour ready money" (McKay 2011: 284).[18]

Sato (1977) and Fujita (1993), however, have raised objections to Marx's definition. Was Proudhon's theory of free credit, like Marx's, something that "directly pursued exchanges based on labor time"? (Sato 1977: 319) As shown in Sect. 2.2, interest-free equivalent exchanges were made on the basis of Proudhon's Bank of Exchange. If supply and demand were aligned as a result of market transactions, then a "proportionality of values" could be maintained. It is possible that the underlying labor amounts included the possibility for exchanges of equal amounts of labor, but they did not proactively guarantee these equal exchanges. In Proudhon's plan, based on the assumption of market transactions, the relationship to the amount of labor was determined *ex post facto* and invisibly, while in the labor money theories of Owen or the Ricardian socialists, products were exchanged after determining labor time *ex ante rem* on the basis of the products. From this viewpoint, the two are decidedly different.

For example, Marx stated in *A Contribution to the Critique of Political Economy*:

> *John Gray* was the first to set forth the theory that labour-time is the direct measure of money in a systematic way. He proposes that a national central bank should ascertain through its branches the labour-time expended in the production of various commodities. In exchange for the commodity, the producer would receive an official certificate of its value [Zertifikat des Werts], i.e., a receipt for as much labour-time as his commodity contains,

labour value is at last a complete and invariable truth. In other words, he must long for a society in which a single law of commodity production prevails exclusively and in full, but in which the conditions are abolished in which it can prevail at all, viz., the other laws of commodity production and, later, of capitalist production."

[18] "Proudhon perceived money as nothing more than a 'bill of exchange written upon solid and durable material and carrying with it its own redemption.' He asserted that 'Labor invented *money*' because its need arose from a requirement to make 'wealth' divisible and 'portable' so that a portion could pass to the hands of the worker" (Knowles 2004: 108).

> and this bank-note of one labour week, one labour day, one labour hour, etc., would serve at the same time as an order [Anweisung] to the bank to hand over an equivalent in any of the other commodities stored in its warehouses. (Marx 1987/1859: 320–321)

This is "the basic principle" of labor money theory (ibid.). Namely, the national central bank would give producers a certificate for labor time spent on production in advance of exchanges. At the same time, the bank would guarantee the value of products at market value.

Under Proudhon's system of the Bank of Exchange, receipts would be given for products guaranteed by current value, thereby realizing an exchange for an equivalent amount of labor. If one considers Gray's model as a typical labor money system, then realizing proportionality according to labor time and cost is clearly different from Owen's concept of labor money, since it does not pursue realization itself, as can be seen in Proudhon's plans to establish the Bank of Exchange (Fujita 1993: 30). In a word, Marx overlooked the fact that the British labor money theory and Proudhon's concepts were not exactly the same. By proceeding with the discussion on this basis, Marx turned the criticism of labor money into a criticism of Proudhon, while confusing the arguments between the two.

But not all of Marx's criticisms are off the mark. According to Marx, labor money theorists must assume a system of production in which each producer's labor must be expended directly as social labor, but also on the basis of commodity production, with the intervention of banks that issue labor money, all of which was preserved by the illusion that private labor can be treated directly as social labor. In other words, the reason why each product must take the form of a commodity in a commodity-producing economy was overlooked.

"Commodities are the direct products of isolated independent individual kinds of labour, and through their alienation in the course of individual exchange they must prove that they are general social labour, in other words, on the basis of commodity production, labour becomes social labour only as a result of the universal alienation of individual kinds of labour" (Marx 1987/1859: 321–322). Even if one posits that Marx asserted "proportionality of values" as a result of market transactions in Proudhon's theory of free credit, the assumption of an exchange of products at a fixed value through banks offering free credit in the circulation process treats currency as an emblem of circulation. This way of thinking does not grasp the characteristics of commodity production, which rests upon the contradiction between private labor and social labor. No matter how much free credit is given, rational economic activity requires a third commodity as a measure of social labor for the other two commodities. In other words, any commodity in the form of money is required. According to Marx, Proudhon thinks that only precious metals are commodities that monopolize the form of money, but even if precious metals are banished from holding monetary status, as long as commodity production continues, new products will have a monetary status. The distinction between precious metals, especially gold, in the seat of money and the form of money itself is unclear within the lens of Proudhon's work. This point will be readdressed in Sect. 2.4.

Marx's criticism of Proudhonism is important for the ways it highlights Marx's own vision of the market, for the gaps this reveals. The first is that the theory of free credit is mistakenly defined as labor money theory. Second, Marx takes the policy proposal based on the contemporary situation in France and uses it to generalize what was specific to the theory of free credit in that context into a global critique of the market.

The chapter money in the *Grundrisse* contains Marx's critique of the "Proudhonian" Darimon (Marx 1986/1857–1858: 51–52). This is worth considering as it corresponds in several ways to what he had to say about Proudhon's theory of free credit.

Marx's criticism of Darimon includes several points, but this text will address the conflict between private labor and social labor, which is of particular theoretical significance. Marx's criticism consists of two points: (a) and (b). First, (a) is the question of whether the private labor time contained in each commodity can be equally measured (or made commensurable), or whether private labor time constitutes a unified measure that reflects the temporal change in labor productivity and the difference in productivity between each producer regarding the production of any given number of the same commodity. The second point, (b), is whether or not labor time is appropriate as a measure for displaying the value of commodities, or whether this can provide for the producer a reliable indicator for being able to determine trends of demand and supply.

With (a), Marx criticizes the assumption made by labor money theorists that the private labor time objectified in each commodity is homogeneous and can be determined equally. The following example will illustrate whether it is possible to say that the labor time objectified in two products is truly equal. Since labor money theory contains a critique of metal money, it is assumed that labor money here is made of paper without the value of money itself. Given a certain labor productivity, each producer will receive labor money written as X number of labor time according to the labor time spent on production. That way, each commodity contains the same value as the labor time spent on its production. Certainly, the exchange in this example is the same as the labor time noted on the labor money held by the producer and the labor time objectified in the commodities, and the labor time of any producer can be set equal. In this example of an exchange, the labor time noted on the labor money held by the producers will match the labor time objectified in the commodity. As a result, each producer's labor time can be equated according to labor productivity, and the theoretical conditions are given for realizing an exchange of equal amounts of labor and rights to whole labor.

However, if we consider the problem of spatial differences in labor productivity for similar commodities, it becomes clear that private labor times are inseparable when there is a difference in productivity. Suppose that at a certain point, producer A produced one unit of a product, a desk for example, in 10 hours. In that case, Producer A would receive labor money labeled for 10 labor time per unit of production. Meanwhile, Producer B, who is twice as productive, produces one unit (or one desk) in 5 hours. Even if Producer B makes the same number of desks as Producer A, they will only receive money for 5 hours of labor. As a result, the labor money that displays the same 10 hours will have two equivalents, one unit or desk and two units, or two desks. If labor money is measured based on the amount of labor commanded by one unit of desks, the labor time of the producer with low productivity becomes double the labor time of the producer with higher productivity. Except when productivity is uniform, in order to equalize private labor time under different productivity, another measure is needed to measure each person's labor time. Moreover, the result is the same even when considering changes in productivity over time. The market economy in which production activities are carried out as a trigger for the pursuit of profit leads to spatial and temporal changes in productivity by using labor time as a measure of value, which is a scale that does not reflect productivity differences. Labor money may be feasible for measuring the production of homogeneous commodities, but the relationship between the amount of labor objectified and the amount of labor commanded will not correspond separately for each producer. Rather than giving rise, therefore, to fair exchange, labor money will promote a sense of unfairness among producers (ibid., 72–74).

The first criticism, (a), points out that private labor time is inadequate as a measure of a commodity's value. In (b), through the assumption of an anarchic system of production based on private ownership, Marx was able criticize labor money theory, in which value and price was equated, because money prices should be required as a measure of value that is tied directly to labor time. Likewise, in (b), Marx criticized labor money theory for its conflation of value and price. He argued that under an anarchic system of production based on private ownership, money price replaces labor time as a measure. "The *value* (the real exchange value) of all commodities (including labour) is determined by their production costs, in other words, by the labour time required for their production. Their *price* is this exchange value... expressed in money" (ibid., 74). Undoubtedly, the "replacement of metallic currency (and the paper or credit money denominated in terms of it) by labour money deriving its denomination from labour time itself, would therefore equate the *real value* (exchange value) of commodities and their *nominal value*, *price*, *money value*. Equation of *real value and nominal value*, *of value and price*. But this would be attained only on the assumption that *value* and *price* are only *nominally* distinct. But such is by no means the case" and that labor money can be expressed directly through labor time as commodity value (ibid., 74–75). Within market economies, however, individual exchanges are based on the system of private property, and demand and supply vary; therefore, social conditions that equate value and price do not exist. Although "Demand and supply continually determine the prices of commodities; they never coincide or do so only accidentally; but the costs of production determine for their part the fluctuations of demand and supply." Eventually, the relationship between demand and supply determines price. Furthermore, the "value of commodities determined by labour time," as imagined by labor money theorists, "is only their *average value*" and in actual market transactions, "But this average is very real if it is recognised as both the driving force and the moving principle of the fluctuations which occur in the prices of commodities during a particular period of time." The average prices of commodities are used as "the basis of commercial speculation" to calculate the probability of speculation. The market value of commodities is always different to the average value of those commodities and emphasizes that speculative transactions based on fluctuations of prices standardized on average commodities prices are a distinctive trait of market economies (ibid., 74–76). Thus, Marx presents the vision of a real market that is overlooked by Proudhon, who had an ideal vision of markets.[19]

According to Marx's *Grundrisse*, money's function as a measure of value, or money itself, is required when private labor time for commodities cannot be equated.[20] Whether a commodity's quality and quantity is in accordance with demand, and whether labor time for commodities is expended on the basis of the socially dominant productivity, cannot be assessed as a direct metric of each commodity's labor time. "Labour time as a measure of value exists only ideally" and "Price as distinct from value" is a metric that can also be referred to as "*money price*."[21] Labor money used as a direct measure of the value of labor time must be "with all the properties of our present money without performing its services." The system of private production gives rise to an anarchic structure of production, which always results in excess or insufficient production, and a continual process of adjustment. When the market is viewed as an anarchic mechanism for the adjustment of production, on the one hand, and as a form in which demand and supply are determined by productive conditions, on the other, it becomes clear how it easy it becomes for mercantile speculation on price differences arising from differences of productive conditions between producers. By questioning the nature of the market in this way, Marx became a critic of Proudhonism, which

[19] Obata (1986: 114) critically examined labor money theory cited in Marx's *Grundrisse* (Marx 1986/1857–1858: 75) and outlined Marx's understanding of markets. Obata commented that "Marx declared that '*Price*, therefore, differs from *value*, not only as the nominal differs from the real; not only by its denomination in gold and silver; but also in that the latter appears as the law of the movements to which the former is subject,' showing the image of an undisciplined market encapsulating movements as 'precisely through continual inequity to itself'." Obata herein clearly explains Marx's peculiar market awareness.

[20] Measure of value includes both showing the value amount and measuring the value of a commodity being purchased. In this book, the former is referred to as "measure of value" and the latter as "the (monetary) function of measure of value."

[21] In the Preface to the first German edition of *The Philosophy of Poverty*, Engels (1999/1885) commented on Rodbertus' labor money theory, declaring that "if price appreciation, or informing producers of world markets in decline in response to competition is forbidden, producers will close their eyes completely." Engels emphasizes that price, for producers, acts as the "sole adjustment" made to determine whether production volume is proportional to social demand.

still clung to an idealistic vision of the market. In other words, for Marx the market is encapsulated by the absence of exchanges based on equal amounts of labor and that it is regulated anarchically by ideal averages; put differently, it is difficult for markets to make adjustments for demand and supply (Marx 1986/1857–1858: 77–78).

2.4 Criticisms of Proudhon in Capital

In *Grundrisse*, Marx's discussion of labor money theory focused on whether labor money as a unit of labor time could function as money. This led him to stress the disjunction between monetary price and labor time and criticized the theory of money as a straightforward measure of value. Assuming a market economy based on private property, labor time cannot be a standard for determining the appropriateness of a commodity's value on the basis of social standards, yet price remains necessary if a commodity is to show its value. Furthermore, labor money that cannot adequately express commodity value cannot become a metric of the social allocation of labor time in a commodity economy.

Furthermore, as is well known, in Chapter 4 of *Capital* Vol. I, "the transformation of money into capital" is referred to as income for producers, including surplus value (or surplus products) from exchanges of equal amounts of labor. Thus, in response to Proudhon, who posited that exploitation would not occur, and the assumptions of labor money theorists, Marx's was a theory of surplus value, with a noted possibility for exploitation in surplus value during the production process, even in a market economy with exchanges of equal amounts of labor.[22] Marx's conceptualization of exchanges of equal amounts of labor sets the stage for the theory of surplus value to criticize labor money as a theory of unfair exploitation. Even so, in Chapter 1 ("Commodities") of *Capital*, based on the assumption of simple commodities in circulation and exchanges of equal amounts of labor, the content on the theory of value form in some ways criticizes "Proudhon's socialism" and deems

[22] Obata (2004) states that "surplus value theory is mostly meaningless when divorced from the object of theoretical criticism of mainstream socialism at the time, such as Ricardian socialism tied to the right to the whole produce of labor, and Proudhon-style market socialism" (4). Perhaps this comment shows a particular aspect of markets similarly assumed in *Capital* with exchanges of equitable value such as were assumed by Proudhon.

labor money theory difficult to comprehend. In keeping with the historical consideration of the criticism of Proudhon's socialism within Marx's *Capital*, a rethinking of the theory of value form and exchange process theory allows a different aspect of the critique of labor money theory to emerge from those found in works written prior to *Capital*.

In the theory of free credit, Proudhon sought to connect the use of precious metals as specie with the power to collect interest in exchanges due to the metallic status of money, thereby drawing the conclusion that this obstructed an ideal market based on equal exchanges. With the Bank of Exchange providing free credit, Proudhon envisioned raising commodities to a status at the same level as precious metals. However, it can be said that Marx's theory of value form rejects Proudhon's claims. This comes out more clearly if we place Proudhon's theory of free credit theory side by side with Marx's view. The Bank of Exchange offers free discounts on commercial bills and interest-free loans secured by products in which labor has been expended. The assumption is that it is possible at some point in time to fix the value of all products and bills, so that they can reflect the value expended in their production. Yet for Marx such an assumption was unacceptable.[23] This is because the fixation value would imply that the result of private labor can be immediately recognized as having intrinsic value without being required to compare it to the standard of social labor. But, for markets to function as a platform where private labor is knitted into social labor, the value of commodities must be allowed to change. In addition to Marx's previous criticism that the theory of value form adjusts labor amounts, his discussion in subsequent paragraphs of *Capital* provides a further analysis of the difficulty of realizing value in terms of constraints to use value. At this point, we can summarize Marx's criticisms of Proudhon regarding the theory of value form by posing two essential questions. First, why is it not possible simultaneously for commodities to take the form of general exchangeability? Second, if we remove metal money from markets, could the form of the

[23] However, "*Article* 40" of incorporation of the Bank of People should be considered. "Up to the expiration of the time fixed by the contract of sale, the consignor is at liberty to repurchase the merchandise, reimbursing the Bank only the amount advanced by it. Upon the expiration of this time, the Bank will sell the deposited merchandise at public auction. The excess of the price obtained at the sale above that fixed at delivery belongs rightfully to the consignor of the merchandise" (Cohen 1927: 103).

market truly take shape without money continuing to obstruct the process of buying and selling?

In Chapter 1 of *Capital* Vol. I, in the notes to the third section of "the general form of value," Marx comments on "Proudhon's socialism" and states the following:

> It is by no means self-evident that this character of direct and universal exchangeability is, so to speak, a polar one, and as intimately connected with its opposite pole, the absence of direct exchangeability, as the positive pole of the magnet is with its negative counterpart. It may therefore be imagined that all commodities can simultaneously have this character impressed upon them, just as it can be imagined that all Catholics can be popes together. It is, of course, highly desirable in the eyes of the petit bourgeois, for whom the production of commodities is the *nec plus ultra* of human freedom and individual independence, that the inconveniences resulting from this character of commodities not being directly exchangeable, should be removed. (Marx 1996/1867: 79)

That is, a commodity in the form of general exchangeability exclusively monopolizes the status of the general equivalent form of value, which is why it is deprived of direct exchangeability. In other words, there must be a group of commodities that are in the form of indirect exchangeability or relative form of value. On the one hand, commodities take the relative form of value, and on the other, money takes the general equivalent form of value. That is, of course, a criticism of Proudhon's assumption that any commodity can be given a form of general exchangeability by eliminating metal money. It is also a criticism of the market view that markets can return to an inherently stable state, with all commodities being exchangeable at any time, if only the introduction of money can be done away with. Disposing of money from circulation and wishing for the direct exchange of products, while still assuming independent small producers and a commodity economy, leads to the loss of an objective basis for determining an appropriate rate of exchange.

Regarding the relationship between the money form and gold, Marx declared that, in the shift from a general form of value to a money form, the "progress consists in this alone, that the character of direct and universal exchangeability — in other words, that the universal equivalent form — has now, by social custom, become finally identified with the substance, gold" (ibid., 80–81). This shows the possibility that the general equivalent form of value that is "a form of value in general...can, therefore, be assumed by any commodity" by social custom (ibid., 80). It is only necessary under certain social conditions that gold is a general equivalent form of value, although the commodity economy inevitably requires a money form, whether commodities settle into a monetary position depends on the historical context and customs of society. Nevertheless, Marx's view was that Proudhon, with his understanding of money being tied to gold, was foolish in his inability to view what had appeared universal in France's situation to be relative and a product of historical context. Therefore, even if gold is expelled from the throne of money as money form, the "equivalent exchange of products" cannot be realized through free credit, which has been proved by equating the money form itself with gold money. The value of one's commodity can be known only by an exchange ratio of the use value of other commodities. Furthermore, a commodity must overcome the constraints of its own use value to realize its value. Although retroactive as a development of the theory of value form, Proudhon's theory of free credit concluded by saying the "whole mystery of the form of value lies hidden in this elementary form" (ibid., 58), thus, questioning the primordial form of the commodity economy.

In the elementary form of value that begins with an exchange between two individuals, the value of the commodities owned by the two individuals is not equated from the outset, as with the homogeneity of human labor obtained as a result of social abstraction. Thus, the value of one person's commodity must be expressed as a mirror of the body of another person's commodity. As an owner of a commodity, it is not possible to recognize the social nature of the value inherent in one's own commodity, so a procedure for expressing value is required. Commodities placed in the equivalent form of value are not only serving as mirrors of value, but are also in a position where they can decide to exchange with commodities in relative form of value. This relationship directly represents the advantage of money placed in a general equivalent form of value. If this point is examined closely, it will result in a theory of the realization of value that demonstrates the conflict between money placed in a general equivalent form of value and commodities placed in a relative form of value. In transactions between individual commodities, the realization of value cannot be guaranteed only by equivalence, not only because of the quantitative relationship of labor behind commodities, but also because products cannot be exchanged without looking at the coincidence of desires between the commodity owners. Therefore, at issue once more is the method of issuing notes by Proudhon's Bank of Exchange.

With Proudhon's Bank of Exchange, it was assumed that the value of products would be fixed and they would be exchanged for equal value. If this assumption is accepted as is, and if the price at the time of the exchange of each product and bill is always maintained, Marx's criticism of the theory of the measure of value may not be problematic for the time being. In the case of free credit, even when considering commercial bills discounted without charge or loans with collateral of deposited products, the value of deposited products or bills held by banks is fixed; thus, these can be seen as safe assets. Nevertheless, was that truly the case? In the theory of free credit, the recipients must settle with banknotes by the date of the bill, even if free credit is given, so the ability to establish a smooth economic cycle depends on the success of sales under the constraints of use value. Free credit provides the conditions for enabling the "equivalent exchange between products" but it does not promise its realization. On the other hand, Proudhon overemphasized the stability of its real asset values (discounted commercial bills and deposited products) and overlooked the uneven change in asset values due to changes in productivity and trends involving demand and supply. After all, since bank credit is given cheaply, even if it is possible to grant purchasing power without being constrained by commercial credit, the opportunity to sell to banknote holders has not changed at all, so the necessity of the money form cannot be demonstrated by the fact that metal money has been excluded from circulation.

Marx disagreed with Proudhon's vision of the market and stressed that anarchy in production would disturb markets. Furthermore, it can be said that Marx's realism (as opposed to Proudhon's idealism), led him to locate the undisciplined nature of markets in the anarchy of production, which rendered the theory of free credit impossible in principle. This is because additional merchant speculation spurs temporary and repetitive discrepancies in the average price of commodities. As shown below, this is related to the philosophy of "genuine globalization" (Graeber 2002: 65), the creation of a market that embodies the ideals of the French Revolution aimed at by Proudhon.

2.5 In Lieu of a Conclusion: The Modern World and Anarchism

We now consider Proudhon's intentions, for which he himself never sufficiently made a case. First, the purpose of the theory of free credit was to provide money to small and medium producers who unable freely to finance their activity. At the same time, it was developed to criticize the privileged position of money gives its holder, who is granted the power to collect interest. It was thought possible to eliminate the inequality of the exchange based on the superiority of money if each producer could obtain money equally through free credit, and thereby achieve a truly free market economy. The markets envisioned in this case were not real markets based on the anarchy of production, but collaborative markets with mutually independent producers who nevertheless were mutually reliant. These markets are not realistic markets that pursue profit amidst uncertainty and dramatic fluctuations, as emphasized by Marx. Rather, they are ideal markets subject to little change and with fixed transactional relationships continually maintained within a narrow range of circulation. Reciprocity of value was nothing more than an ideological representation of this type of market vision. In other words, while Marx emphasized that value in actual markets is not fixed, Proudhon maintained that market deficiencies should be corrected to create relationships where value can be fixed. Marx's focus was on the world of capitalistic markets, whereas Proudhon continued to pursue the ideal vision of a local market economy, based not on capitalists but on small producers such as artisans and farmers. In this way, their respective visions of the market are divided into distinctly different forms. Yet the question of how to understand the market was common to both Marx and Proudhon, and the controversy this gave rise to has continued to influence labor money theory, especially as subsequent thinkers have sought to develop a more realistic theory of the market. Returning to Marx and Proudhon, their respective visions of the market were clearly presented as fundamental investigations of the nature of money. Arguments around labor money theory and labor note theory have developed out of this duality and continue to be shaped by it.

We can see this clearly when looking at contemporary forms of anarchism, which owe much to Proudhon's vision of the market and his theory of money and credit reform. For example, according to Graeber (2002), the anarchist movement is more of a "globalization movement" than an "anti-globalization movement," meaning it is a movement of "the effacement of borders and the free movement of people, possessions and ideas" (Graeber 2002: 63). In addition, even though local currencies seem to point in the opposite direction, by denying the rights to positive interest rates and the monopoly of issuing notes by the central bank, they envisage the possibility of creating a medium that includes their claims and values. Such views rely upon the same ideals of a free and equitable market network rather than a capitalistic market economy. This is also shown in the organizational forms of the groups spawned in the globalization movement. In other words, the Proudhon's philosophy is reflected in Graeber's description of contemporary anarchism which, "is about creating and enacting horizontal networks instead of top-down structures like states, parties or corporations; networks based on principles of decentralized, non-hierarchical consensus democracy" (ibid., 70). These ideals, which deny the state and monopoly, exist across history and share common ground with those of Proudhon. Therefore, in Chapter 3, the focus will turn to non-market areas by considering the relevance of modern local currencies, while taking into account Marx's critique of labor money theory.

In this chapter, we have explored Marx's critique, by stressing two key aspects to his theory. The first aspect can be seen in his works up to *A Contribution to the Critique of Political Economy*, which states the substance of the value of a commodity is labor, which can serve as the measure of value; commodity value cannot be expressed in private labor time but must be expressed in terms of money price. The second is that the anarchy of production in the market economy inevitably creates difficulties in the realization of sales (or realization of value). Labor money theorists, including Proudhon, overlook both of these aspects. Nevertheless, Marx's theory is not without room for reconsideration. Proudhon's narrow understanding of market relationships, and the fact that social relationships are not encapsulated in market relationships alone, are issues with similar roots. This is because Marx's theories of the measure of value and the inevitability of money are constrained by the same problematic setting that is criticized in Proudhon's theories that assume a rigid commodity production system. This leads to marginalize Marx's concept of the historical realities of social reproduction. For example, this partial interpretation of Marx's theories does not demonstrate the idea that the market cannot include the entire social reproduction process and that it constantly leaves behind fragments. In addition, the exogenous nature of markets that have developed through history, such as trade relationship between communities, are not theoretically incorporated. Without questioning these shortcomings in Marx's work, discussions of the problems of realizing value and the quantitative relationships of labor assumed in a market economy are insufficient for a critique of the whole social system. At the same time, the debate between Marx and Proudhon cannot serve a sufficient theoretical framework to examine local currencies and other movements when their activities are looked at in non-market areas.

If one considers the current circumstances, the metabolic cycles of regional economies have been broken down owing to bloated financial markets and the burden of interest rates on small producers and workers. Despite this, neither Keynesian doctrine nor Soviet-style socialism are viable alternatives. Attention has been paid to Proudhonian ideals, such as the elimination of increased unearned income, including interest and rent, so as to bring about fair market economies, coupled with an aversion to implementing state policies or making large-scale changes to economic systems. The approach of setting market ideals and criticizing real markets has been inherited by various recurring movements within anarchism, such as the recent WTO protests, and by movements in favor of local currencies. More than these being an inherent market ideal, it may be more appropriately to say that that certain people's ideals are being incorporated into markets. In this sense, is it appropriate to continue incorporating such ideals as a method for counter-positioning ideals to reality within a normative theory? The idea of ideal markets functioning as alternatives is one that merits further research.

Bibliography

Cohen, H. (Ed.). (1927). *Proudhon's solution of the social problem.* Vanguard Press.

Engels, F. (1999/1885). Preface to the first German edition. The poverty of philosophy: Answer to the philosophy of poverty by M. Proudhon. *Marx/Engels Internet Archive (marxists.org).* http://www.marxists.org/archive/marx/works/1847/poverty-philosophy/pre-1885.htm

Fujita, K. (1993). *Purūdon to Gendai* [Proudhon and our time]. Sekai Shoin.

Graeber, D. (2002). The new anarchists. *New Left Review, 13*, 61–73.

Grubacic, A., & Graeber, D. (2004). Anarchism, or the revolutionary movement of the twenty-first century. *ZNet*. http://www.zcommunications.org/anarchism-or-the-revolutionary-movement-of-the-twenty-first-century-by-david-graeber

Knowles, R. (2004). *Political economy from below: Economic thought in communitarian anarchism, 1840–1914*. Routledge.

Koga, E. (1964). Furansu Shihonshugi to Ōto Banku [French capitalism and "la haute banque"]. *Shakaigaku Kenkyū [Hitotsubashi University Research Series. Social Sciences], 6*, 73–259.

Marx, K. (1976/1847). The poverty of philosophy: Answer to the philosophy of poverty by M. Proudhon. In *Marx & Engels collected works* (Vol. 6). Lawrence & Wishart.

Marx, K. (1978/1850). The class struggles in France, 1848 to 1850. In *Marx & Engels collected works* (Vol. 10). London: Lawrence & Wishart.

Marx, K. (1986/1857–1858). Economic manuscripts of 1857–58. In *Marx & Engels collected works* (Vol. 28). Lawrence & Wishart.

Marx, K. (1987/1859). A contribution to the critique of political economy. In *Marx & Engels collected works* (Vol. 29). Lawrence & Wishart.

Marx, K. (1996/1867). Capital, Vol. I. In *Marx & Engels collected works* (Vol. 35). Lawrence & Wishart.

McKay, I. (Ed.). (2011). *Property is theft! A Pierre-Joseph Proudhon anthology*. AK Press.

Mendelson, L. A. (1960/1959). *Kyōkō no Riron to Rekishi* [The theory and history of crisis] (Vol. 2). Aoki Shoten.

Mori, T. (1967). *Furansu Shihonshugi to Sozei* [French capitalism and taxation]. University of Tokyo Press.

Morino, E. (1997, 1998a, 1998b, 2001, 2002). Purūdon no Kōkanginkōron (1)–(5) [On the Exchange bank of P. J. Proudhon (1)–(5)]. *Jiyū Keizai Kenkyū* [Study for Free Economy] (Vols. 11, 12, 13, 20, 21).

Motoike, R. (1979). *Furansu Sangyōkakumei to Kyōkō* [French industrial revolution and crisis]. Ochanomizushobo.

Obata, M. (1986). Shijō no Mukiritsusei to Kahei no Kakusan: Marx Kahei Chikuzōron no Kanōsei [Undisciplined nature of market and diffusion of money: A possibility of Marxian theory of the money hoarding]. *Shisō* [Thought], *748*, 111–132.

Obata, M. (2004). Grōbarizumu to Genriron [Principles of political economy under globalism]. *Political Economy Quarterly, 41*(1), 16–27.

Oishi, T. (1989). Kachigainen to Burujoateki shokankei no Rekishisei oyobi Tōitsusei haaku: "Tetsugaku no Hinkon" niokeru Purūdon "Sōgōkachi" ron hihan wo chūshin toshite [A study of Marx's concept of value: With special Marx's critique on Proudhon's value concept in "the poverty of philosophy"]. *Takushokudaigaku Ronshu* [The Review of Takushoku University], *176*, 59–87.

Proudhon, P. J. (1849). *Les Conffessions d'un Révolutionnaire pour server à l'Histoire de la Révolution de Février* [Confessions of a revolutionary for the history of the February revolution]. au Bureau Journal la voix du Peuple.

Proudhon, P. J. (1888/1848). *System of economical contradictions: Or, the philosophy of poverty*. McMaster University.

Proudhon, P. J. (2007/1851). *General idea of the revolution in the nineteenth century*. Cosimo.

Sato, S. (1977). Purūdon no Kōkanginkōron [P.-J. Proudhon and his project of "Bank of Exchange"]. *Keizai Kenkyū* [The Economic Review (Hitotsubashi University)], *28*(4), 319–327.

Tsugita, K. (1972). 19 seiki niokeru Furansu no Tetsudōkensetsu (1) [Railroad policy of French governments in the 19th century (1)]. *Osakadaigaku Keizaigaku* [The Economic Review of Osaka University], *22*(1), 58–87.

Tsugita, K. (1973). 19 seiki niokeru Furansu no Tetsudōkensetsu (2) [Railroad policy of French governments in the 19th century (2)]. *Osakadaigaku Keizaigaku* [The Economic Review of Osaka University], *22*(2), 39–61.

Yamanobe, T. (1974). Marukusu ni totte Purūdon hihan ga imishita mono [Marx's critique on Proudhon: An interpretation]. *Kanazawa Daigaku Hōgakubu ronsyū Keizaigaku hen* [Studies and Essays by The Faculty of Law and Literature, Kanazawa University, Economics], *21,* 111–134.

Yamamoto, Y. (1989). Marukusu *Keizaigakuhihanyōkō* niokeru Kaheiseiseiron to Purūdonshugi hihan [Geldableitung und Proudhonismus-Kritik in Marx' "Grundrissen der Kritik der politischen Ökonomie"]. *Shōdai ronsyū* [Journal of Kobe University of Commerce], *41*(2–3), 273–293.

CHAPTER 3

Theoretical Connotations of Marx's Critique of the Theory of Labor Money: *On Socialism and Local Currencies*

As noted in the previous chapter, an important implication of Marx's critique of the theory of labor money is that the instability triggered by markets is due to the anarchic nature of commodity production, a phenomenon that is difficult to overcome. Added to this is the behavior of subjects who seek to reap windfall profits by exploiting price fluctuations in the market. Therefore, the question of stabilizing markets is a false one. It is vain hope to seek to control market fluctuations through monetary reforms. As long as anarchic commodity production remains the locus of markets, fluctuations will be an intrinsic and unavoidable feature of their functioning. However, trying to achieve a stable economic society is not a hopeless endeavor. In social conditions where the conceptual triad of commodity–money–price no longer holds sway, it should become possible, at least, to avoid the economic instability inherent to markets. The first half of this chapter outlines the version of socialism derived from the logic of Marx's critique of labor money. This explains his view that labor money, while being logically unfeasible under commodity production, could be established in a communal system of production. The latter half of the chapter goes on to suggest that, by subtly tweaking Marx's vision of socialism as the replacement of the market with communal social production, the contents of his critique of the theory of labor money could be applied more broadly to local currencies used in non-market

© The Author(s), under exclusive license to Springer Nature Switzerland AG 2021

T. Yuki, *Socialism, Markets, and the Critique of Money*,
Marx, Engels, and Marxisms,
https://doi.org/10.1007/978-3-030-80408-4_3

realms. One such local currency, "Time Dollars," for instance, shares a common trait with labor notes in that it uses labor time as a measure and unit of economic calculations. However, it differs greatly from labor money in that its use is limited to non-market labor. As in the case of time dollars, examples of the application to different realms of monetary media that use labor time as the same unit of measure can provide us with a new frame of reference for reconsidering labor money, besides its relation to socialism, and this chapter will consider that point to the extent necessary for the subject at hand.

The content of this chapter is as follows. Section 3.1 reviews the critique of the theory of labor money founded on practices of independent small producers, drawing on passages from Marx's writings. An examination of his critique reveals that a system of production based on the common ownership of the means of production is required. The labor money used by the New Harmony community, which has the same theoretical character as the system of production that complies with the reasoning presented in Sect. 3.1, can be grouped under the category of "certificates" or "tickets," for it had lost its essential character as money. Next, Sect. 3.2 looks at the significance and the problems of the bookkeeping-based labor notes system that the cooperative community of New Harmony attempted to use to demonstrate the superiority of this method compared to a method founded on independent small producers as the subjects. The first advantage of this system is that it overcomes the systematic limitations of the labor note model based on independent small producers, where members of society cannot receive products from the circulation process without first supplying labor time on the basis of the social surplus accumulated in the community (to redistribute income to those members of the community who are unable to provide labor in return for labor money). Second, this method does not pivot on the equivalence between the labor times (measured by the market) that are inputted by each community member, but rather has its basis in the mutual recognition of equal labor time expended by people who share the same standpoint as community members. Finally, the chapter suggests, in relation to these two points, that a modern approach to local currency is required.

3.1 Presenting Labor Certificates as a Consequence of the Critique of Labor Money Theory

Labor Time as a Measure of Distribution

Marx's method of treating labor time within his critique of labor money has two aspects, each of which rely upon different premises. (a) The first aspect is premised on the market economy, with Marx pointing out that labor money cannot function as a measure of value for the private labor time objectified in a product, and that even if certificates existed that indicate the private labor time objectified in a product, they could not function as an indication of an excess or deficiency in demand or supply at the social level of productivity. The content of this criticism is developed, for example, in Marx's critique of labor money in *Grundrisse* and *A Contribution to the Critique of Political Economy*. (b) The second aspect is elaborated from the "double part" (Marx 1996/1867: 89) of labor time in a future society in which certain social conditions have been fulfilled. Labor time, in this case, is a measure of the planned allocation of labor and a measure of the distribution of products. Since Marx's vision of a future society ideologically presents an ideal society, it could be thought of as fulfilling the role of historically relativizing the current stage of capitalism, so that this method itself is an expression of a normative or critical attitude toward the current situation. The issues regarding Marx's critique of labor money have already been dealt with in the previous chapter, so in this chapter they will only be reconsidered to the extent necessary for development of my arguments.

With regard to point (a), Marx, in *A Contribution to the Critique of Political Economy*, criticized the theory of labor money advanced by Gray, who insisted that it was possible for paper certificates indicating the private labor time expended by each producer to be directly used as a means of exchange.[1] Petty-bourgeois socialists like Gray argued that if products were exchanged using labor money indicating the labor time actually expended by each producer to produce products, then exchange could be carried out on the basis of an equal amount of labor so that the income of each of the producers would be proportionate to their

[1] Marx's critique of labor money theorists includes J. Gray (1799–1883), Proudhon, J. F. Bray (1809–1897), A. Darimon (1819–1902), and J. K. Rodbertus (1805–1875).

labor time, bringing about the equal exchange of labor quantities and the right to one's full produce of labor, which in turn would bring about an equal society. Marx criticized this view by pointing out that if labor money was used on the basis of the anarchic system of production centered on private property, it would be impossible for the labor time expended by producers to be recognized as having social validity, given the private character of the labor time indicated by the labor money (Marx 1987/1859: 320–323). The petty-bourgeois socialists envisaged independent small producers as the appropriate subjects to participate in the processes of the market using labor money, privately owning their means of production and freely disposing of their labor products as their own property. The labor money system introduced by Owen that was used in the National Equitable Labour Exchanges was also based on small producers, which became one reason his theory of labor money or labor certificates was conflated with an ideal of a society of small producers.[2]

Marx's criticism has two other aspects. (i) First, in the market economy premised on an anarchic system of production, production plans are made in line with the expectations and decisions of individual producers, which result in the supply of products not being appropriate to the overall social demand. Under the market economy, given the anarchic manner in which production is carried out, the difficulty of socially adjusting the volume of production to levels of social demand is a situation that can generally occur.

(ii) The second aspect, as clarified in the previous chapter, is that since labor money is a medium of directly representing privately expended labor time, it encompasses the coexistence of similar types of products with different quantities of labor time owing to differences in the productivity

[2] For example, Marx writes: "*Equitable-labour-exchange bazaars* have been set up in London, Sheffield, Leeds and many other towns in England. These bazaars have all ended in scandalous failures after having absorbed considerable capital. The taste for them has gone for ever. You are warned, M. Proudhon!" (Marx 1976/1847: 144). Moreover, the claim that "Marx's criticism is aimed at Owen, not Bray and Gray" (Tezuka 1926: 355) risks confusing Owen's proposal for labor money with those that are based solely on small producers. Hardach and Karras characterize Ravenstone, Hodgskin, and Proudhon as "individualist anti-capitalists," stating: "We thought that a nation of craftsmen and farmers based on private ownership was closest to the ideal state of society"; therefore, they were not interested in Owen's community construction plan (Hardach et al. 1978: 15). According to Hirao, even among the Ricardian socialists, the plan was divided into "envisioning a society of free and equal independent small producers," and "planning the construction of a communal society" (Hirao 1975: 123).

of labor. Labor money representing private labor time is unable to discern whether an appropriate quantity of labor was expended with regard to social demand, or whether it was a quantity of labor expended according to the social level of productivity. In other words, when there is a market producing the same kinds of products under different degrees of labor productivity, labor money cannot function as a measure of value in the Marxian sense of the term.

In the market economy, the function of money as a measure of value operates as a mechanism to socially evaluate private labor time that is objectified in each commodity and thus concerns those two aspects (i) and (ii). In other words, in the case of privately produced commodities, it is only through the external measure of value, whereby price is indicated through a fixed rate of exchange with money, that the social appropriateness of the quantity of labor as the substance of value can be verified with regard to the given level of demand and supply and the social level of productivity. Moreover, in sales and purchases where money price is an indicator, the social allocation of labor is adjusted on the basis of the results of market transactions, so that labor money, in deciding the quantity of labor objectified in a product prior to the market transactions, receives a reverse determination. Marx criticized the labor money of Gray for being a utopian creation that cannot guarantee social validity because it indicates labor time does not reflect the imbalances between supply and demand or the social level of productivity.[3]

However, with regard to the second point (b), Marx, as the logical outcome of his critique of the theory of labor money, also understood that labor money or labor certificates could be used in a future society that put in place certain social conditions through the transformation of the anarchic system of production that is premised in Gray's theory of labor money. For example, in the first volume of *Capital* as well as in the *Critique of the Gotha Programme*, there are the famous passages on the social roles of labor time. In *Capital*, Marx states that, assuming "a community of free individuals, carrying on their work with the means of production in common, in which the labour power of all the different individuals is consciously applied as the combined labour power of the

[3] Saad-Filho (1993) points out that Gray's labor money does not fulfil the function of money, viewing the market as a logical process to verify whether the labor time bestowed on commodities is appropriate from the perspective of social demand, and whether labor is expended under a system of socially standardized labor productivity.

community," "Labour time would, in that case, play a double part." The first role of labor time is described as "Its apportionment in accordance with a defined social plan [that] maintains the proper proportion between the different kinds of work to be done and the various wants of the community." This first role of labor time, unlike the case of private labor time in a market economy, is useful as a measure of the planned allocation of labor because the labor time of each individual can be grasped directly as social labor time. This means that the private character of labor time vis-à-vis demand and supply and productivity under a market economy is transformed into the representation of the social quantity and level of labor within a "community of free individuals." The extent to which labor time can be directly used in adjusting the allocation of social labor can be understood through an indication of the extent to which the allocation of labor would have shifted from an unconscious relation determined *ex post facto*, against the backdrop of the market economy, toward production that is consciously managed according to a priori production planning (Marx 1996/1867: 89).

Marx goes on to describe the second role of labor time as "a measure of the portion of the common labour borne by each individual, and of his share in the part of the total product destined for individual consumption" (ibid., 89–90). Marx revisited this point in his *Critique of the Gotha Programme*. In this essay, he states that, "Within the collective society [*Genossenschaftlichen*] based on common ownership of the means of production, the producers do not exchange their products; just as little does the labour employed on the products appear here *as the value* of these products, as a material quality possessed by them" (Marx 1989/1875: 85). This statement rests on the same assumptions that underlay the passage quoted from Capital; namely, there is no longer a characteristic of the commodity economy in which individual labor time is understood as the value of a commodity. However, removing the concept of value does not remove the concept of labor time from the intrinsic properties of the commodity produced. Rather, instead of determining commodity value through an economic "roundabout way" by an exchange with other commodities, individual labor time objectified in each product can be treated "directly as a component of total labour" (ibid.).[4] Moreover, in such a "collective society," "the individual

[4] Engels mentions that in the society of a commodity-based economy, where the social labor time objectified in products cannot be directly measured, labor time for products

labour time of the individual producer is the part of the social working day contributed by him, his share in it" (ibid., 86). In other words, labor time that can be treated "directly as a component of total labour," as described here is not individual labor time in which individuality must be eliminated through market transactions, but is a labor time which is a portion of the total social labor time, regardless of the type of work that is carried out. In addition, Marx refers to labor certificates as follows, "He receives a certificate from society that he has furnished such and such an amount of labour (after deducting his labour for the common funds), and with this certificate he draws from the social stock of means of consumption as much as the same amount of labour costs. The same amount of labour which he has given to society in one form he receives back in another" (ibid.). This sentence indicates that the distribution of individual means of consumption is carried out in proportion to the worker or producer's contribution measured by the amount of labor he has expended. This can be understood through the statement, "the same principle prevails as that which regulates the exchange of commodities, as far as this is the exchange of equal values" (ibid.). The specific form of the distribution method not involving exchange is not the primary issue here, but there may be an aspect that is similar in form to the distribution or benefit from the allocation of shared consumption.[5] The use of labor certificates implies that the expansion of joint consumption will broaden the scope for freedom of choice in the means of consumption and services, and a social relationship will be created enabling provision of equal amounts of labor.

In the same part of *Critique of the Gotha Programme*, Marx also enters into a detailed discussion of distribution measured by labor time in a future society. He divides this society into a lower and a higher stage and indicates the problem of rights related to distribution that could arise in the lower stage, where products are distributed in line with the contribution of labor. Marx says that the right of each member of society to receive products in line with the amount of labor provided is an "*equal right* [*gleiche Recht*]" (ibid.) from the perspective of each

is measured "in a roundabout way, through the medium of exchange, relatively" (Engels 1987/1878: 292).

[5] It should be understood that distribution here is based on the socialization of donations or gifts in that it does not depend on the tax collection function of the nation.

individual's social contribution, measured equally. But this right "tacitly recognises the unequal individual endowment and thus productive capacity of the workers as natural privileges. *It is, therefore, a right of inequality, in its content, like every right*" (ibid.). Under social conditions where these inequalities are tolerated, "*equal right*" equates to an "inequality of results." In this way, Marx, in discussing this "*equal right*," is focused solely on the labor capacity of the individuals who form society and can perform a variety of social roles and indicates the limit of only understanding them in their quality as workers.

Therefore, Marx presents "unequal rights" under which non-workers receive a share of the distribution as well. For instance, he speaks of "*funds for those unable to work,* etc., in short, for what is included under so-called official poor relief today" (ibid., 85). Furthermore, the part of "*the common satisfaction of needs,* such as schools, health services, etc." should also be deducted from the "the *total social product*" (ibid., 84–5). This sentence suggests the possibility of socialization regarding the necessary labor time. Therefore, under "unequal rights," a relatively high amount of individual labor time is considered to be deducted "for the common funds" (ibid., 86), which provides a degree of social freedom, including redistribution function of income in dealing with a surplus.[6]

In addition, Marx disapproves of the equivalence of labor, saying that in order for "labour, to serve as a measure, [it] must be defined by its duration or intensity, otherwise it ceases to be a standard of measurement" (ibid.). Marx's social theory regarding a future society entails the problem of complex or skilled labor as an unresolved conundrum, but if it is possible to reduce complex labor to its simpler form (even if complex labor remains), then the problem of adjusting demand and supply can be solved through social regulations on labor allocation. Further, by expanding social discretion through the formation of a common fund that responds to the various living conditions of its members, the problem of complex labor is treated as a distribution problem at the lower level, and

[6] Itoh postulates the distinction between surplus labor and necessary labor in a "cooperative society," noting that "the meaning should be clearly different from the division in a class society, in that surplus labor does not stand opposed to necessary labor, but certainly complements it," thus indicating the change in the social nature of surplus labor. He adds that, "socialism includes flexible freedoms which can be left to cooperative and democratic decision-making," suggesting the possibility of "unequal rights" that Marx notes (Itoh 1995: 133–134).

then at the higher level is resolved through the basic communistic principle of "From each according to his abilities, to each according to his needs!" (ibid., 87). For this to be a reality, the only solution left is an increase in productive forces.

On the other hand, Marx says that "Any distribution whatever of the means of consumption is only a consequence of the distribution of the conditions of production themselves" and criticizes those who consider "distribution independent of the form of production" as "vulgar socialists" (ibid., 87–8). In addition, he speaks of prescriptive ideas, such as the right to the "undiminished proceeds of labour," as "ideas which in a certain period had some meaning but have now become obsolete verbal rubbish" (ibid., 87) and emphasizes the special historical character of such prescriptions, thus warning against any simple universalizations.[7] In this regard, we must consider that it is necessary to understand the special historical limitations that the analysis of the time was based on, particularly with regard to the lower level of the Marxian future society.

While Marx criticizes individualistic and enlightened socialism, the first volume of *Capital* acknowledges some agreement between his future form of socialism and that of Owen.[8] Having said that, we need to consider why Owen thought it possible to use labor notes for confirming

[7] Obata criticizes enlightened socialists and says, "human nature is not a universal idea that transcends history, rather it is temporary appearance, an ensemble of social relations that is socially formed and is in flux" (Obata 2004: 16).

[8] As a consequence of Marx's criticism of Gray's labor money theory, Itoh expressed the view that "if social relations are formed in which the foundation of commodity production is changed, capital and land are transferred to national ownership, and labor is directly treated as social labor, the concept of labor money or labor notes can be fully utilized." This is mentioned in "R. Owen's *Report to the County of Lanark*, etc., since the labor note theory is combined with the idea of transformation into a cooperative society of agriculture and industrial enterprises... it escapes from the utopia of Gray's theory of labor money" (Itoh 1995: 56). With regard to this, Yoshida draws on "Owen's 'labor money' as not being 'money,' just like a theatre ticket is not money" from Marx's description and states that, "the emphasis here is on 'not being money,' not on 'being like a theatre ticket'." Since labor money based on individual labor does not solve "qualitative challenges," such as the demand for commodities deposited at the labor exchanges, it naturally must turn into "the ultimate challenge of abolishing 'money' which is, rather the defeat of labor money, and an abolition of the 'exchange'" (Yoshida 1995: 63–67). Yoshida's view suggests that "qualitative challenges" at labor exchanges can also arise in a "cooperative society" developed under a common ownership system. In this case, the better question is: How can "qualitative challenges," such as demand issues adjusted through the market mechanism, be managed in a "co-operative society"?

"the part taken by the individual in the common labour, and of his right to a certain portion of the common produce destined for consumption" (Marx 1996/1867: 104). Here, we will take a closer look at Owen's theory of labor notes.

From the Critique of Labor Money Theory to Owen's Valuation

As summed up in the previous chapter, Marx states, the "answer can often consist only in the critique of the question, can often be provided only by denying the question itself" (Marx 1986/1857–1858: 65). That is, Marx's critique indicates that the problem with labor money lies less in the abstract concept and more in terms of its application, and that it is a fallacy to identify labor money with monetary reform. A system of anarchic commodity production—wherein private commodity producers perform distributed activities of production that are adjusted for supply and demand after the fact—inevitably requires money. Therefore, to abolish gold money and replace it with labor money, it is necessary to construct a production system that corresponds to labor money.

However, if a production system were to overcome the anarchy of production, the bank that issues labor money would have to become not only "the bank that is both general buyer and seller in one person" of the commodity, but would also have to define the socially necessary quantities of production and standard of productivity, and allocate workers to each sector of production (ibid., 92). Thus, "In fact, it would be either the despot governing production and managing distribution, or indeed nothing more than a **board** to carry on the bookkeeping and accounting for society working in common" (ibid., 93). However, if social conditions are established where private labor time remains homogenous and equivalent to forms such as "communal labour time" or "labour time of directly associated individuals," labor money is no longer just an assumption or dogma (Marx 1987/1859: 322).[9]

Marx goes further by making the following assumption: "Let us now picture to ourselves, by way of change, a community of free individuals [einen Verein freier Menschen], carrying on their work with the means of production in common, in which the labour power of all the different

[9] Marx ridicules the contradictory attitude of changing the basics of production by only changing the form of money, referring to this as "smart gimmicks in the sphere of circulation" (Marx 1986/1857–1858: 60) or a "pious wish" (Marx 1987/1859: 322).

individuals is consciously applied as the combined labour power of the community," with participants in this community using labor time as a measure of the distribution of means of consumption and the planned allocation of labor (Marx 1996/1867: 89). Thus, how does this perspective of a "community of free individuals," which is considered close to what might be called the "theatre-ticket" society discussed as an assessment of Owen, differ from "a tyrannical administrator of production and trustee of distribution"—referred to as a logical consequence of the criticism of the labor money theory based on small producers?

In a note in Volume 1 of *Capital*, Marx states:

> The question — Why does not money directly represent labour time, so that a piece of paper may represent, for instance, x hours' labour, is at bottom the same as the question why, given the production of commodities, must products take the form of commodities? This is evident, since their taking the form of commodities implies their differentiation into commodities and money. Or, why cannot private labour — labour for the account of private individuals — be treated as its opposite, immediate social labour? I have elsewhere examined thoroughly the Utopian idea of "labour money" [Arbeitsgeld] in a society founded on the production of commodities.... On this point I will only say further, that Owen's "labour money," for instance, is no more "money" than a ticket for the theatre. Owen pre-supposes directly associated labour, a form of production that is entirely inconsistent with the production of commodities. The certificate of labour is merely evidence of the part taken by the individual in the common labour, and of his right to a certain portion of the common produce destined for consumption. But it never enters into Owen's head to presuppose the production of commodities, and at the same time, by juggling with money, to try to evade the necessary conditions of that production. (ibid., 104)

Therefore, Owen's labor money "represent[s] money, but only at ... this particular theatre." Marx says that the "bank ticket would have ceased to conform to the requirements of money" (Marx 1986/1857–1858: 92) and "the bank ticket would not be money, or would be money valid only by convention between the bank and its customers." In other words, Owen's labor money is like a ticket that can be used only by a specific theater where the audience gathers to watch the same performance. Such money can be considered as a ticket that can only be used by those who share a purpose and a place.[10] Such a theater-like society, wherein that tickets (circulating among the audience in the theater) can no longer be called money, is excluded from Marx's criticism.

Finally, it should be noted that Marx and Owen have different theoretical and ideological grounds regarding why labor time should be used as a measure of distribution. For Owen, the notion of labor time is deeply connected with the problems with human nature, which Marx denies.

The next chapter is devoted to a detailed development of Owen's concept of value, which is a confrontation between the natural and the artificial regarding value, but here the focus is on the criticism of civilization in *The Social System* (1826–27). There are basically two points of criticism of the artificial, or of civilization, in *The Social System*. The first is that his theory of value, which most likely has been strongly influenced by Rousseau.[11] The second point of the criticism of the artificial or civilization lies in what it can tell us about the acquired character of human influence on character formation, which leads to Owen's theory of character formation.[12] The logic approaches the theory of human nature, seeking the original image of the human being unexposed to the adverse effects of civilization; this method may be based on Rousseau's methodology, which assumes a "natural person," which is to say, a person who

[10] Nishibe states that, in "communities or cooperatives like 'theaters'," "the labor of all participants are considered to be 'socialized' and 'equivalent' from the beginning, so it is not necessary to demonstrate equivalence through exchange. Labor notes are not money that mediates 'exchange' in the market between individuals, rather, those should be understood as certificates that represent the share of contributions to the cooperative communities or the producers' co-operatives," thus explaining the connotation of a certificate without the character of money (Nishibe 2002: 268).

[11] Hijikata sees the commonality between the theories of Rousseau and Owen in the idea of a confrontation between the natural and the artificial, but their direction is quite the opposite. In other words, while Rousseau's "'natural person' is conceptually drawn from a longing for the beautiful natural state of the past," Owen thought that, "If science and technology are used reasonably, in the not too distant future, we can be 'rational beings' leading to happiness" (Hijikata 2003: 67). Even though Owen had a strong inclination toward the Enlightenment, he is more or less approaching a realist way of thinking.

[12] Owen's environmental determinism is expressed in *A New View of Society*, which was subtitled "Essays on the Principle of the Formation of Human Character," directly expressing that "*the character of man is, without a single exception, always formed for him*" (Owen 1993a/1813–1814: 62). The same applies to the proposition "[t]hat the character is formed *for* and not *by* the individual" (Owen 1993b/1821: 330).

exists in a state of nature.[13] Second, Owen states that "All things will be estimated by their intrinsic worth, nothing will be esteemed merely for its cost or scarcity, and fashion of any kind will have no existence" (Owen 1993c/1826–1827: 70). From such an explanation of intrinsic or natural value, it can be understood that Owen's ideal image of a human being is close to Rousseau's "natural person." Further, he develops a criticism of civilization, arguing that such ideas as "cost, rarity, and fashion" are only artificially created in "commercial societies." Owen criticizes the pursuit of artifice and artificially created value as a deviation from human nature, and he emphasizes the view of living a materially modest life that values inner and mental fulfillment. Furthermore, this perspective influenced statements such as: "'by the right application of the illimitable powers of science to enable society united to produce a vast superfluity of wealth for all.' The question now is, not how are we to become rich, but how are we to attain happiness, and secure it permanently throughout our lives?" (Owen 1993d/1842–1844: 127). Clearly, therefore, Owen was pursuing happiness in a dimension separate from wealth.

Through these views of nature, Owen advocates labor time as a standard for measuring the "natural value" of wealth. Labor notes as securities, which use a measure or unit, have "labor time" as the "natural standard of value." Owen sought to test two systems of labor notes: the bookkeeping and the paper-money methods.[14] Based on his account the *Report to the County of Lanark* Owen mainly used the paper-money

[13] As Smith describes "In that early and rude state of society which precedes both the accumulation of stock and the appropriation of land, the proportion between the quantities of labour necessary for acquiring different objects seems to be the only circumstance which can afford any rule for exchanging them for one another" (Smith 1976/1776: 65). However, the abandonment of "the accumulation of stock and the appropriation of land" through the abstraction of "early uncivilized condition of society" has much in common with Rousseau's assumption of the "rude state of society" abandoning civilization. Therefore, the "rude state of society" can be regarded as almost identical to Rousseau's "state of nature." Presupposing the "early uncivilized condition of society," Owen shared Smith's assumption that "different objects" had to be exchanged according to labor quantity. In addition, according to the Japanese translator's note in *The Wealth of Nations*, the "manner of perceiving civil society in contrast to a primitive society is... a basic view of society common to thinkers of the Scottish historical school, and a method of analysis" (Ōkōchi 1978: 81).

[14] Refer to Maruyama (1997) for the activities of the Equitable Labour Exchange in 1832–34.

method, but the bookkeeping method was also implemented.[15] In any case, this does not contradict Owen's claim that money should be non-metallic. The reason he gives for this claim is that the value of a product should not be expressed as the material value of money, but rather as a representative for expressing its intrinsic value. Therefore, the labor note can consist of any material and method, as long as it is an accurate representation of the labor time of the product.

From 1825, Owen spent two years on the New Harmony experiment in the United States. Although the experiment was unsuccessful, it is in accord with the lower stage of communism demonstrated in the *Critique of the Gotha Programme*. An account type labor note called the "time-credit system" was adopted in the community,[16] and it is interesting to note how the account method moved away from the original concept. However, as elucidated in the next chapter, the account method of labor notes was adopted at the beginning of the experiment, and was introduced as a mechanism for aggregating information on the entire community and performing production management. Under the account method, all transactions within the community were recorded in labor time. Then, to express the "intrinsic value" of all products and services in labor time, labor time for production had to find a commensurate measure and unit; in other words, the labor spent by each member would have had to be considered as being equivalent. Owen did not clearly develop the theory from which he derived equivalence of labor time, but its constituent elements can be listed as: (i) mechanical equivalence of each worker's labor, (ii) character formation theory, and (iii) wealth source theory. (i) Although there are clear differences in the labor power expended by each individual worker, when understood as a collective force on the premise of co-operation, the difference of each individual's power may be averaged and disregarded, which is known as the mechanical equivalence of labor.[17] (ii) The "character formation theory"

[15] Regarding Owen's plan in 1821 in *the Report to the County of Lanark*, he said that the "paper representative [of] the value of the labour" would be used in the community he proposed.

[16] Hijikata suggests that the bookkeeping method at New Harmony was an imitation of the "time-credit system" that had been conducted in the Orbiston community, an experiment that began in March 1825 (Hijikata 2003: 130).

[17] Assuming the counter-argument "that human labour or power is so unequal in individuals, that its average amount cannot be estimated," Owen said, "the average physical

stated in *A New View of Society* (1813–14) that the character and nature of human beings have been acquired or artificially distorted. According to Owen, the differences in the skills and proficiencies of each worker were formed posteriorly, not by innate or intrinsic differences. If the social conditions and social environments of each worker were improved, each worker would be free of differences, such as skills and proficiencies acquired through education. This would establish the fact that the factors causing differences in evaluating labor time of each worker are not essential, thereby establishing the equivalence of each worker's labor. (iii) In a roundabout way, this can be considered as the basis of the equivalence theory, and the idea of labor as a source of wealth can also be viewed as the equivalence of labor as a creator of wealth. Owen understands the problem of complex labor as a problem of skill formation and skills acquired through education and training, and that it is not necessary to evaluate the difference in labor based on complex labor when the opportunity of education and training was granted equitably and the cost was borne socially.

3.2 Relationship Between Labor Certificates and Local Currency

From Realizing Equal Quantities of Labor Exchange to Accepting Exchange of Unequal Labor Quantities

Incidentally, as long as one remains within the scope of the anarchic production, the difference between "a community of free individuals," a "society working in common," and "the despot governing production and managing distribution" is unclear. Thus, in the following section, I will focus on another aspect of New Harmony, as a "society working in common," which is its built-in function of income redistribution, unlike other cases of labor money based on independent small producers. The aim is to broaden my study of labor money by using this redistribution function.

One basic difference between the New Harmony model and the independent small producer model of labor exchange lies in the question

power of men as well as horses (equally varied in the individuals,) has been calculated for scientific purposes, and both now serve to measure inanimate powers" (Owen 1993b/1821: 292).

about whether the products of individual labor are viewed as social relations or personal income. When understood as personal income, labor money is a medium for realizing the rights to the whole produce and for the exchange of equal amounts of labor, but the situation is different in the case of labor that is understood as a branch of social reproduction. Societies include people unable to engage in labor, people receiving education, people engaged in labor that is not valued in the market, and those who work in interpersonal services. The labor of such individuals cannot be handled at labor exchanges, which employ a method of issuing labor money with labor products as collateral. This is because labor exchanges only understand labor as the process of physical production. On the other hand, in communities such as New Harmony, it is necessary to accumulate and share the social surplus for a system to assess the labor of these members, provide social security for the members not engaged in labor, and supplement for the depreciation and expansion of the means of production.

Although there are no provisions for supplementing or expanding the means of production in the constitution of the "Community of Equality" in New Harmony, it is stated that providing sufficient protection to those unable to work or those getting an education is necessary. The constitution states that "All the members of the Community shall be considered as one family, and no one shall be held in higher or lower estimation on account of occupation" (*New Harmony Gazette*, Vol. 1, No. 21, February 15, 1826, p. 162) and declares that the shift from distribution of labor notes proportional to labor time, to the ideal of distribution according to living needs. Such a view seems to be consistent with the description of labor certificates in Marx's *Critique of the Gotha Programme*. According to Marx, the "*equal right*" of distribution according to labor time is equal if humans are evaluated only as workers, which is a question of rights related to equality of opportunity. On the contrary, considering other social conditions, such as the circumstances of the individual workers, each individual needs to be given "unequal rights." The circumstances of individual workers include family structure, age, and gender (Marx 1989/1875: 87). Such "unequal rights" could be guaranteed through the accumulation of social surplus and joint funds. In terms of its content, it is equivalent to the unequal exchange of labor among its members. As a basic condition of social participation (if necessary for social reproduction and the accumulation of a surplus), the quality and output of products with the same amount of labor time must be unequal, in line with the type of labor expended and degree of skill—even though each member has to provide the community with the same amount of labor time. However, Marx's "unequal rights" are not a result of labor expenditure, but an exchange of unequal labor time treated as equal, consequential to evaluation from the perspective of the co-operation of participants and the universality of human labor in "communal societies" or "theaters." In other words, "unequal right," through a redistribution mechanism, will be implemented by exchanging the quantity of labor for equivalent labor.[18]

If the participants can accept such "unequal rights" and build a social relationship in which "the labour power of all the different individuals is consciously applied as the combined labour power of the community," it is no longer under the tyrannical control of production. In that sense, the distinction between a society controlled by "the despot governing production and managing distribution" and a "society working in common" may entail the participants' independent involvement and acceptance of the idea of participation with a joint purpose and place and an equal exchange of each person's labor. Homogeneity of labor stretches as far as the market views it and renders it unnecessary to recognize the criteria of the market in an economic system that does not entrust resource allocation to the market. Hereafter, "equivalence" is used to signify that components of heterogeneous labor are treated as equal. However, "homogeneity" may amount to the reduction of different kinds of heterogeneous labor to homogeneous labor. Unlike reduction, which attempts to bring heterogeneous labor units down to homogeneous units, the process of equalizing heterogeneous labor entails building consensus to acquire social acceptance. The relationship between time dollars and labor money and labor notes, as explained in the following section, will supplement the points stated so far, to a certain extent.

[18] After all, exchanging equal labor for labor quantities is nothing but replacing it by equal quantities of labor measured by external time (un-abstracted labor time). However, it does not imply a simple comparison of the amount of labor bestowed; rather, it evaluates labor leading to unequal commodity value as equivalent labor from the perspective of social necessity and community co-operation, and it exchanges unequal labor in terms of external time. In this text, the exchange of equal labor for equal labor is referred to as "exchange with equal quantity of labor."

Relationship with Local Currency (Time Dollars)

Briefly, the three aims of the time dollar are to correct social inequality, rebuild the community by evaluating non-marketed labor, and establish the equivalence of labor in marketed and non-marketed areas (Cahn 1999a: 499–500; 1999b: 43–45). In the following paragraphs, this subject has been discussed, taking a leaf out of Cahn's book, *No More Throw-Away People: The Co-Production Imperative* (1999b).

First, Cahn says that we should evaluate labor in non-marketed areas as that which creates the same value as created in marketed areas. Positively evaluating such a wide range of labor will make it possible to discover labor capabilities not used in the market, despite the prevalent ability to work, and open ways to use these capabilities. This is because time dollars and compensation are provided to people who provide labor in non-marketed economic areas, and this system, albeit with restrictions, can generate purchasing power. Furthermore, in using time dollars, since the value of labor is measured by participants' duration of work, the rarity of the product does not disrupt its value, thus ensuring stability of value.

One characteristic of the time dollar is that the focus of labor valuation has been expanded from the market to a non-market domain. Thus, time dollars are used as a monetary medium that can handle any form of labor and product.[19] The labor evaluated by the time dollar does not depend on the kind of object produced or the intensity and productivity of the labor expended. Thus, since each participant accepts the equivalence of labor, labor time may be mutually exchanged as a measure or unit, and goods and services may be exchanged for the time dollar regardless of the content of labor. If labor money theorists have a somewhat narrow understanding of labor as being something that only produces, Owen's ideas and the conception of the time dollar expand the purview of labor beyond the market domain or the capitalist production process to include non-marketed labor. This concept of labor also includes labor in the process of living—both non-capitalist production and consumption processes—rather than defining labor as just in a process of production. Moreover, it is not possible to support the exchange of units of labor time for each other with an equal quantity of equivalent labor while maintaining the

[19] For now, we can consider it to functionally have a measure of value, means of circulation, and means of hoarding. However, these functions are restricted so they are not fully exhibited.

concept of labor time, which otherwise emphasizes the act of production in the market area.

The concept of labor time for Owen and the idea of time dollars seem to emphasize time itself rather than production and labor. In other words, it is not a labor-qualified time. Labor-qualified time is that which can be understood as the time of life or livelihood that should be given equally to all people according to distinct lifespans. We suppose a certain period of time, and as each person can only have the same amount of time, the potential unit of time is a finite resource for contributing labor. If labor as this socially finite resource is narrowed down to labor in the process of production, the whole quantity of its expenditure will become the quantity necessary to maintain and reproduce society. However, it is not possible to narrow down the amount of labor necessary for production to merely productive labor in the market domain. From the perspective of social necessity, it is natural to attempt to conceptualize non-marketed labor and labor involved in life processes as an essential economic principle. Indeed, it is not enough just to expand the concept. It is the concept of production rather than the concept of labor that ought to be expanded. As has been mentioned before, non-marketed labor is labor if it is related to the concept of social reproduction through the commodity exchange process, and the non-marketed labor as it is a contribution to the others.[20] Therefore, what matters is not self-preservation but labor for the preservation of other people, and non-marketed labor can only in that sense appear in the process of exchange. Non-marketed labor cannot help being excluded from the category of productive labor owing to the capitalist production process. However, for supporting the process of reproduction in the commodity economy, it is undeniably labor. Labor expended for the repetitive maintenance of human society, whether marketed, non-marketed, in the production process or the consumption process, can be included in the inclusive domain of labor notes, as long as it is spent as socially indispensable labor.

[20] Areas of labor in non-marketed domains, including consumption and life processes, are called areas of reproduction. The labor involved in it is known as reproductive labor, and it is sometimes referred to as being inadequately captured in terms of the concept of production. However, beyond the conceptual sphere of political economy, the term reproduction is used in the sense of regeneration or sexual reproduction and cannot be considered inadequate.

Can it be said that, then, that time dollars are, as Marx noted, just "smart gimmicks in the sphere of circulation" that are labor money rather than a "certificate" or "ticket."? Labor money theorists argue that the goal was to transform society as a whole and to replace money entirely. In other words, society was supposed to be organized through the consistent principle of labor money; but this was not so for the time dollar. They acknowledge that money is an economically rational measure for achieving cost minimization in some respects. The ambiguous stance of the time dollar, which, on the one hand, identifies money as rational, while, on the other hand, criticizing the "external costs" resulting from a monetary economy is not what Marx and labor money theorists had assumed in their pursuit of logical consistency.[21] In this case, a space in circulation is still considered to exist between "tickets" and "certificates" on a certain scale, such as in time dollars.[22] The target area of labor notes seems to have been transferred from the market production domain that considered it a fundamental aspect of social reproduction to areas located on the outer periphery of the market-oriented production domain that is necessary to maintain society. Understanding the relationship between local currencies and labor notes will also prompt a reflection on economics that excludes the areas of reproduction outside of the market from consideration. The idea based on labor time was passed over to the modern time dollar, leading to the discovery of a new sphere of existence, a "variant of 'labor money'" (Maruyama 1997: 3).

Summary and Remaining Issues

Based on Marx's text, this chapter summarizes the inherent problems pertaining to the labor money theory and indicates that the economic system inferred from the logical consequences of the critique of the labor

[21] External costs of money constitute the according to Cahn (1999b: Secs. 7–8), can of selling and buying that result from the general availability of money, the outflow of money from the region resulting from free transportability, and the gap between the market price defined by its rarity and the need in people's lives.

[22] Time dollars adopt the method of replacing money issuance by recording an account of transactions on a PC. In this method, the basis for the issuance of money which appears as an asset of the bank is the absence of a requirement of commodity economic collateral at the time of issuing money, something that strengthens the relationship of trust between the community members (ibid., 97–99).

money theory is consistent with the idea of the New Harmony Community. However, the actual functioning of economic calculations using labor time as a measure/unit did not work well in New Harmony, and there was no planned allocation of labor. In addition, it swayed the normative ties in a community accepting the equivalence of labor. The next chapter addresses this point. Additionally, the constitution of the "Community of Equality" that embodied the equality of distribution did not necessarily insist on distribution according to labor time or exchange of equal labor amount. Similarly, Marx stated in his *Critique of the Gotha Programme* that the "*equal right*" gained by participation and contribution in labor—perhaps in the process of production—is a narrow concept that only accounts for those able to work, and "unequal rights" ensure distribution to members of the community according to their needs.

However, when considered within the framework of Engels' (1989/1880) utopian socialism, Owen's theory of labor notes was evaluated by Marx as a petit-bourgeois variant. First, it tries to scrap the private ownership system as the basis of the commodity economy. Second, while claiming to use labor time as a measure of distribution, it does not provide the right to the whole produce of labor, something which falls under the ambit of the petit bourgeoisie with claims to "unequal rights." And to add a point from the author's perspective, Owen was not merely a dreamer, but a man of action.

Although these issues have focused solely on socialist theory in previous research, this chapter reconsiders labor money theory and the labor note theory in relation to the local currency known as "time dollars." Not only do time dollars accept Marx's "unequal rights" in some respects, but also develop a new area, a non-marketed area, as a subject of the theory of labor money. This encourages a reconsideration of the traditional, narrow debates over labor money theory, and it also avoids a conception of the market as the main area of social reproduction, which was also an important concern in labor money theory.

Bibliography

Cahn, E. S. (1999a). Time dollars, work and community: From 'why' to 'why not?' *Futures, 31*(5), 499–509.

Cahn, E. S. (1999b). *No more throw-away people: The co-production imperative.* Essential Books.

Engels, F. (1987/1878). Anti-Dühring. In *Marx & Engels collected works* (Vol. 25). Lawrence & Wishart.
Engels, F. (1989/1880). Socialism: Utopian and scientific. In *Marx & Engels collected works* (Vol. 24). Lawrence & Wishart.
Hardach, G., Karras, D., & Fine, B. (1978). *A short history of socialist economic thought*. Edward Arnold.
Hijikata, N. (2003). *Robāto Ōen* [Robert Owen]. Kenkyusha.
Hirao, S. (1975). *Ricārdoha Shakaishugi no Kenkyū* [A study of Ricardian socialism]. Minervashobo.
Itoh, M. (1995). *Shijōkeizai to Shakaishugi* [Market economy and socialism]. Heibonsha.
Maruyama, T. (1997). Ōen to Zenkoku Kōseirōdōkōkanjo [Robert Owen and the national equitable labour exchange]. *Oitadaigaku Keizaironshū* [Oita University Economic Review], *49*(3–4), 1–32.
Marx, K. (1976/1847). The poverty of philosophy: Answer to the philosophy of poverty by M. Proudhon. In *Marx & Engels collected works* (Vol. 6). Lawrence & Wishart.
Marx, K. (1986/1857–1858). Economic manuscripts of 1857–58. In *Marx & Engels collected works* (Vol. 28). Lawrence & Wishart.
Marx, K. (1987/1859). A contribution to the critique of political economy. In *Marx & Engels collected works* (Vol. 29). Lawrence & Wishart.
Marx, K. (1989/1875). Critique of the Gotha Programme. In *Marx & Engels collected works* (Vol. 24). Lawrence & Wishart.
Marx, K. (1996/1867). Capital, Vol. I. In *Marx & Engels collected works* (Vol. 35). Lawrence & Wishart.
Nishibe, M. (2002). Shakai Kigyōka Ōen [Social entrepreneur Owen]. *Jūryoku 01* [Gravity 01], 256–293.
Obata, M. (2004). Gurōbarizumu to Genriron [Principles of political economy under globalism]. *Political Economy Quarterly, 41*(1), 16–27.
Owen, R. (1993a/1813–1814). A new view of society; or, essays on the principle of the formation of the human character. In G. Claeys (Ed.), *Selected works of Robert Owen* (Vol. 1). William Pickering.
Owen, R. (1993b/1821). Report to the county of Lanark. In *Selected works of Robert Owen* (Vol. 1). William Pickering.
Owen, R. (1993c/1826–1827). The social system. In *Selected works of Robert Owen* (Vol. 2). William Pickering; *The New-Harmony Gazette* (Vol. 2. No. 8, 14, 15, 17, 18, 19, 20, 21, 22, 23, 24).
Owen, R. (1993d/1842–1844). The book of the new moral world. In *Selected works of Robert Owen* (Vol. 3). William Pickering.
Saad-Filho, A. (1993). Labour, money and "labour-money": A view of Marx's critique of John Gray's monetary analysis. *History of Political Economy, 25*(1), 65–84.

Smith, A. (1976/1776). *An inquiry into the nature and causes of the wealth of nations* (R. H. Campbell, A. S. Skinner, & W. B. Todd, Eds.) (Vol. 1). Oxford: Clarendon Press (Ōkōchi, K. 1978. *Kokufuron* (Vol. 1). Chukobunko [Japanese Translation]).

Tezuka, T. (1926). Robāto Ōen no Rōdōkōkanginkō [Robert Owen's Labour Exchange Bank]. *Shogakutōkyū* [The Economic Review], *1*, Gesatsu [second part of two], 317–59.

Yoshida, K. (1995). Kahei "Gainen" toha nanika: Robāto Ōen to Rudorufu Hirufādingu [What is the concept of money]. *Robert Owen Kyōkai Nenpō* [The Annual Report of the Robert Owen Association], *19*, 53–75.

Newspapers, Magazines, Etc.

New Harmony Gazette (Vol. 1). New York: Greenwood Reprint, 1969/1825–1826].

CHAPTER 4

Labor Note Theories of Robert Owen and Josiah Warren

4.1 The Forgotten Stage—Labor Note Theories in America

In this chapter, we will be focusing on the development of labor note theories in America. Before doing so it is first worth recapping on the discussion so far. The theory of labor notes as developed by Robert Owen in the early nineteenth century was inherited by a variety of thinkers including Ricardian Socialists, Proudhon and other anarchists as part of their critique of money. Proudhon's adoption of labor note theory was set out in two major works, *System of Economical Contradictions: Or, the Philosophy of Poverty* (1888/1848) and *The Poverty of Philosophy* (1976/1847). Both books sparked controversy, and spurred Marx into developing a critique of labor note theory which remains influential to this day. Most notably Marx pointed out how labor note theories had focused exclusively on money, and not on the system of commodity production, based on private ownership that underpinned the market. Furthermore, that it would not be possible to displace money with labor notes without changing the mode of production. As a result of Marx's critique, labor note theory has become a neglected field of research in its own right, and thinkers like Owen have been too easily assimilated to the likes of Proudhon and other "petty-bourgeois socialists," who clung to a form of private property and market exchange.

© The Author(s), under exclusive license to Springer Nature Switzerland AG 2021

T. Yuki, *Socialism, Markets, and the Critique of Money*, Marx, Engels, and Marxisms,
https://doi.org/10.1007/978-3-030-80408-4_4

Such failure on the theoretical front was compounded by the political setbacks experienced by those movements that had experimented with forms of labor notes. Owen's New Harmony, the National Equitable Labour Exchange, and Proudhon's concept of the People's Bank had all run their course, and it is easy to see why collective term "utopian socialism," as deployed by Marx and Engels, had a ring of truth.

Under these circumstances, labor note theories had become to fall out of favor, but as we turn to the United States, things begin to look different. Josiah Warren (1798–1874) was a former resident at Owen's New Harmony who, despite some departure's from Owen's ideas, did much after the dissolution of New Harmony; he continued to maintain its legacy, by exploring the way he worked with Owen's legacy; we will hope to cast new light on how labor note theory lived on, and how America has come to be a "forgotten state" for theories of labor notes. But to do this we have to see people like Warren, not merely as the heirs of Owen, but as developing their own critical paths.[1]

As we have seen, labor note theories are based on the notion that there is a natural equivalence between all forms of human labor and this should be fairly recompensed. The theories assume that individual labor times can be uniformly compared and treated as the standard for the measurement of value. There are four critical issues that any labor note theory needs successfully to address: (1) its place within the system ownership (Marx's classification forms the standard here), (2) its ability to measure actual labor time and make it commensurable with other labor times, (3) the process by which labor notes could be issued, and (4) the relationship with the evaluation of products and labor in the market economy, or with monetary value. These four features are not always rigid, and various ideas were also proposed and tried by various theorists who inherited labor note theories. Yet as criteria for any viable theory of labor notes, these four issues have retained their validity and can be used as a framework for evaluating individual labor note theories.

[1] It is worth noting the bulk of studies into Owen are overly biographical, or that they fall into a tendency to think in terms of Owen's influence domestically in the UK and "foreign" adaptations of his thought and practice. Japanese studies of Owen and Warren include Tezuka (1928), Kasugai (1930) and Uga (1976). Tezuka (1928) and Kasugai (1930) refer to the Warren in terms Owen's heir, though he does admit that Warren was a pioneer in some respects, especially in terms of theories of labor exchange (Kasugai 1930: 18; Tezuka 1928: 83–84).

4.2 Owen's Theory of Labor Note—Proposing Labor Time as a Natural Standard of Value

Owen's theory of labor notes started out as a proposal for monetary reform as described in his *Report to the County of Lanark* (1821). From being proposal, it turned into a practical idea that he was able to trial himself in the 1820s and 1830s. These ideas gained currency in the period immediately after the Napoleonic Wars, in which the economy of the UK was blighted by overproduction, a steep rise in the collapse of small producers, and the deprivation of the working class, who had been hit especially by high food prices. Owen sought to address these challenges by developing his vision in "A View and Plan of the Agricultural and Manufacturing Villages of *Unity* and *Mutual Co-operation*" (Owen 1993b/1817a: 148). Owen's vision was based on the dual concept of "community construction" and "money reform," and the labor note would act as an internal currency that could be used solely within this community.

According to Owen, society was guided by the wrong principles. He noted how the Industrial Revolution had dramatically increased the productive forces of society, but none of this wealth had been used to improve the conditions of the working class. For Owen, the emerging "commercial system" (Owen 1968/1821a: 95), or "individual system" (Owen 1969/1825: 1) had to confront this question of how the jump in productivity could result in a better standard of living. His analysis focused on three features of the economic system, namely, (a) the wage system, (b) the money system, and (c) the commercial principle.

a. According to Owen, the direct cause of the economic depression in Britain after the end of the Napoleonic War lay in the sudden contraction of sales channels, making it difficult to adjust production activities that had expanded toward wartime demand—in other words, it created a crisis of overproduction. Moreover, as a subsequent response, capitalists, on the one hand, carried out a policy of devaluing wages and, on the other hand, shifted to labor-saving production methods, thus increasing unemployment. However, according to Owen, when overproduction is the problem, these measures to reduce demand are erroneous. Owen's view was that the best means for resolving a crisis of overproduction lay in the consumption power of workers who can stimulate demand if they have higher wages and a stronger purchasing power. Thus Owen can be credited for producing an early version of the underconsumption theory[2] (Owen 1993b/1817a: 143–144).

b. Owen considers money as a problem of the current social system, in which working people cannot enjoy the wealth enriched by workers, as can be judged from the contradictory phenomena of the increase in wealth and the overproduction depression that occurred simultaneously with the Industrial Revolution. According to Owen, the reason why the purchasing power of workers is not created is that there is a structural flaw in the monetary system in addition to the poor response of each capitalist. And, fundamentally, the reason for the limited purchasing power of workers is that the volume of banknotes issued by the issuing bank, the Bank of England, is constrained by gold reserve. Since the Bank of England is obliged to have a certain amount of reserves, it is not possible to increase the issuing volume alone beyond a certain ratio. According to Owen's analysis, the money supply has fallen into an absolute shortage due to the reserves of the issuing bank. Owen then stated that precious metals were ineligible for the preparation of money, based on the 1797 suspension on cash conversion. He added that it would be dangerous for the one-profit company, the Bank of England, to monopolize the discounting business that influences "the prosperity and wellbeing of community." Owen concludes that precious metals are called "artificial standard" of value and that "Money is the root of all evil" because it impedes the development of society (Owen 1993d/1821b: 290–291).

The precious metal, which is an artificially distorted "a standard of value altered the *intrinsic* values of all things into *artificial* values." What kind of "a standard of value" should be sought in place of precious metals? According to Owen, the redemption method to replace the English banknotes based on gold reserves is that means of exchange must be issued based on **"human labour,"** which is **"the natural standard of value"** of "its value in every article of produce." Therefore, it is necessary to define "the average of human labor or power" in order to use

[2] According to Nishizawa, "the problem for Owen is the danger of overproduction and underconsumption" (Nishizawa 1994: 149).

"human labor" as "a standard of value." Owen defines the nature of "*the natural standard of human labor*," that is, the "power of creating new wealth," and "the average physical power of men as well as horses ... has been calculated for scientific purposes, and both now serve to measure inanimate powers." Since "human labor" is a measurable force as described above, "its value in every article of produce may also be ascertained." Based on this "its value in every article of produce," the "exchangeable value" with other products is also determined. The value of "human labor" in things is also "the whole to be permanent for a given period." From this perspective of Owen, "human labor" is the power that humans spend. It can be understood that the value of "human labor" in a product is the amount of labor expenditure objectified to the product (ibid., 290–292, 301).

In another section, Owen said that "the amount of it [labour] in all articles" is "denoted by what in commerce is technically termed 'the prime cost,' or the net value of the whole labour contained in any article of value." He further states that "labour is the foundation of all values" and that "The profit of production will arise, in all cases, from the value of labour contained in the article produced," and "Its exact amount will depend upon what, by strict examination, shall be proved to be the present real value of a day's labour; calculated with reference to the amount of wealth, in the necessaries and comforts of life, which an average labourer may, by temperate exertions, be now made to produce." From the above, "the value of the labour" in a product is (i) the amount of labor expenditure, (ii) the portion corresponding to cost, and (iii) the amount of physical wealth produced by average labor expenditure. The corresponding part, three rules are given (ibid., 302–303).

Owen's conceptualization for "the value of the labour" also reveals the scale and units for measuring labor value. The "*intrinsic* values" in each product is formed by the labor of the producer, and "the value of the labour" in the product is the appropriately expended amount of labor included in the product.[3] Because it is possible as a measure and the unit

[3] However, if labor is not expended properly, it will diverge from the average amount of labor expenditure. Regarding this point, Maruyama mentions that "Owen calculated the average amount of human labor of various qualities, and measured the human labor of various qualities based on the average human labor" (Maruyama 1999: 62), considering the problem of "reduce to simple labor from complex labor." Certainly, there is respect which can be understood that it was working on the problem of complex labor by considering the divergence from "average amount of human labor," but the author thinks

when the amount of labor spent on each product exchanges, the value per unit of labor must be the same to serve as a "natural standard of value" for determining the exchange rate of products. The unit of measure for labor is time, as Owen proposes labor notes that displays the face value by labor time as an exchange method that adopts the "natural standard of value."

c. Owen explains that profits earned by reselling commodities whose supply is below demand and exchanging unequal amounts of labor under the "commercial system," even though equivalent amount of labor exchange is the only fair principle of exchange. This is because "a profit upon price can be obtained only, when *the demand is equal to, or exceeds, the supply*" (Owen 1968/1821a: 94). This commercial principle, on the one hand, includes the utilitarian goodness of "to produce or procure every article at the *lowest*" amount of labor, but on the other hand it also includes the injustice of acquiring "in exchange, the *highest* amount of labour" (Owen 1993d/1821b: 302). Therefore, even if the pursuit of individual profits in the commercial system provides the maximum benefit for a particular individual, it does not improve the benefit as a sum of the whole society. Therefore, it was necessary to devise a system where the benefit for the individual and the social benefit did not conflict. As described later, labor note theory guarantees personal benefits by preventing the fraud by the merchant beforehand, and it was proposed as a system where the benefit with others would not conflict by "equivalent amount of labor exchange."

Let us continue the examination a little more because the logic of this merchant criticism is the one to show Owen's market vision frankly. In order to make a profit in a competitive market where the price difference

that the face value of the labor note is only a detour indication of the market price, and the meaning of the labor time indication may be lost if only the market evaluation is reflected in the face value of the labor note in a form like piece wage payment. In addition, Owen might have assumed the tendency which converged to average labor by mechanization and large-scale industrialization while observing factory labor of New Lanark as an objective condition for the establishment of the average theory. Owen believed that the rational use of "British industry aided by its scientific improvements" (Owen 1993d/1821b: 291), such as machinery, could not only enable work beyond the limits of human physical strength, but also lower the degree to which individual skills must be relied upon.

due to resale is contested, there is an incentive to keep the supply of goods scarce with respect to demand. However, despite the inherent "*while the real interest of society requires that the supply should, at all times, exceed the demand*," merchants always scarce merchandise through acts such as buying and selling. Inevitably, it appears as a disruptor that prevents the fair distribution of wealth (Owen 1968/1821a: 94). The principle of commerce eliminated the inconvenience of bartering and motivated the pursuit of egoism and inventions and innovations, but on the other hand sharpened the interests of people. It also created the negative effect of pushing for deceptive product production methods.

One of the measures to eliminate such commercial deception is labor notes for fair trade, but as introduced at the beginning, Owen's social reform plan is integrated with "community construction" called "Villages of *Unity* and *Mutual Co-operation*." Here, we must explain the nature of the community as a recipient of "money reform." First of all, the "Villages of *Unity* and *Mutual Co-operation*" is the "Report to the Committee of the Association for the Relief of the Manufacturing and Labouring Poor" (Owen 1993b/1817a) and the "New State of Society—Address delivered at the City of London Tavern, on Thursday, August 21st" (Owen 1993c/1817b). As the title indicates, it was a measure to meet the immediate challenge of bailing out poor workers. It is a farmer-industry integrated community where 500–1,500 members live together on 1,000–1,500 acres of land. Owen does not directly apply labor notes to a society organized by the market. Despite admitting the market society to the outside, the inside has used the cooperative community organized by labor notes as the injection point of the fair principle. The inside of the collaborative community is organized as follows.

> By this arrangement they will receive all their external supply, and thereby render money, and all money transactions, wholly unnecessary; their labour by these arrangements will require no other representative than notes or vouchers, to be given when the articles are delivered at the appointed depot; these notes or vouchers will designate the exact amount of labour contained in such articles, which amount will be estimated upon equitable principles, ascertained and fixed by the Communities. Thus all bargaining, and *its degrading effects on the human character*, will be obviated.
>
> But even this stage of society will be but temporary; for, by the most simple arrangements, which will be beneficial to all, supply may be made so far to exceed any possible demand, that it will be discovered, in a comparatively short time, that all may use whatever they desire, without

the necessity existing for the intervention of any immediate or direct equivalent. (Owen 1968/1821a: 102–103)

"It is evident that the members of these communities *will be able, with facility, to create a considerable surplus beyond their own consumption*; this surplus produce they will exchange for the surplus produce of other similar Communities, by estimating the value of such surplus produce *in labour*, and *not in money*, as at present," he said that a co-operative community of the same type will expand in parallel and reciprocate surpluses with each other. In addition, in the early stage of the community, since it is not possible to be completely self-sufficient, they have to rely on an external market for supply, and "Their transactions with present society will, of course, be carried on by means of the usual circulating medium" (ibid., 102).

Because of this, it is not possible to completely escape the disruptive effects of the markets. However, once the community becomes large and wide enough, it will be less dependent on the market and will gradually secure internal stability.[4] Not only that, but because the community has a mechanism to create the demand amount corresponding to the production amount, it is possible to inform one's superiority "by means of competing for a short time with the existing commercial system" (ibid., 97). Therefore, on the one hand, each community has a policy of exiting other companies while acting as a company that is competitive with the external market, and on the other hand, it embraces a cooperatively organized internal society.[5] This is Owen's community strategy.

Labor notes are used within such communities and their name comes from the fact that labor time is the "standard of value." In the transaction using labor notes, the value of the product is measured and displayed by the hours worked in production. When each producer brings self-produced products to the community warehouse, they can receive labor notes for the labor time required for production. The products stored in the warehouse are displayed in stores at their value in labor time.

[4] Owen believed that labor notes could not be used in the "*old society*," that is, outside the community, as a guarantee that no external incentive to violate the inside of the community (Owen 1993d/1821b: 326–327).

[5] Owen's community is understood by multiple researchers as a company that operates an internal organization cooperatively (Nagai 1992: 63–65; Nakagawa 1984: 14; Nishibe 2002: 289–293).

The producer who receives the labor notes can use the labor notes to purchase the products produced and delivered by other producers from the warehouse, but in that case, they will receive the products of others that include only the same labor time as displayed on their labor notes. Through this mechanism, each producer first receives a labor note as a result of self-labor, so they can claim a legitimate share of all production results.[6] Then, when exchanging with the products of others, it is possible to realize equivalent amount of labor exchange through a labor note. For this reason, labor note theory is an idea that can include two ideas: "fair income" and "fair exchange." Owen claimed that the crisis based on the theory of underconsumption could be avoided if the issue of labor notes could give workers sufficient purchasing power.

The characteristics of Owen's theory of labor note can be summarized in four points: (i) Build a community based on common ownership as the basis of fair social life. (ii) Since human labor is understood as the natural and original creativity of wealth, and the unit of measurement of labor is considered to be time, each person's labor time should be treated equally. (iii) Issuing labor notes out of paper notes. (iv) Using labor notes as internal currency of the community. By the way, as far as it can be understood from *Report to the County of Lanark*, "In transactions using labor notes, the value of a product is measured by the labor time in production." The following actual operational problems may be hidden here. It is a question of how to measure the labor time of each person and to ensure the transparency of the measurement. If the measurement of the labor time of each person is self-reported, the suspicion of false declaration cannot be dispelled, and the standard will be a problem when measured by others. This issue is a subject that should be considered in the next section. Through examination, it will be clarified that the problem of measuring labor time is included as particular issue in the theories of labor note.

[6] Owen said, "Of this new wealth, so created, the labourer who produce it is justly entitled to his fair proportion" (Owen 1993d/1821b: 301–302), or "because labor is the foundation of all values, and it is only from labour, liberally remunerated, that high profits can be paid for agricultural and manufactured products" (ibid., 303). From what he said, "if we were to claim that Owen was demanding the total amount of labor he had bestowed, that would lead to the right to the whole produce of labor, but he was affirming his profit, the claim was invalid" (Maruyama 1999: 106). Rather than deny the profit category, Owen aimed to raise real wages by improving generous remuneration, improving the living conditions of workers, and increasing consumption expenditure accordingly.

From the above, it can be considered that Owen had prepared a program to annihilate money and implement labor notes through four processes. The first is that by changing the standard of value, which was likened to a standard of measurement, from a precious metal basis to labor, we denied the need for a third product to measure the value of the product. As a result, Owen's focus on money is not deepened enough, and his interest shifts to the distribution problem. However, the money problem, which is the main cause of the supply and demand discrepancy in the market at the static analysis level, will be avoided by changing this standard of value. Second, since labor notes can promise equality of demand and supply within the community, it is possible to provide conditions for continuing to increase productive forces without being restricted by underconsumption. Once the increase in productivity has reached the point where it exceeds the consumption desires of its members, the selfish motive for individual members to pursue money should also disappear (Owen 1993e/1826–1827: 68). Owen believed that it would be easy to exceed the consumer demand and to solve the problem of scarcity of commodities if the productive forces after the Industrial Revolution were used rationally for social prosperity. In excess of wealth, people will lose the motivation and need to have the means to purchase commodities. Third, Owen believed that private ownership encourages personal hoardings based on selfish motives, and thought that changing the ownership system to a community-based common ownership system would reduce the motive for private wealth accumulation. Finally, it is a collaborative idea that hopes to overcome selfishness and transform into a mutually beneficial person. Owen demanded that he be "*a rational being*" (Owen 1993d/1821b: 321) by explaining the need for human change, which is responsible for social change. It was not an image of a person, but rather an image of a human being guided by fellowship such as co-operation and philanthropy, and was a person who pursued social rationality rather than individual. Owen discovered money at the root of various social harms created by the market society and was trying to eliminate the social conditions that required money through community construction and labor notes.

4.3 Experiment of BookKeeping Method in New Harmony—Failure of Idealism

Owen's theory of labor notes was first practiced in New Harmony. Labor note theories criticize merchant behavior for pursuing "profit based on price differences" and promises "fair income" and "fair exchange," but that is not enough. Although the labor notes system is a condition that enables a fair relationship between members, it would be premature to think that a monetary system reformation alone would establish a cooperative relationship. This is also the reason why Owen was particular about the social form of a community based on a co-ownership system. Since money is a medium that represents the relationship between members of a community, the nature of the community can change greatly. Therefore, it was essential for Owen to build a community that would establish a labor note.

New Harmony was founded on May 1, 1825, with Owen purchasing the land and equipment of the Harmony Community, which was run by Rappites. In the New Harmony, Owen's thought was embodied in the constitution, and at the same time, it was set as a common goal of its members. The constitution can be understood as something like a movement policy, not just a statement of ideals. At the beginning of "The Constitution of the Preliminary Society of New-Harmony," it was declared that "*The Society is instituted generally to promote the Happiness of the World.*" After mentioning the purpose and obligation of the community, the labor notes system was mentioned as follows (*New Harmony Gazette*, Vol. 1, No. 1, October 1, 1825, p. 2).

> Each Family and individual Member shall have a credit and debit account, in which they will be charged with what they receive, at the prices the Harmonians usually charged for the same articles, and credited by the value of their service, to be estimated by the Committee, assisted by the persons at the head of the departments in which the respective individuals may be employed; the value of their services, over their expenditure, shall be placed at the end of each year to their credit, in the books of the Society; but no part of this credit shall be drawn out, except in the productions of the establishment, or in store goods, and with the consent of the Committee. (ibid., 3)

From this section, the characteristics of labor note theories in the "preliminary society" are as follows: (1) Common ownership system, (2)

The "value of the labour" of each member shall be evaluated by the committee, (3) A book method that does not use paper notes, (4) Internal currency. This can be understood, for example, "the value of the labour" of each member is arbitrarily ranked by the committee of the community. It seems to be inconsistent with the view in the *Report to the County of Lanark*, which states that "the value of the labour" can be measured by the labor time of the average worker. The ambiguity about the evaluation of this labor time is deeply related to the position of the community of "preliminary society." "Preliminary society" is given a transitional social nature to prepare for the transition to a "community of equality," which is a more "perfect community" (Brown 1827: 12–13) that Owen aimed for. In order to measure the value of labor directly by the labor time of each member, it is necessary to build a human-social relationship that regards "the value of the labour" of each member as equal. However, there will be no base where each person's labor time are considered equal for the member who behaved accustomed to the monetary evaluation in the market economy. Considering that it has become common knowledge that rewards can be given according to the result of labor under the market economy; "the value of their service, to be estimated by the Committee, assisted by the persons at the head of the departments in which the respective individuals may be employed."

On the other hand, if a social relationship is established in which labor notes directly indicate the labor value of each member by labor time, then according to Owen's doctrine, it can be said that the situation is the most equitable with regard to "acquisition of self-labor achievements" and "exchange of self-labor with labor of others." However, in a community surrounded by the market economy of circumference, the labor notes system for equity included the risk of transforming the system of unfairness based on commodity economy or monetary values, if it did not meet the share of normative values within the community and a certain standard of living. Therefore, in the "preliminary society," rather than implementing rapid equalization with respect to the decision of the labor evaluation, it took a cautious stance, and it provided as follows. In other words, it would be a lack of standard compensation for obtaining "the aid and assistance of men of science, and of great experience, as instructors and directors in the various departments, in which superior qualifications are requisite," so "for a time, a certain degree of pecuniary inequality." In addition, the "The Constitution of the Preliminary Society of New-Harmony" said that "But to change from the individual to the social system[7]; form single families with separate interests, to communities of many families with one interest, cannot be accomplished at once," adding that it would take two to three years to complete the transition, which is "the intermediate measures" designed to anticipate various resistance associated with the transition. And, it was understood that the inequality between members was decided by the inequality of the environment given to each person based on Owen's character formation theory, and the community where "we shall speedily lose every idea of personal inequality, except that which naturally arises from age and experience." These measures would have been a compromise, because the nature of the community as an isolated island floating in the ocean called the market economy would have required financial motivation (*New Harmony Gazette*, Vol. 1, No. 1, October 1, 1825, pp. 1–3).

However, this preparatory period exposed the structural difficulties in maintaining community reproduction. First of all, there were about 900 participants at the beginning. It was certainly due to Owen's fame that this number of people could be gathered at once. However, despite the fact that the scale of 900 people was larger than that of coexisting communities, it can be said that the productive capacity of the community was too large from the start. With regard to the number of members, not only the number of people but also its quality became a problem. The acceptance of the enormous number was based on the lack of understanding of what skills and how many people to hire for the operation of New Harmony.[8] As a result, they had an excessive working population and functioned as a workhouse for those who could not but be called "black sheep" or "idle persons" (Noyes 2002/1870: 35). These events

[7] According to Harrison, the term "socialists" by the Owenites "*emphasized a social, as opposed to an individual, approach in all fields of human endeavour—including, though not limited to economic organization.*" The term "socialists" also had the implication of "friendly" behavior and "*the purest principles of charity and good will*" (Harrison 1969: 46).

[8] In the *New Harmony Gazette* of 22 October 1825, only 137 artisans were actually employed. Only 36 of them were farmers. In addition, Bestor said that despite the industrial equipment provided by Rappite, the villagers are not using those equipment due to lack of engineers, and some production departments are producing more than they need (Bestor 1970/1950: 163–164).

confirm Owen's lack of preparation, which is a sign that New Harmony is a community that suddenly appeared. Rather than, as it was originally intended, labor notes correct the overproduction situation of "poverty in abundance," production could not cover the consumption needed in New Harmony at all. First and foremost, it was necessary to raise the internal productivity of the community to the level of England at the time, which Owen had presupposed to.[9]

William Owen (1802–1842) has complained to his father Owen about the plight of overpopulation and lack of housing and supplies (*Co-operative Magazine*, January, 1826, pp. 15–16). However, Owen was carelessly out of New Harmony and was not involved in the actual operation. While continuing the paternalistic governance that Owen's private expenses cover the financial loss of having a large number of redundant workers,[10] the "Constitution of the New-Harmony Community of Equity" proposed by Owen on February 5, 1826 is unanimously adopted. This constitution is based on "Community of Property," which states principles such as equality of rights and obligations (*New Harmony Gazette*, Vol. 1, No. 21, February 15, 1826, p. 161).

In addition, in "Articles of Union and Cooperation," economic reform of New Harmony is discussed. There, the equality of labor evaluation is stated: "All the members of the Community shall be considered and family, and no one shall be held in higher or lower estimation on account of occupation." By this provision, the "equal society" has the same function as the labor notes of the "preliminary society," but it provides the basis that the work of each member can be directly measured by labor time. It is then shown that the community is organized centrally. Specifically, "the duty of the Executive Council to make all contracts, to carry into effect all general regulations, and generally to conduct and superintend all the concerns of the Community." Then, the economic organization of the community is divided into six departments or sub-communities, under which groups for each occupation are formed. "The

[9] Owen generalized the dramatic increase in productivity of the cotton industry at the time, and assumed that the production capacity was rising in all industries, and therefore made a huge plan. The development of production technology had just started from the spinning industry (Asai 1953: 95).

[10] On June 5, 1825, Owen left New Harmony for publicity, and by the time he returned in January of the following year, he had already had a deficit of $30,000. Moreover, Owen was responsible for all the deficit (Bestor 1970/1950: 180).

Executive Council shall be reported, weekly, to the Assembly all the proceedings, accounts, receipts, and expenditure of each Department and Occupation," and any excess or deficiency will be adjusted based on the report, "all the accounts of the Community shall be balanced at least once in each month." Reorganization into an "equal society" centralizes labor and resource allocation to stimulate stagnant economic activities, eliminate inefficiencies in each department, and at the same time, it was a radical attempt to achieve economic and social equality all at once[11] (ibid., 162).

However, despite the constitutional stipulation that New Harmony is an equal society based on common ownership, most of New Harmony's property effectively belongs to Owen's privately. And the conversion of New Harmony from Owen's private ownership to co-ownership by the residents actually meant that the residents bear a huge debt and an annual interest rate of 5%. There was person using a "stern look" to write down the actual situation of Owen's rule, including this transfer of property. That person is the dissident anarchist Paul Brown.[12] Brown has been interested in New Harmony through the recordings of Owen's lectures and has participated in New Harmony since April 2, 1826 (Brown 1827: 14). It records the inside of New Harmony in Brown's book *Twelve Months in New-Harmony* (1827). He harshly criticizes this property transfer process as a betrayal of people who came from afar in sympathy with Owen's ideal (ibid., 31–32). According to Brown, Owen "was very anxious to secure by contract the value of the land, which profits on what he had paid, and the interest" (ibid., 20). What can be understood from these Brown's records is that there must have been a challenge of how

[11] Ueda called the labor allocation system that occurred after the adoption of the "Equal Community Constitution" as "a compulsory labor allocation system that rarely considers individual labor abilities." From the travel record of K. Bernhard, who observed New Harmony for a week from April 14, 1826, "Skilled workers quickly became frustrated with a simple accounting system that cannot evaluate individual work ability correctly. The labor quota system, which is implemented in the name of equality, caused the feud among the villagers as a whole" (Ueda 1984: 296–297).

[12] Hijikata defines Brown, a dissidentist in the New Harmony, as "anarchist" (Hijikata 2003: 119). Brown calls Owen's social criticism as in "religion or superstition, individual exclusive property, and political or legal marriage founded on one or both of the former, as the tripleheaded case of the moral evil and misery of the earth." The fact that he was a person with an anarchist tendency after William Godwin and Mary Woolstoncraft (Brown 1827: 33–34).

to transfer the New Harmony property to a common ownership system before the difficulties that the common ownership system had occurred.

The rapid equalization procedures associated with these top-down reforms by Owen led to some residents' opposition. Warren may have been included in this group of opponents, but it did not appear in the records at that time. Therefore, let us guess the real image of how the labor notes were operated based on Brown's records.

Regarding the bookkeeping method, Brown makes the following statement. Despite the direct democracy, the "Meetings were held every evening; and often several meetings in a day" have been a burden to the activities of its members, "what must have made it tenfold more wearing, was the monstrous undertaking of keeping book accounts, and rounding the incomes and outgoes of the whole, every week, in dollars and cents." In addition, Brown stressed the complexity and irrationality of the method, the "keeping accounts of every pennyworth that was consumed, and of every hour's labour that was done, provided it chance to be *proved* or came under the eye of a reporter, setting them down as debt and credit, ranking persons in certain degrees of character according to the number of hours' work that appeared against their names on paper, was the sterile and tasteless drudgery of a number of intelligent persons, who otherwise might have been productive of the necessaries of life." Originally, even though it was a labor note that was given the role of deepening friendship among its members, it was actually too complicated. Moreover, because the obsessions with "Mercantile ideas" and "some sorts of legal or mercantile instruments" that all balances were evaluated in dollars. It was said that the book-type labor notes "can never inspire a real community spirit" (ibid., 16–17).

From another statement, it can be pointed out that there are two levels of utilization of labor notes. Labor notes were not only used by individuals, but also between divided sub-communities. Each sub-community trades through labor notes, and the surplus remaining after offsetting credits and debts is stored in "a general merchant-magazine." Only the "society of external commerce" that oversees this "general merchant-magazine" was responsible for trading with the outside community for the purpose of cashing surplus products. Therefore, when sub-communities store their products in their warehouses, labor notes are paid in return. Since this passage clearly states "*labor notes*" rather than "account book," it can be pointed out that the book method and the banknote method may have been used together (ibid., 24).

Brown points out the following problems with the book method. First, there was a problem that the ownership of property in New Harmony is unclear, and co-owned farmland and privately-owned farmland were mixed and not clearly divided. As a result, sometimes it can be considered that one's own labor is not carried out on a common property, and only about three-fifths of actual labor time were recorded. The reason why the labor time were not properly recorded is that the right people were not monitoring who worked and how much. Second, in order to use the book method, (a) a record of the labor time spent in producing the product, (b) delivery and recording of the product to the warehouse, (c) withdrawal of the product from the warehouse and recording. It was said that the harvested vegetables had already withered by the time they reached the table because they had to go through the "ten thousand unnecessary steps" of bookkeeping (ibid., 26).

What can be understood from the first problem pointed out by Brown is that in New Harmony, each person's labor time were measured and monitored by others. If it were self-reporting, it would not have happened that it "had no credit given me (as I suppose) in the general reporting office for three-fifths of what I [Brown] did" (ibid.). Second, what Brown has repeatedly pointed out is that the implementation of labor notes in a book method complicates administrative procedures. What can be understood from Brown's record is that the transparency in operating the system was not ensured, although it was the theory of labor notes that should realize "fairness of income and exchange." And the paperwork of measuring and recording labor time would have been too complicated due to the technical level at that time.[13]

The change to equal distribution requires material conditions to be met. Moreover, it is considered necessary that the consciousness of the participants is changed to fraternity in which mutual labor is recognized as equivalent. Owen's decision was far from the reality of New Harmony, and it was too much for the residents to keep up with. Owen was "almost lunatic hurry" to move to a "Community of Equality" (Cole 1953: 155). His leadership was criticized for being patriarchal and dictatorial,

[13] Owen, after returning to England, inherited the co-operative movement that had already been in full swing in the UK, and started a shop in London in 1832 to trade the products produced by the co-operative, called a labor exchange. It is similar to Warren's Time Store in that it takes the form of a store without forming a community. This labor exchange used labor notes for transactions (Cole 1953: 180–184).

causing complaints that the residents criticized their personality. Especially, it was said that the opposition to the egalitarian distribution was great (Maruyama 1994: 11). In the first place, labor notes that receive a distribution in proportion to labor time are only meant to ensure the fairness of labor per hour, and it would not have been understood as to intend equality of results.

Owen's most important contributor, William Maclure (1763–1840), wrote in the *New Harmony Gazette*, May 17, that:

> To accomplish this object it has been tried, by individual reports of production, and making public the number of hours each was occupied in a day; the practice of which was rather invidious, and difficult impartially to be executed; and even if it were possible to get correct returns, it was liable to injustice; as one willing workman might do more in an hour than another without the same good will or industry, would do in four.
>
> It is perhaps better to divide the community into departments and occupations, allowing each to regulate the quantum that every individual in the department or occupation ought to perform, only fixing the aggregate quantity that the department or occupation ought to produce, as their share of the amount of property necessary to enable the society to fulfil their engagement. (*New Harmony Gazette*, Vol. 1, No. 34, May 17, 1826, p. 268)

As Maclure points out, the New Harmony "Executive Council" does not work at all, labor and resource allocation were not socially adjusted. Therefore, even if the same work was done, the labor productivity was different between members, and the worker who worked more efficiently would be undervalued, and that caused the sense of unfairness. It was even more difficult to secure fairness in labor evaluation between different industries. In addition, Maclure's recommendation that social allocation must be adjusted from the technical relationship between the social requirements of the products and the amount of work needed to produce them, which made us strongly aware that production plans are necessary to operate communities without market.[14] New Harmony's efforts resulted in some theoretical and practical challenges in introducing labor notes for fairness.

[14] Owen aimed to create an environment in which production capacity was the sole determinant, not sales potential, because the community would determine production plans based on necessity rather than profitability (Pollard 1986: 16–17).

New Harmony then split and reorganized several times, but on April 13, 1828, Owen admitted that the practice of this community had failed, and summed up the fact that the participants' individualistic behavior could not be changed by education as a major cause of failure. Owen expected that "moral qualities of forbearance and charity for each other" would grow (*New Harmony Gazette*, Vol. 3, No. 26, April 23, 1828, p. 402). However, such a man never appeared. Owen was originally claimed in the character formation theory that reciprocal people would grow only after improving their living environment, but the failure cause of New Harmony had contracted to the problem of the education and the cooperative thought. Thus, it was not able to recognize the allocation problem of labor and the resource to maintain and re-produce the securing of the material necessary for the member to live. As a result, Owen could not consciously grasp the problems including his own money and market vision, and in the community where money and the market were lost as a reflection of those visions. It could be said that it was not possible to proceed with the question of how to construct a framework that replaces the market mechanism.

4.4 Warren's Theory of Labor Note—Critical Inheritance of Owen's Thought

Warren's Biography

Warren was called "an inventive genius, a social philosopher, and a peaceful revolutionist" by sociological biographer Bailie (1972/1906: 1). He was born in 1798 in a Puritan family as a descendant of General Joseph Warren, a famous hero of the American Revolutionary War. He made a living playing in a band with his brothers, but married at the age of 20 and moved to Cincinnati. Even in that area, while working as a conductor of an orchestra and a music teacher, he ran a lamp factory and succeeded in obtaining a patent in 1823. However, when he listened to Owen's public speech in 1824, he was impressed by Owen's idea of human liberation in both moral and economic terms, and said, so then "Warren became a devoted student of Owen's theories" (ibid., 3). Owen's speech was also a publicity stunt for the New Harmony project, which began in 1825, so Warren soon decided to join with his family in New Harmony and sold the lamp factory the following year. However, after two years of experiments with New Harmony, Warren left New Harmony when he realized the obvious failure of Owen's plan. But rather dismissed the experience of New Harmony as a mere failure, he summed up the cause of the failure and found more appropriate ways of social change (Wunderlich 1992: 17).

Warren became disillusioned with the reality of New Harmony and began to severely criticize "the inadequacy of communism to correct the evils of private property, and the failure both of paternal authority and majority rule as forms of government" (Bailie 1972/1906: 4–5). This new harmony "two stormy years" (ibid.) is burned into the mind as an intense experience, Warren strived to overcome Owen-type communism for his whole life. He sought the cause of the failure of the New Harmony from the lost "the absolute **sovereignty of every individual**" (Warren 1967/1852: 18) and insisted on the revitalization of the community based on individual rehabilitation. Warren's theory of labor note reinforces the individualistic color in this context. Bailie, who wrote Warren's biography, described him as "*the first American anarchist*" (Bailie 1972/1906: xi), and Mill ranks among a group of liberal thinkers (Mill 1981/1873: 260–261). Warren independently improved the Owen-type labor notes used in New Harmony, tested it for two years from 1827 at the Cincinnati Time Store. The Time Store has gained momentum from its commercial success and will continue to be involved in community building.

After leaving New Harmony, Warren immediately took action and in May 1827 opened a store in Cincinnati called the Time Store that can use labor notes. After confirming the user's response to the Time Store, Warren was confident in his direction and closed after a two-year experiment. In 1833 he moved on to writing a magazine called *The Peaceful Revolutionist*, and at the same time, a community activity called Equity Village (1833–1835) was carried out. After the dissolution of Equity Village, he started his own business again. He focused on printing industry for 15 years, and received a patent for printing technology in

1846.[15] After that, he was involved in communities and was active energetically, such as Trialville, Ohio (1847–1858), sometimes called Utopia, and Modern Times, New York (1851–1863).[16] In addition, labor notes were used in Utopia and the Modern Times, and Utopia resident E. G. Cubberly said, the "labor notes put us into a reciprocating society — the result was, in two years twelve families found themselves with homes who never owned them before" (Bailie 1972/1906: 55). Among these activities, Owen's idea of the theory of labor note was clearly inherited. And it is interesting that the activities were enthusiastically carried out while making modifications to the content. It can be said that Warren's ideological maturity period is the most prolific period from the late 1840s to the 1850s, when he was actively involved in community activities. He left the Modern Times around 1860–1861 and spent the rest of life in his hometown Boston, but he continued to write until shortly before his death in 1874. In this chapter, along with Warren's theory of labor note, let us consider the case of the Time Store, which is thought to have opened up the beginning of these community construction activities and left various community activities for future research.

The Concept of Individuality and the Theory of Individual Sovereignty

Warren concluded that "all modifications of the plan were unsuccessful" due to the philanthropism that he experienced in New Harmony. He appealed for the need for "new principles" to replace Owen's ideas (common ownership, egalitarian distribution, and paternalistic governance) (Warren 1967/1852: 9). And Warren has developed the theory of *Equitable Commerce* (1852), which is composed of "five principles." The "individual sovereignty theory" and the "labor cost theory" described below are the two main pillars of "equitable commerce."

While investigating the cause of New Harmony's failure, Warren began to go back and consider what "individuality" was. "Individuality" is the

[15] The development of printing technology is closely related to Warren's theory of individual sovereignty. In order to establish individual sovereignty, "To be one's own banker, however, was not enough. A sovereign individual must be able to promulgate his views without the threat of censorship from the public press. A sovereign individual must therefore also be his own printer" (Stern 1980: 11). The development and popularization of cheap and easy publishing machines have been a challenge that Warren has continued to pursue since the New Harmony.

[16] For each community, refer to the dictionary study by Fogarty (1980).

"first principle" in Warren's claim of "equitable commerce." According to Warren, "diversity is *inevitable*" that arises from "the peculiarities or Individualities of persons," and this difference establishes a boundary with others (ibid., 15). And, due to "indestructibility or inalienability of this Individuality" such as preferences and sensitivity, "grows the **absolute right** of its exercise, or the absolute **sovereignty of every individual**." This is the "second principle" (ibid., 18). In the following, we will discuss in detail the development of ideas from the "first principle" to the "second principle" along with Warren's text.

First, Warren described "Society is a complicated machine" at the beginning of Chapter 2 "**Means for the Attainment of Our Proposed Ends**" of *Equitable Commerce* and developed a kind of mechanism theory. Then, it shows the recognition that the new elements making up modern society are the drivers of social transformation. For example, he states that while the inventions of steam engines and spinning machines materially change the working class, the invention of printing technology is creating the conditions that enable the peaceful transformation of human beings. While he notes that ideas such as peace and love for humanity transform the lifestyles of people, new academic discoveries such as neurology are becoming more important as constituents of society. However, it states that "**the Study of Individuality**" is the "first element of Equitable Commerce, or rather the foundation of the whole subject" (ibid., 14–15). According to Warren, the fundamental social element is individuality, and the concept of individuality consists of three points. These are individuals' (a) differentiation, (b) individualization, and (c) boundaries, respectively. Therefore, in the following, it is necessary to consider not only the theory of individual sovereignty but also Warren's concept of individuality, which is the basis of the whole "equitable commerce theory."

a. Warren begins with an explanation of the ambiguity of words to illustrate the first aspect of individuality. "It assumes different significations in different cases. We sometimes use it as a substantive, sometimes as an adjective, sometimes as a verb. Different persons understand it differently in either form; and the same person will understand and appreciate it differently at different times, according to different degrees of development and different states of mind, under different circumstances. Such is the indefinite diversity that will spring up out of the peculiarities or Individualities of persons, times, and circumstances, when the word is used; and this diversity *is inevitable*" (ibid., 15).[17] In addition, personal characteristics such as taste, poetic emotions, aesthetics, and sensibility are formed through "nature's constant production" (ibid., 17); if it is inevitable, human differences will inevitably occur. If environmental differences are inevitably given to individuals, human differences would also be inevitably occurred. Because the differences are natural to human beings, "Out of the indestructibility and inalienability of this Individuality grows the **absolute right** of its exercise, or the absolute **sovereignty of every individual**" (ibid., 18). Here, Warren described the characteristics of individuality as an "indefinite" and "subtle" difference, which can be understood that they are indefinite and difficult to capture (ibid., 15–16). Individuality is a fundamental element of society, but because it has a fluid and uncontrollable nature, it has the inviolability that cannot be touched by each other and the individual is clearly separated from the others. The diversity of human individuality makes it difficult to model a specific human image from a simplified lifestyle and behavioral pattern, thus denying the viability of laws and institutions designed on the basis of certain human behavior. Therefore, it can be said that individual sovereignty is the absolute right for an individual to act freely according to their individuality.

Regarding the deductive logic of such a concept of individuality, it is possible to observe the ideological succession relationship with Owen. The point is that Warren did not confer human personality innately, but rather differentiated due to constant influence from the environment. This environmental determinant is reminiscent of Owen's theory of character formation, "That the character is formed *for* and not *by* the individual" (Owen 1993a/1820: 330). Owen emphasized the acquired

[17] Owen discusses "the Formation of Human Character" in which the difference in human character is formed by the acquired influences such as the environment. Owen claimed that human differences are not intrinsic by emphasizing the acquired nature of character formation and considering natural states with little human influence. In contrast, Warren stated that human differences may be considered to be intrinsic. Because human differences inevitably occur, if the natural effects on humans are unequal. It is the denial of Owen's view of humanity.

character of environmental influences on character formation. While interpreting that human innate differences can be ignored, he pursued the original equality of humans, and at the same time pointed out the possibility of human transformation by creating an ideal environment. On the other hand, Warren said that even though the environment forms the character of human beings, the way in which the environment has an impact is so diverse. It argues that human character and differences will inevitably occur, which takes Owen's argument to the contrary.[18]

Moreover, since the inviolability of individuality is the basis of individual sovereignty, individual sovereignty forms its own institution and custom and is incompatible with other authorities and laws. Since all laws and institutions are predicated on individual "obedience" to laws and institutions and individual "uniformity," they cannot match human nature. Thus, it can be said that "a fundamental error [of society] in human legislation" (Warren 1967/1852: 19). Therefore, by law or institution "as it is both inexpedient and impossible to overcome this Individuality, we must *conform our institutions* **to it**!" (ibid.).

b. Warren presents a question using the following example to explain the second aspect of individuality. That is, "When one finds his different papers, bills, receipts, orders, letters, etc., all in one confused heap, and wishes to restore them to order, what does he do but *separate*, *disconnected*, *divide*, and *disunite* them—putting each *Individual* kind in an *Individual* place, until all are *Individualized?*" (ibid., 20). Warren pointed out metaphorically that the cluttered situation of various types of documents piled up in piles is like the diversity of the participants who gathered at the New Harmony created the confusion in the community.[19] The situation

[18] This point is related to the understanding of the environment. Warren considered the existing environment to be self-explanatory, and thought that differences in the environment create individuality of human beings, so the environment is natural. However, Owen thought that the current environment is a civilized society, and the general environment cannot be regarded as natural. Therefore, in the environment of civilized society, Owen diversifies humans due to differences in environment, and at the same time creates a conflict of religious and economic interests. But in a natural and ideal environment, it was inferred that humans would regain their original harmonious form and become "*a rational being*."

[19] For the confusion caused by the participation of people with diverse tendencies, refer to Lockwood (1971/1905: 82–83).

in New Harmony is like a mess caused by "If a multitude of ideas crowd at once upon the mind of a speaker or a writer." In order to prevent such confusion, "*divide* his subject, *disconnected*, **disunite** its parts, giving to each an *Individual* time and place" (ibid.). In other words, Warren clarifies the differences in views by recognizing the individuality of each individual, avoiding confusion and standardization of each individuality, emphasizing the point of establishing individual autonomy. In addition, Warren draws an example like a musician, in which a chord consists of sounds that are independent of each other. That is to say a sequence of identical notes does not play any music, which states that social harmony also consists of independent individuals (ibid., 22).

c. Third, Warren discusses the definition of the boundaries and areas of individuals or individuality, based on the illustration of individual differentiation and individualization. According to Warren, the process of political progress is reflected in the demarcation and separation of various elements. For example, the separation of politics and religion is based on the freedom to interpret the Bible according to a personal view, which is a remarkable achievement of the Reformation for freedom and harmony. Furthermore, whereas the combination of interests involved in various collective forms of organization obscures individual responsibility, individualization of interests makes individual responsibilities clear. Therefore, "Responsibility must be *Individual*, or there is no responsibility at all" (ibid., 23). As described above, if we recognize the differentiation and individualization of individuals illustrated by Warren, "the *right of supreme Individuality must be accorded to every one*" (ibid., 24). On top of that, there is a reservation "each can exercise his right of individuality *at his own cost*" without repressing the individual's freedom and sovereignty (ibid.). In other words, "cost" is the only standard that can be quantified for each individual to enjoy absolute sovereignty and to harmonize with the sovereignty of others. The "cost" of each person, which is determined based on the individual's sovereignty, defines each person's boundaries, or areas of sovereignty.

From the above study of the concept of individuality and the theory of individual sovereignty, Warren's consciousness of society can be summarized as follows. First, uniform legislation and institutions that do not recognize human differences impair individual independence and the right to self-determination. Second, Owen-type communities and organizational forms based on the combination of interests such as governments and companies obscure individual responsibility in order to bury individual interests in the interests of the group. This point is also related to individual decision making. Third, based on the above two points, it is necessary to determine the sovereignty domain and boundaries of each person in order to avoid mutual conflict and personal harmony of individual sovereignty. Starting from the awareness of issues, Warren questioned the existing organizations, and based on consideration of individual peculiarities, was eager for a society where individual freedom could be maximized.

Pare, a theorist of Owenite, explained Warren's "doctrine 'the Sovereignty of the Individual'," saying that "individuality can only become the law of human action by securing to each individual the sovereign determination of his own judgement." However, the scope of "the Sovereignty of the Individual" must be defined in relation to others, "the prerogative of others whose sovereignty the doctrine equally affirms" (Pare 1856: 129). And the limits of "the Sovereignty of the Individual" are defined by whether an action brings "*agreeable* consequences" to others. If you want others to do something that you do not agree with, it imposes "endurance, or burden" on others, and "the term '*cost*' is elected as a scientific technically" (ibid., 130). Based on this understanding of "individual sovereignty," any institution or government will be denied by Warren because it will suffocate the diversity of individuality and the independent decisions of individuals. Therefore, it can be said that the harmonious principle of society is only required for "the Sovereignty of the Individual" or "absolute personal liberty" (ibid., 131). Warren says that "**Liberty** is the vital principle of human happiness; and human nature seeks its *liberty* as the magnet seeks the north, or as water seeks its level" (Warren 1967/1852: 12). It would also be a backlash against Owen's governance of New Harmony that had undermined the autonomy of its members.[20]

[20] According to Wunderlich, Owen's "top-down leadership" and "cohesion principle" suffocated the independence of individual members. And the turmoil of New Harmony has made Warren an "extreme anti-communist," and Warren's construction of the Modern Times community was guided by the "rejection of the New Harmony," not by scientific evidence (Wunderlich 1992: 17–18).

According to Bailie, "Accounting for the shattered hopes and unrealized aspiration at New Harmony, Warren believed that the chief causes were the suppression of individuality, the lack of initiative and responsibility" (Bailie 1972/1906: 6). In addition, "consistent interests for all members do not imply responsibility for all members" and criticized that a majority decision would suppress individual will, and claimed that humans have a "propensity for freedom" by nature. It can be presumed that "consistent interests of all members" refer to the responsibility structure in the joint ownership system of New Harmony. Warren said, "Responsibility must be *Individual*, or there is no responsibility at all," he said, adding that the theory of individual sovereignty also included the meaning of attributing interests to individuals and clarifying individual responsibilities.

Cost Concept and the Theory of Labor Note

As studied in "*The Concept of Individuality and the Theory of Individual Sovereignty*" of 4.4, individual sovereignty is established based on the inviolability of individuality, and the area is defined by the "third principle" of "**cost the limit of price**" (Warren 1967/1852: 11), or "labor cost theory." In this section, we will examine Warren's cost principles and then consider the theory of labor note as the development of a concrete system based on the cost principle. There are three derivation paths in cost concepts. The first point is based on the request that the area of individual sovereignty be decided. Second, it is based on the criticism that the transaction based on the market price is unfair. The third point is a criticism of Owen's concept of fairness. Since the first request theory has already been considered, let us clarify the reality of the cost concept in this section through discussions on "The proper, legitimate, and just reward of labor" among the "**problem to be solved**" in Chapter 1 of *Equitable Commerce*.

Warren said that "It is now evident to all eyes, that labor does not obtain its legitimate reward" due to the rapid decline in wage levels over the last 20 years, presenting a situation in which productive workers are being forced to live a difficult life because they are unable to get their own products. He said that it is important to consider "a discrimination, a *disconnection*, a **disunion** between **cost** and *Value*" in order to address "the great problem of its just reward," to defend "the right of labor," and to get out of poverty. Warren thinks the root cause of the problem lies in the injustice of the exchange. To start with, "*value*," despite the fact that labor is not objectified, is defined as being "*what it will bring*." In turn, "*The price of a thing should be what it will bring*." This definition is abstract and difficult to understand, so Warren uses concrete examples of water. In areas where water is plentiful, the value of water is equal to zero, but it is self-evident that it has great value for those who suffer from drought. Therefore, because the value is decided regardless of the amount of labor bestowed or real inputs put into the product, it reflects only the rarity and urgency of demand for individuals (consumers). The value not only varies depending on the psychological and material condition of the individual, but also the problem of demanding more money for those who are urgently in need.[21] Price-based transactions representing this value inevitably become speculative because they benefit more by artificially creating desires and cravings in the community. Let us assume that such a transaction is done to a certain amount of bread which makes a major item of the wage basket for instance. In that case, "The *value* of a loaf of bread to a starving man, is equivalent to the value of his life." Thus, because the bread value is enlarged by his poverty, it will make "his whole future life in servitude as the price of the loaf!" This "value principle" is the motto of the current commerce, and the price determined by "its *value* to the receiver [buyer]" rather than "its cost to the producer" is the basis for speculative trading because it fluctuates in the short term due to changes in demand. The buying out and holding off on the selling would result in destabilization the lives of workers. Warren accuses that the modern way of commerce demands unjust profits by looking at the feet of people who suffer from deficiency. It is not an exaggeration to say that is "civilized cannibalism." Furthermore, "value" without an objective principle of determining labor is a volatile standard of exchange, including the uncertainty of trading. Therefore, under the current commercial, producers must live in accordance with merchant transactions that pursue price differences in the future and cannot escape poverty (Warren 1967/1852: 40–42).

Warren then presents a "cost principle" instead of "value principle." Warren's "cost" means "labor as a sacrifice" objectified at a product.

[21] Of course, Warren admits that music and information are also valuable, and that it has a lot of value compared to its usefulness. However, no matter how useful they are to consumers, it does not involve any cost in terms of the bestowal of labor as well as the real input. Warren calls emotional exchanges such as music "*moral commerce*," and talks about conversations and provided useful information as "*intellectual commerce*," and distinguishes them from general commercial transactions (Warren 1967/1852: 44).

If the price is decided according to the amount of sacrifice associated with production, the merchant loses the basis of speculation because "costs" are fixed and price fluctuations are eliminated, and the exchange of "*equivalent* labor" (ibid., 42) will be conducted between producers and merchants. Warren argues that this "cost principle" makes speculative transactions impossible, and at the same time solves the needs of producers. But for Warren, who counts "*hour for hour*" exchange as one of the causes of New Harmony's failure, he could not claim "equivalent amount of labor exchange," which simply regarded the labor time of each person as equivalent.[22]

So, what kind of deal is fair? As in the previous example, "If the producers and venders of the bread had bestowed one hour's labor upon its production and in passing it to the starving man, then some other articles which *cost* its producer and vender an hour's *equivalent* labor, would be a natural and just compensation for the loaf" (ibid.). He said that the idea of "*equivalent* labor" is the point to emphasize, "because it appears that we must *discriminate* between different kinds of labor, some being more disagreeable, more repugnant, requiring a more **costly** draft upon our ease or health than others. The idea of *cost* extends to and embrace this difference. The most repugnant labor being considered the most **costly**" (ibid., 42–43).[23] Here, the meaning that Warren emphasizes the uniqueness of the concept of equivalent labor is clearly linked to Owen's criticism for the concept of fairness. As mentioned in the preface to *Equitable Commerce*, even though it contains Owen's criticism throughout, the point is not clearly stated, so it is hard to understand what Warren is developing such a discussion with just reading it.[24] However, in *Practical Details in Equitable Commerce* (1854), the idea

[22] Hall notes that Warren "was aware of the usefulness of different wages as an incentive mechanism" (Hall 1974: 99). However, Warren's interests are limited to the evaluation of heterogenous labor, and "labor cost theory" brings a difference to the evaluation of different types of labor does not necessarily admit the wage gap, because he considers "labor cost theory" as a standard for fairness. Because not only is the wages decided in the labor market determined based on "value principle," but also Warren's consideration is that, unlike wage labor and corporate organizations, they are aimed at independent producers in the community.

[23] Warren's concept of cost was then organized by S. P. Andrews into three elements, "intensity ('amount of repugnance overcome'), time, and skill" (Schuster 1970: 110).

[24] Warren had to come up with a new principle, since the plan proposed by pure philanthropism failed, as the New Harmony's two years of experience showed in the

of Owen's equivalent amount of labor exchange is not a fair exchange because it does not consider the concept of cost (Warren 1854: 14).[25] When Warren understood the theory of labor note as a means of fair exchange, Owen considered each person's work to be equivalent, but "the proposition of Robert Owen to exchange *hour for hour*. This was seen not to be perfect, because some labors were harder than others," Warren emphasizes the "toil and trouble" of labor. It is an argument that labor is not something that can be uniformly evaluated by labor time, because the labor burdens on workers differ. Therefore, according to Warren, "fair exchange" is not based on equal amount of labor, but "an exchange for *equivalents—Labor for Labor*" including equal burden (ibid., 13–14). This is the third rationale for the deduction of Warren's cost concept. Therefore, fair exchange in equitable commerce is equivalent labor in a sense different from equal amount of labor, in other words, labor exchange involving the same amount of cost and sacrifice. Therefore, according to Warren's description, the labor cost is defined by "labor time × labor discomfort," and this labor cost determines the "**cost the limit of price**" (Warren 1967/1852: 11).

From the above explanation on the "cost principle," "**circulating medium founded on the cost of labor**" as the "fourth principle," that is, Warren's theory of labor note (ibid.). This is the most minimalist system that constitutes equitable commerce. The mechanism of labor notes was an idea proposed by Owen in 1821 to solve the unemployment and poverty of workers. Although it has the same name by Warren, it has different principles and methods.[26] As pointed out earlier, Owens thought that the principle of fairness was equality of each person's labor

preface to *Equitable Commerce* (Warren 1967/1852: 9). From this perspective, it can be inferred that Warren's proposals underlie the criticism of Owen.

[25] It is worth noting that Warren understood Owen's theory of labor note as a concept of equivalent amount of labor exchange, which did not consider the burden and difficulty of labor. It cannot be said that Owen consistently insisted on equivalent amount of labor exchange as "*hour for hour*" exchange. There are historical materials that can be used to confirm whether equivalent amount of labor exchange was carried out at New Harmony. Because it had been scattered, it was unclear how Owen emphasized equivalent labor exchange. But Warren's discourse could be read as a valuable resident testimony, suggesting that Owen emphasized "*hour for hour*" exchange in New Harmony at least in theory.

[26] Owen says that "A paper representative [of] the value of labour, manufactured on the principle of the new notes of the Bank of England, will serve for every purpose of their domestic commerce or exchanges, and will be issued only for intrinsic value received

and equivalent amount of labor exchange, while Warren argued that the cost of labor should not be measured solely by time, but must take into account the degree of burden, including pain and intensity. By the way, Warren makes a statement as if he/she accepts the disparity in the homogeneous labor by using the expression of the difference in burden, but this is not the case. The degree of labor burden is considered to be almost constant from job to job. Therefore, the difference in the degree of labor burden can be expressed as the difference in occupation and work.[27]

Owen and Warren also differ in the method of issuing and using labor notes. First, in the case of Owen, all the products of the community are once stored in the warehouses and banks of the community, and in return, each member receives a labor notes commensurate with the time worked. Each member uses the received labor notes to consume the products of the community. Through this issuing process, it is possible to confirm the equality of the labor time of each person and carry out production management and welfare business for the whole society. It can be said that this method is based on egalitarianism and emphasizes supply and demand management and sharing of a sense of purpose throughout society.

However, Warren's diagnosis has the drawback that the issue of notes and the social management of production and distribution create a combination of interests and impair individual responsibility. It is synonymous with the loss of individuality or sovereignty. Therefore, the functions of issuing and production need to be put back into the hands of individuals. In addition to acknowledging the difference in burden between occupations, there is also the view that admitting any difference by profession in the exchange rate of labor time recognizes the individuality of the individual. Based on the above arguments, labor notes are issued as follows. That is, when producer A purchases product B' from producer B, A enters his job type and labor time in the notes as a promise of future payment, and then the seller of product B' must sign and judge the validity of the

and in store" (Owen 1993d/1821b: 326). This intrinsic value is the amount of labor measured by labor time.

[27] The calculation method of labor cost is as follows. When producing a certain product, the labor time spent by the producer is the basis, and the labor time is multiplied by the labor cost associated with a specific occupation (including burden such as unpleasantness and discomfort). Various expenses will be added, and the training period for skill formation will be added as a weight of cost. Since the monetary price is basically used for the raw material cost part, the labor cost is calculated only for the labor directly bestowed for production (Warren 1967/1852: 42–45).

consideration written on the notes. For example, if a carpenter warrants ten hours of carpentry labor to be paid in the future to purchase a product from another producer, it needs to be written on the labor notes, "*Due to the bearer, ten hours' labor in carpenter work, or three hundred pounds of corn.*" A transaction is completed by adding the signatures of the buyer (carpenter) and the seller to this. Through this transaction process, individual sovereignty of self-issuing notes and decision-making regarding production is secured. Grain volume and labor costs together on the note because carpenter labor may not meet the needs of bearers, and at the same time, a standard is needed to compare the costs of carpenter labor and other labor. The reason why grain is chosen as a real criterion is, in addition to the fact that it constitutes a major part of livelihood, and the "labor cost" for grain production is fixed on average in a certain area. Besides, it is actually inconvenient to pay a bearer of labor notes in "*ten hours' labor in carpenter work*," and it is more convenient to show the equivalent of the same labor. The "labor cost" of a carpenter is also calculated as a standard for comparing the difficulty of this type of grain production labor between different types of labor. In this example, two minutes of labor per pound of corn are covered, so ten hours of carpentry work is equivalent to ten hours of grain production labor (ibid., 107–108, 116–117).

Above, let us sort out the meaning of the fixed cost concept and labor note theory. First of all, the value that fluctuates according to the urgency of personal demand is the basis of speculative transactions and cannot be the principle of equitable commerce. Secondly, labor is not average and homogeneous as Owen envisions, because each occupation has different pains and labors. It is necessary to have a cost concept that can be weighed considering the extent of those burdens. And this cost became the principle of equitable commerce that also determines the domain of individual sovereignty. Thirdly, transactions based on the cost principle must be done through labor notes. This is because, if individual sovereignty is incompatible with sovereignty of different instances, money and notes must be issued individually. At that time, the creditworthiness of the labor notes issued by each person will be secured by the certainty of payment by the payer and the integrity of the labor paid (and the resulting labor product). It can be said that it is decided within the scope of self-responsibility. The theory of individual sovereignty developed in "*The Concept of Individuality and the Theory of Individual Sovereignty*" of 4.4 was expanded to the area of exchange by meeting others through the mechanism of labor notes. Warren further indicates various methods of application, assuming that individual sovereignty and costs can be applied to other areas as a social formation principle of equitable commerce. In addition, as will be described later in the next chapter, Pare clarifies that Warren's labor notes are issued by individual responsibility and credit. This may be different from Owen's theory of labor note, which seeks to socially control and adjust production and volumes of issued notes.

Finally, as the "fifth principle," Warren describes "**adaptation of the supply to the demand**" (ibid., 11). This is the utilization of labor notes, a practical application of the "cost principle" which defines "competition" (ibid., 85) within the community that should be constructed in the future. First, when forming a community, summarize a list of requirements from each individual and family and what they can provide into a list, and create a supply and demand table for the entire community. Next, for each product or service, create three items of (a) demand, (b) supply, (c) price/labor time, and these become the basic data of production activities in the community. Production is the responsibility of each individual. Besides, equalization of productivity differences as well as adjustment of labor allocation caused by individual production activities are achieved through "competition" within the community. It is clearly different from market competition. For example, if producer A takes 50 hours to produce one coat, while producer B only takes 30 hours to produce a similar product, then only producer B's coat will meet the demand. And then, the producer A must move to the sector with insufficient production according to the supply and demand table. In the Warren community, "each individual being the only deciding power for the estimate his own labor, and *competition* being the regulator of all" (ibid., 108). Since the products produced with the minimum labor time are always selected according to the supply and demand table, it is devised so that lazy producers cannot engage in production activities.[28]

[28] The current profit-seeking commerce is "destructive" competition, but the "competition" in "equitable commerce" is a harmonious "competition" that always promotes production with a minimum labor amount. Furthermore, the advantages of conducting production activities based on the "report of supply and demand (i) eliminates speculation and the oppression of volatile prices, (ii) aids people in finding a new employment for which they are better suited, and (iii) aids those with specific talents in finding certain jobs and communities in which to locate themselves." It facilitates "the mobility of labor into all employments," through "competition" within the community. "Competition" within the community, which always regulates to produce at the lowest labor cost, has become a "strong incentive" for the most appropriate labor allocation. Warren also claims that

This innovation is based on the "*hour for hour*" exchange carried out in the New Harmony and the reflection that Owen's paternalistic governance ruled on the contrary reduced the willingness of each producer to work. However, it is also related to how the community envisioned by Warren is closed to the external market. Is it possible that it will be difficult to distinguish between the relationship consisting of "labor costs" inside the community and the relationship defined by the market price or "value" outside the community? By using the market price as the second reference standard, the supply–demand relationship within the community reflects the market supply–demand relationship. However, there may be a risk that speculative transactions will be involved over the price difference between inside and outside the community.

Let us summarize Warren's theory of labor note. (1) Warren, unlike Owen, does not have a clear definition the community ownership. However, it seems unlikely that they are supporting a co-ownership system, as they criticize it for damaging the creativity and responsibility of its members. Judging from the context of Owen's criticism, it is probable that Warren had envisioned a loosely connected local community of individuals via labor notes. The participants will be small producers. (2) Labor time of heterogenous labor are unequal based on the "labor cost theory," (3) paper-made labor notes, and (4) reference to market prices when determining product prices. The most notable point in comparison with Owen is that he actively appealed that it is necessary to make a difference in labor evaluation for equitable exchange while making full use of the concept of "labor cost." It's not just about incorporating the problem of calculating heterogenous labor, but also from the perspective of demonstrating the creativity of producers and clarifying their responsibilities.

Time Store Operation Status

In the following, we will introduce a practical example of Time Store.[29] Time Store is a store that handles labor notes and is Warren's first experiment with labor notes. Regarding the results of the operation for Time

due to the vocational training for the members who had to change their profession by "competition," the apprenticeship system must be changed at the same time (Hall 1974: 99–103).

[29] The name "*Time Store*" came from the fact that there was a clock inside the store to measure the labor time of the clerk (Warren 1854: 19).

Store, which opened on May 18, 1827, Warren wrote *Practical Details in Equitable Commerce* (1854). In this book, the Time Store is described as having a commercial success, operating under Warren's "cost principle." Warren chose a location away from New Harmony in order to avoid the bad reputation of labor notes in New Harmony, but at the beginning of the store, he was ridiculed as "some new visionary Utopian scheme." Although he had difficulty understanding how to use labor notes, he patiently explained, and user reviews gradually increased the number of customers. Thus, it is possible to gather people in the store within three months after the store opened. Furthermore, a store owner in the next corner said, "I can sell nothing. I must either open a store or shut up. I wish you would tell me how to do it." Warren then agreed to open the second time store. It is said that both stores did not lose their customers (Warren 1854: 17–19).

The secret to the success of the Time Store is the cost transaction using labor notes. In other words, profit-free pricing and cash savings for buyers. The product price at the store consisted of "cost + clerk's labor cost + miscellaneous expenses (cost × 4%)." Expenses include interest, rent, shipping charges, damage compensation, leakage, etc., and the cost is multiplied by a fixed rate. As a result, the cash payable by the buyer will be significantly reduced compared to regular merchandise. Labor notes are used as a compensation for the clerk's labor among the components of the commodity price and as a certificate of the buyer's labor to be paid in the future. In the Time Store transaction, clerk labor and buyer labor are equivalently exchanged, and the portion of the cost and overhead is paid in cash. Then, a "*report of the demand*" is posted every morning at the store to let you know which products are currently in demand. The producer refers to the report and considers delivering the product to the store, and then the store employee purchases the product from the producer using the labor notes (ibid., 16).

According to the transaction record in June 1827, Mr. M., a blacksmith, purchased various daily necessities from the Time Store and paid $1.485. If he buys the same item at "Common price," he has to pay $2.625. In other words, he has saved $1.14 in cash, which is equivalent to his 20 minutes of labor. In addition, Mr. M paid "20 minutes of blacksmith labor" in labor notes in exchange for one day of clerk's labor, which worth $1.14. It is said that the labor of a blacksmith is much more repugnant than the labor of a clerk, so it includes about 30 times the "labor cost." Also, Mrs. S. bought a "Common price" of $5.31 for a "cost price, or *Equitable* price" of $1.81, saving $3.50 in cash. This $3.50 savings is worth about 14 working days of sewing work, so Mrs. S pays 14 working days of sewing work for about 40 minutes of clerk labor equivalent to the same amount (ibid., 21–22).

Given that Warren expects one working day to be 9–10 hours, it can be seen that the valuation gap in "labor costs" between different types of work is quite large. Regarding the fairness of the "labor cost" assessment, Warren says that if a job's labor rating is too high or too low, it must be corrected. He says it must be revised to "Equilibrium," but the criteria for correction are not clear. Probably, Warren's "Equilibrium" was to adjust inventory based on store demand reports, or was a revaluation of "labor costs" based on a subjective sense of fairness between the exchange parties. But at the same time, since labor notes can only be used for transactions through the store, the store's owner, Warren, has decided on the correction of the "labor cost" valuation. Perhaps he was calculating the labor discomfort by referring to the market price of each product. In any case, the "labor cost theory," which leaves the arbitrariness of labor evaluation, may not necessarily be fair compared to Owen's theory of labor equivalence (ibid., 22).

Time Store was an experimental store to test if Warren's "cost principle" was really tolerable, so Warren was happy with his two-year commercial success. After fulfilling his purpose, the store was closed to prepare for the grand ideal. And, according to Noyes's view, the success of the Time Store has an impact on Owen and inspired the idea of labor exchanges attempted in London (Noyes 2002/1870: 95). After closing the Time Store, Warren set up local communities, while British Owenites separated from the community construction based on the co-ownership system, branching into a cooperative direction. This contrast is also an interesting subject for the future.

4.5 Historical Significance and Problems of Theories of Labor Note

As discussed through this chapter, the theories of labor note devised by Owen were carried out in the New Harmony by the book method. Furthermore, after the dissolution of the New Harmony, it was critically inherited by Warren and developed in three aspects: theory, thought and practice. It is no exaggeration to say that the theories of labor note in the nineteenth century in America are based on Warren, rather than Owen's, when evaluated in terms of the operating period of labor notes. In the following, instead of a summary, let us sort out the historical meanings and problems of theories of labor note developed by both parties.

First of all, as the "natural standard of value" is the cornerstone of theories of labor note. So what was the theory behind "human labor"? Through the criticism of metal money based on the theory of underconsumption, Owen derives "the reason of value theory" that demands the source of wealth from labor. Then, "human labor" or "power" is defined as a constant measurable force through analogy with machines. Based on the average amount of labor expenditure, the product value can be measured by the amount of labor.

This "human labor" is not merely given the role of a "natural standard of value" for measuring the value of products. In order for "human labor" to be a measurement and unit, that labor must be a fixed amount dictated by the average amount of expenditure. And by comparing the equivalence of each person's labor on the basis of this average amount of labor expenditure, it will also offer a wide range of normative perspectives that go beyond the measure of value.

However, there were some difficulties when trying to implement labor notes based on the "natural standard of value" in New Harmony. Brown points out that even if exchanges based on labor time were fair, it was difficult to measure labor time accurately. If labor time are measured inaccurately, the transparency of the measurement cannot be ensured, resulting in fatal difficulties in the criteria for fairness. And the book method chosen in New Harmony also posed a challenge. If they want to deny metal money and establish a labor-based economy, they can use either notes or books as an alternative exchange and distribution means. However, the selection of book method based on the state of the art at the time, which results in a disadvantage of increasing complicated paperwork. Of course, from the perspective of remembering the trend of transactions in society as a whole through the bookkeeping of books, it is important to remember the aspect that was used to manage production and distribution.

Regarding Owen's theory of labor note, Warren emphasized the individualistic point of view and inherited it critically, and then developed his own ideas. According to Warren, there is a lack of "individual sovereignty" and "responsibility" in New Harmony. Labor notes must be issued by individuals in order to take advantage of the individual's creativity and independence. Labor time must be measured by the producers themselves instead of others. Based on that, "labor cost" must be determined through self-evaluation by producers and objective comparison of production results. It can be said that by using the concept of "cost," Warren did not question the norm of fairness itself, but rather renewed the concept of fairness proposed by Owen. Warren's "labor cost theory," on the one hand, contains criticisms of Owen's overgeneralization of the labor concept and the uncertainties of various labor differences. On the other hand, it contains criticisms of speculative market transactions based on the "value principle," which is thought to include the theory of utility and the theory of supply and demand.

Next, let us examine the applicable law of Warren's labor theory of cost. Warren criticizes the equivalent amount of labor exchange as a measure of fairness, as well as the speculative nature of the market. From this two-sided criticism, Warren needed to consider a production/distribution system that is neither a communal control nor a market, but that respects individual decisions. What is proposed there is "competition" within the local community based on small producers as "the adaptation of the supply to the demand." How does the "competition" proposed by Warren differ from the New Harmony production system or market competition? To begin with, it clarified individual responsibility for production, which tends to be unclear under a joint ownership system. Second, the supply–demand relationship of the market economy is adjusted only after the result of market transactions, but Warren tries to collect information on supply–demand in advance in order to eliminate this anarchical production as much as possible. This supply and demand table forces people to produce in minimum labor time, and encourages labor mobility through self-responsibility. Third, since the ratio between price and labor time is a problem, it suggests that economic activities were not limited to the local community but were aware of external trade. Perhaps, to some extent, it was not possible to achieve self-sufficiency in the internal society completely, thus some areas had to rely on external supply constantly. The smaller the scope of the communities connected by labor notes and the smaller the production scale, the greater the dependence on external markets. As a result, labor mobility will not be carried out smoothly, and restrictions will increase. If the dependence on the external market is high, the relationship that "the limit of price" is defined by "labor cost" is weakened, and the attractiveness of labor notes as internal currency is diminished. Diverse human desires or the increasing gap between the demand and the limit of the supply items that can be produced in the local community increases the attractiveness to the external market, and increase the demand for the general currency as a foreign currency. The existence of an external market and the difficulty of self-sufficiency may be a bottleneck for Warren's theory of labor note.

Bibliography

Asai, K. (1953). *Eikoku Shakaishugi: Robāto Ōen* [British socialism: Robert Owen]. Shakaishisō Kenkyūkai Shuppanbu.

Bailie, W. (1972/1906). *Josiah Warren: The first American anarchist, a sociological study*. Arno Press and The New York Times.

Bestor, A. (1970/1950). *Backwoods utopias: The sectarian origins and the Owenite phase of communitarian socialism in America: 1663–1829* (2nd ed.). University of Pennsylvania Press.

Brown, P. (1827). *Twelve months in New-Harmony*. W. H. Woodward.

Cole, M. (1953). *Robert Owen of New Lanark*. The Batchworth Press.

Fogarty, R. S. (1980). *Dictionary of American communal and utopian history*. Greenwood Press.

Hall, B. N. (1974). The economic ideas of Josiah Warren: First American anarchist. *History of Political Economy, 6*(1), 95–108.

Harrison, J. F. C. (1969). *Quest for the new moral world, Robert Owen and the Owenites in Britain and America*. Charles Scribner's Sons.

Hijikata, N. (2003). *Robāto Ōen* [Robert Owen]. Kenkyusha.

Kasugai, K. (1930). Bunpai no Kōsei to Rōdōhoni-kaheian: Ōenisuto oyobi Rikarudian-sōsharisuto no shuchō [Fairness of distribution and a proposal of labor standard money (1): Claims of Owenists and Ricadian socialists]. *Meidai Shōgaku-ronsō* [The Bulletin of the Faculty of Commerce Meiji University], *8*(4), 1–25.

Lockwood, G. B. (1971/1905). *The New Harmony movement*. Dover.

Maruyama, T. (1994). Ōen to Nyū Hāmonī: Shisō no Nashonariti to Cosumoporitanizumu (2) [Owen and New Harmony: Nationalities of thought and cosmopolitanism (2)]. *Oita University Economic Review, 45*(4–5), 1–28.

Maruyama, T. (1999). *Ōen no Yūtopia to Kyōseishakai* [Owen's utopia and symbiotic society]. Minervashobo.

Marx, K. (1976/1847). The poverty of philosophy: Answer to the philosophy of poverty by M. Proudhon. In *Marx & Engels collected works* (Vol. 6). Lawrence & Wishart.

Mill, J. S. (1981/1873). Autobiography. In *Collected works of John Stuart Mill* (Vol. 1). Routledge & Kegan Paul.

Nagai, Y. (1992). *Robāto Ōen to Kindai Shakaishugi* [Robert Owen and modern socialism]. Minervashobo.

Nakagawa, Y. (1984). *Igirisu Kyōdōkumiai Shisō Kenkyū* [Studies in British cooperative thought]. Nihon Keizai Hyoronsha.
Nishibe, M. (2002). Shakai Kigyōka Owen [Social entrepreneur Owen]. *Jūryoku 01* [Gravity 01], 256–293.
Nishizawa, T. (1994). *Itan no Economisuto Gunzō: 19 seiki Bāmingamu Gakuha no Keizai Shisō* [Ensembles on heterodox economists: The Birmingham School of economic policy thought in the 19th century]. Iwanami Shoten.
Noyes, J. H. (2002/1870). *History of American socialisms*. University Press of the Pacific.
Owen, R. (1968/1821a). An explanation of the cause of the distress. *Economist, 2*(32), 92–104.
Owen, R. (1969/1825). Address delivered by Robert Owen, of New-Lanark, on Wednesday, the 27th of April, 1825, in the hall of New-Harmony, Indiana; Together with the Constitution of the Preliminary Society, founded 1st May, 1825. *The New-Harmony Gazette*. Vol. 1. No. 1. Greenwood Reprint.
Owen, R. (1993a/1813–1814). A new view of society; or, essays on the principle of the formation of the human character. In G. Claeys (Ed.), *Selected works of Robert Owen* (Vol. 1). William Pickering.
Owen, R. (1993b/1817a). Report to the Committee of the Association for the Relief of the Manufacturing and Labouring Poor. In *Selected works of Robert Owen* (Vol. 1). William Pickering.
Owen, R. (1993c/1817b). New state of society—Address delivered at the City of London Tavern, on Thursday, August 21st. In *Selected works of Robert Owen* (Vol. 1). William Pickering.
Owen, R. (1993d/1821b). Report to the County of Lanark. In *Selected works of Robert Owen* (Vol. 1). William Pickering.
Owen, R. (1993e/1826–1827). The social system. In *Selected works of Robert Owen* (Vol. 2). William Pickering; *The New-Harmony Gazette*. Vol. 2. No. 8, 14, 15, 17, 18, 19, 20, 21, 22, 23, 24.
Pare, W. (1856, June). Equitable commerce as practised in the equity villages of the United States of North America. *Journal of the Statistical Society of London, XIX*, 127–143.
Pollard, S. (1986). Robāto Ōen no Keizaishisō: Orutanatibu heno Kōken [Robert Owen's economic thought: Contributions to alternative thinking]. In C. Tsuzuki (Ed.), *Igirisu Shakaisyugi Shisōshi* [A history of British socialist thought]. Sanseido.
Proudhon, P. J. (1888/1848). *System of economical contradictions: Or, the philosophy of poverty*. McMaster University.
Schuster, E. M. (1970). *Native American anarchism: A study of left-wing American individualism*. Da Capo Press.
Stern, M. B. (1980). Every man his own printer: The typographical experiments of Josiah Warren. *Printing History, 2*(2), 11–20.

Tezuka, T. (1928). Ōen ga naseru Kinzokukahei haishi no Kokoromi to sono Shippai no Igi [The significance of Owen's attempt to abolish metal money and its failure]. In *Robert Owen 70 shūnen kinen ronbunshū* [Robert Owen Seventy Year Anniversary Essay Collection]. Chūōshakaijigyōkyōkai.

Ueda, C. (1984). *Ōen to Nyū Hāmonī* [Owen and New Harmony]. Minervashobo.

Uga, H. (1976). *Shakaikagaku kara Shakaigaku he: America Shakaigaku Shisōshi Kenkyū* [From "social science" to sociology: A study of the history of American sociological thought]. Koseisha Koseikaku.

Warren, J. (1854). *Practical details in equitable commerce*. Fowlers and Wells.

Warren, J. (1967/1852). *Equitable commerce: A new development of principles as substitutes for laws and governments, for the harmonious adjustment and regulation of the pecuniary, intellectual, and moral intercourse of mankind*. Burt Franklin.

Wunderlich, R. (1992). *Low living and high thinking at Modern Times, New York*. Syracuse University Press.

Newspapers, Magazines, etc.

Co-operative Magazine (Vol. 1). Ann Arbor: University Microfilms International, 1966/1826.

New Harmony Gazette (Vols. 1–3). New York: Greenwood Reprint, 1969/1825–1828.

CHAPTER 5

William Pare's Theory of Labor Notes: *From an Analysis of Monetary Functions to a Vision of Markets*

5.1 Origins and Branches of the Theory of Labor Notes

First, this chapter will examine changes to Owen's theory of labor notes as a result of his experiences in the United States during the 1820s and 1830s, and the significance of these changes to the evolution of local currencies among attempts to find an exchange mechanism for labor. The argument will then move on to examine William Pare (1805–1873), most notably his paper "Equitable Commerce as Practised in the Equity Villages of the United States of North America" (1856). The aim will be to demonstrate Pare's role as an intermediary in the evolution of theories of labor notes in terms of the development of a labor exchange. As will be shown, for Pare the importance of labor notes as organized through a labor exchange lay in the question of purifying the functions of money into the means of exchange that would prevent the means of payment and hoarding.[1]

[1] Pare was an Owenite who played a leading role in the trade union and cooperative movement in Birmingham. According to Nishizawa, Pare played a major role in "establishing the Birmingham branch of the Equitable Labour Exchange in 1832–33" and "was a strong link between Owen and Attwood in thought and movement." Additionally, he

© The Author(s), under exclusive license to Springer Nature Switzerland AG 2021

T. Yuki, *Socialism, Markets, and the Critique of Money*, Marx, Engels, and Marxisms,
https://doi.org/10.1007/978-3-030-80408-4_5

The idea of labor notes first appeared in Owen's *Report to the County of Lanark* but he did not mention the form of a labor exchange. The labor notes described there are used in a community of integrated agriculture-industry model based on a common ownership system and were akin to the "wage tickets" used at the stores in the New Lanark spinning mill run by Owen (Donnachie 2000: 84, 172). Of concern for Owen was the increasing social division of labor between agriculture and industry that he hoped to overcome, via the creation of small communities that could operate within a larger market society. The establishment of the National Equitable Labour Exchange in 1832, though a modest attempt for Owen, was to serve as a hub for a coalition of Owenite cooperatives, and trade unions, and the labor exchange movement sought to expand upon and develop many of the ideas inherent in Owen's initial projects and theories.

Even when considering the offshoots of the various Owenite movements, it is not fundamentally possible to ignore the influence of *Report to the County of Lanark* to the theoretical and ideological foundation of labor notes. Subsequently, a community building movement that traditionally inherited the view of the *Report to the County of Lanark* was actively developed during the 1820s. However, since Owen himself failed to run New Harmony during 1825–1827 in the United States, the community route came to a standstill. When Owen returned to Britain in 1827 disillusioned by his experiences, he was surprised to find an upsurge in the Owenite movement that had developed independently. Within the British Owenite school, a triple movement of cooperative shops, labor exchanges and exchange bazaars, and trade unions developed under the name of Owenism, despite the disagreement on whether the community route was to be included (Oliver 1958: 355–358).[2]

Confronted with these developments, Owen's obsession around community building was fired as he went about searching for the capital to fund the various project he had in mind, which led him to the idea

was "charmed by Warren's 'equitable commerce,' he was an ardent promoter of monetary reform and equitable labor exchange" (Nishizawa 1994: 156).

[2] The report on the management status of the Ralahine Agricultural and Manufacturing Co-operative Society at the Third Co-operative Congress generated a great deal of interest from the participants of the convention. Within this community was a "cooperative store" that used "labour notes." Furthermore, they reported the existence of a facility like a labor exchange, called a "labor exchange bank." However, in reality, it was a "savings bank" that saved a portion of wages rather facilitating labor exchange (Nakagawa 2002: 121–128).

of trying to develop a unified national organization based on an amalgamation of the movements he found in operation. This would finally result in the reimportation of certain key ideas developed in the United States, most notably the Time Stores based on "equitable commerce" as implemented by Warren in the United States after the New Harmony setback.[3]

A systematic description of the function and structure of labor exchanges is provided in *Crisis* dated June 30, 1832. According to this chapter, a labor exchange called the "Equitable Bank of Exchange" was being established to promote education, improve welfare, and eliminate unemployment and poverty associated with the crisis of overproduction. Based on the analysis that "*universal distress, occasioned by ruinous competition and over-production,*" the goal of the Exchange was to eliminate the discrepancies in demand and supply and microscopic production that creates "*ruinous competition*" and the lack of purchasing power giving rise to overproduction. Therefore, the first thing to note was the attempt to exclude the entry of merchants whose manipulation of discrepancies between demand and supply resulted in profiteering and speculation. This was achieved by stipulating that all transactions would be carried out in branches of the exchange spread across the country, and the shortfall and surplus of products in each region were to be adjusted nationwide. Then, at each branch of the exchange, the products produced in each region would be deposited, and deposited products evaluated solely in terms of the labor time required for production—rather the monetary value they can accrue due to temporary scarcity. The value of a product was calculated in hourly units by converting the "*cost price*" of the raw material part, with the wage valuation of six pence for every hour of labor added to it. In addition, an exchange maintenance fee of "a per centage of one halfpenny in the shilling" of transaction was added. At the same time, the depositor would receive the valuation of the product in the labor time denominated security. This labor note could be used only between the exchange and the producer (depositor), and it was not allowed to be circulated in the city (outside the exchange), since this would breach the national structure put in place to manage temporal discrepancies between demand and supply. Using notes with a limited circulation range, the total

[3] See Chapter 4 for the realities about Warren's *Equitable Commerce*.

demand and supply could be matched, and crises brought about by overproduction could be eliminated. At that time, the system was designed to forestall hoarding and the establishment of any system of credit, in the hope of preventing the impact they would have on the equilibrium of supply and demand. Through exchanges and labor notes, it was hoped that money would be converted into a pure means of exchange and thus realize a smooth match between total demand and total supply (*Crisis*, Vol. 1, No. 15 and 16, June 30, 1832, pp. 59–61).

The question of the influence of developments in the United States in Britain has continued to be a subject of scholarly debate in the field and was notably initiated in 1870 with the publication of a work by John Alfred Noyes, which implied that Warren's experimental Time Store inspired the idea of Owen's exchange (Noyes 1870: 95). However, even if Noyes's research is limited to the testimony of contemporaneous communitarians, researchers remain skeptical because it lacks a sufficient empirical and historical basis.[4] However, even if the extent of the impact is uncertain, it is at least possible to point out the existence of historical documents that may indicate that Warren had some influence on the British Owenites.

The first mention of Time Stores can be traced to a relatively early article in the *New Harmony Gazette* of 12 December 1827: "For an equal exchange of Labor as valued by Time, now in successful operation, at the corner of Elm and Fifth street, Cincinnati" (*New Harmony Gazette*, Vol. 3, No. 12, December 26, 1827, p. 94). According to this chapter, the Time Store was "Where *labor* buys *labor* for that *sum* of *time*, (From one to another) in which it was done," and where any labor could be purchased, but it could only be exchanged for "*same time*." In this account, the Time Store is based on a "*Bill of all Wants*" known as the "*Time-Magazine*" in which the cost of those products in units of time was posted. Customers could peruse the Time Magazine and deliver favorable products to the store and purchase products from the

[4] However, I could not find the literature that explicitly criticizes or denies the Noyes' study. Moreover, Schuster and Podmore support Noyes' suggestion (Podmore 1923/1906: 404; Schuster 1970: 95). According to Podmore, the "idea of a labour currency" was tied to the experience of the "Exchange Bazaars," which had already been tried at the Time Store. "From the fourth quarterly report of the British Association for promoting Co-operative Knowledge, published early in 1830, we learn that Owen, no doubt with Warren's experiment in his mind, had advocated the use of labour notes at the Greville Street Bazaar."

store by using labor notes received as consideration. The article in the *New Harmony Gazette* went on to state that "When the standard or labor by time is displayed; / When the value of money shall decline, / Since *Labor* and *Time* are the *Medium* of trade," and praised Warren for demonstrating the principle of an exchange that should replace money. Warren's Time Store opened in May 1827, so it would be introduced in New Harmony, less than a year after it opened.

Furthermore, *Crisis* in 1832 described the situation in the Third Co-operative Congress of the "Exchange Labour Banks" (*Crisis*, Vol. 1, No. 5, May 5, 1832, p. 20). The article reports that Pare "proceed[ed] to read the following extracts from the *New York Free Enquire*, for the purpose of showing the operations and results of the system of exchanging labour for labour in some part of America." Pare introduced community education by Mrs. Charity Rotch of the Society of Friends, following which Owen drew attention to, "the facilities of learning a trade when taught by scientific principles," and "he remarked that Josiah Warren, the person mentioned in the *Free Enquire*" (*Crisis*, Vol. 1, No. 6, May 5, 1832, p. 21). This article, if genuine, is a historical source suggesting Owen's reception of the ideas of Warren, who was a severe critic of Owen. However, other records doubt the authenticity of this article. According to the *Proceedings of the Third Co-operative Congress* compiled by Carpenter, Owen introduced Joseph Warrington (*Proceedings of the Third Co-operative Congress*, 1832, p. 31). It is difficult to validate which record is correct, but another issue of *Crisis* contains the rest of Pare's quote from *Free Enquirer* at the Third Co-operative Congress (*Crisis*, Vol. 1, No. 8, May 19, 1832, p. 31). This article, entitled "The Equal Exchange of Labour," referred to Josiah Warren of Kendal and the schools he observed. The reporter said, "I am a convert to his system of reform, comprehending as it does a gradual departure from the old system of speculation and counteraction," and that if possible he "would try the experiment of a practical school based on the principle of an equal exchange of labor, on a small scale" with his own hands. Warren's biography contains no allusions to the truth about the *Crisis* article, or how he was involved in the Kendal community, or whether labor notes were used (Bailie 1906; Wunderlich 1992). Even so, there is a clear indication that Warren's "principle of an equal exchange of labor" or his theory of labor note was favorably received by a segment of the British Owenites. If the journalist confessed to a switch, it is implied that the Exchange needs to be converted into a gradual, small-scale movement, and it is no longer possible to just find a community building route. It is believed that Warren's ideas were publicized in Britain by Pare, who was later fascinated by Warren (Nishizawa 1994: 154). Therefore, Warren's ideology was presented in Britain through Pare and thus it should be understood as being presented as Pare's theory of labor notes.

As shown above, labor exchanges have several offshoots which developed as a consequence of the evolution of Owen's ideology. The next section highlights the realization of Pare's theory of labor notes by examining Pare's introductory paper on Warren's theories, and how Pare laid stress upon gradual and small-scale initiatives as opposed to large-scale labor exchanges.

5.2 William Pare's Theory of Labor Notes

Pare's Interpretation Warren's Theory of Labor Notes

In many respects it is possible to view Warren's initial decision to open a Time Store in Cincinnati, in 1827 as something of a challenge to Owen's approach in New Harmony. Though it was only in 1854, with the publication of *Practical Details in Equitable Commerce*, that the principles of the Time Store were set out along with the basis on which they differed from experiments such as New Harmony.

Warren had several objections to Owen's project. Firstly, he was concerned that the model of community management based on the common ownership system would undermine the dignity of the individual. He was also concerned that Owen's principle of the equal exchange of "time for time" is unable to account for the exchange between different kinds of labor that vary in terms of skill, and complexity. Concerning the question of "individuality" and "individual sovereignty," Pare's model served as a medium to carry on Warren's ideas in two respects: first, in terms of its model of ownership, based on independent small producers, and second, as a method of evaluation in terms of labor and raw materials (Warren 1854: 14). To address this difference, Warren sought to replace Owen's slogan "time for time" with "labor for labor" in the hope that it would produce a system which would more fairly recognize the individual's expenditure of labor.

Pare sought to bring out these differences in his own interpretation of Warren, by implying the way in which Owen's method of evaluation actually reduced the scope for individual autonomy in New Harmony. In his view, a system of fair exchange could only be constructed by paying attention to individual differences between labors. He further said that the "Infinite diversity" of humanity makes it impossible for laws and institutions which treat humans uniformly and which reduce them to interest groups to exist in harmony with human needs. In stating this, Warren was guided by the "Sovereignty of the Individual" that must rest with all individuals if any one individual is to benefit. Warren's "equitable commerce" held it paramount that individuals maintain freedom of decision-making as sovereigns. As Pare stated: "the doctrine of 'Individuality,' and 'the Sovereignty of the Individual,' involves two of the most important scientific consequences" as follows. "[A]bsolute personal liberty" becomes a "guiding principle" toward a fair society, and simultaneously, is a goal for achieving the objectives. As described below, to implement this liberty, labor notes are viewed as an intermediary "a scientific, gradual, and perfectly peaceable substitution of new and harmonious relations." Liberty, in principle the liberty of a sovereign, may be understood as the freedom of independent small producers or the freedom of production and consumption, for the time being. Next, if an individual is understood as a small producer, conducting a fair transaction becomes an issue. The "cost principle" of exchanging equal costs of labor is raised to address this issue (Pare 1856: 128, 131).

While Warren conceptually sought to distinguish "cost" from "value," Pare stated that "Value is a consideration for the purchaser alone" and criticized the demand theory that "*value* is the limit of price." Political economists have so far the "only question discussed has been, what it is which *now* regulates price—never, what should regulate it." The analysis of "value" is based on how current prices are regulated and a consciousness of the present situation, while "cost principle" is a proposition as to what should regulate prices (ibid., 132–133).

"*Cost* is the only equitable limit, and by cost is meant the amount of *labour* bestowed on its production, that measure being again measured by the *painfulness* or *repugnance* of the labour itself." The exchange of labor or labor products contained in equal amounts of "cost" is a simple "*principle* of equity." The amount of labor of each individual is measured according to the "cost principle" in two ways. First, "if all labour were equally repugnant or toilsome," it can be measured by the "length of time." Second, since the degree of effort required by labor depends on the individual, there are cases "that equity in the exchange of labour, or the products of labour, cannot be arrived at by measuring the labour of different persons *by time* merely," so objective standards are necessary for comparing the efforts and sacrifices in labor (ibid., 133–135).

A comparison of different kinds of labor requires the following three conditions:

> 1. That some method must be devised for comparing the relative repugnance of different kinds of labour.
> 2. That in making the comparison, *each individual* must make his or her own estimate of the repugnance to him or her of the labour which he or she performs, &c.
> 3. That there should be a sufficient motive in the results, or consequences, to insure an honest exercise of the judgment, and an honest expression of the real feelings of each, in making the comparison (ibid., 134).

For the first condition, "All that is required is to agree upon some particular kind of labour, the average repugnance of which is most easily ascertained, or the most nearly fixed, and use it as a *standard of comparison*, a sort of *yard-stick* for measuring the relative *repugnance* of other kinds of labour." In western American states, if corn production labor is assumed to be suitable for comparative standards, the standard one-hour labor in the region is equivalent to 20 pounds of corn. Second, equitable trade must be established recognizing sovereignty of every individual under the principle that all decisions should be self-determined. The third condition requires honest declarations to be made. Such actions are motivated by having a bird's-eye view that each person will make honest declarations and repeating equitable transactions, which will make the business relationships of society equitable. Since participation in "equitable commerce" is voluntary, the surrounding producers are expected to gradually participate due to the "attractive nature" of various principles that "equitable commerce" includes (ibid., 134–135).

Furthermore, Warren establishes a central apparatus to lead the price and quantity of products traded to converge at a certain level. For instance, Warren provides for "a book" that records demand and supply, and the ratio of price to the labor time within a community in which members loosely cooperate (Warren 1967/1852: 80); or, when "equitable commerce" has been applied on the premise of a market, a "*report of the demand*" could be used instead, presenting the price and quantity of the product needed by Time Stores that accept labor notes (Warren 1854: 16). It was expected that transactions would be conducted fairly by having a central apparatus to indicate internal standards for labor note trading.

Pare sought to iron out some of the functional aspects of labor notes that were unclear in Warren's *Equitable Commerce*. According to Pare, the function of money is "a standard of value" and "a circulating medium." However, he said that, "money, as at present used, is rejected as being too uncertain and fluctuating in its nature to be a *standard*; and (so far as gold and silver are concerned), as not being convenient as a circulating medium." He held corn, to be a better standard of "labor costs," and that it would be appropriate as a standard of value. In addition, "paper" was viewed by Pare to be well suited as a means of circulation because the use value of the material is independent of the standard of value and can function as a substitute for the product "cost." However, the labor that produces the corn was chosen as a standard in order to adapt to the local circumstances of western America and should only be approved that specific region. Therefore, wheat might be taken as a standard in another region, and something completely different might be adopted in a third (Pare 1856: 139–140).

However, Pare's perception of money included more than just is function as a medium of circulation and a standard of value. Pare sought to emphasize the local and ad hoc aspects of trade with money:

> Now, if an exchange could be always made and completed on the spot, each party giving and receiving an equivalent in labour or the product of labour, the whole problem of exchanges would be solved by this simple method, and there would be no necessity for a circulating medium, or for anything to perform the part which is performed by money in our existing commerce. But such is not the case. Ordinarily the exchange is only partially completed on the spot, the remaining part *waiting to be completed at some future time*, by the performance of an equivalent amount of labour, or the products or commodities having in them an equivalent amount of labour.

On top of this, Pare identified the following four points as characteristics of labor notes:

1. Its cheapness and abundance.

2. Being based on individual credit it makes every man his own banker.
3. It combines the properties of a circulating medium, and a means of credit.
4. It represents an ascertained and definite amount of labour or property, which ordinary money does not (ibid., 140–141).

As clarified by Pare, trading in the market cannot conclude all transactions at once and is always done locally and partially. There is a segment prepared for future transactions, in the form of stock and funds, and another segment that has a decentralized nature that remains in the portion not been paid by credit transactions. Given the decentralized nature of such markets, "the labor note" or "Equitable Money" is "*an evidence of his obligation to do so at some future time*" (ibid.). This led Pare to develop a model of a market where money divides sellers and buyers in time and space, and based on this, he demands labor notes for its functions and issuing methods. In Pare's model, labor notes are not issued as consideration for deposits like in labor exchanges, where the buyer of the product issues the note as a promise of future payment to the seller. Pare's theory of labor note does not assume the organization of markets or exchanges and actively promotes transactions based on free circulation of notes and the creditworthiness of the payer. As previously stated, for Pare labor notes, "being based on individual credit it makes every man his own banker," and involve the circulation of debt securities based on the payer's credit, i.e., labor and production capacity, assets, and transaction performance of the payer. This is different from the labor exchange method, which is based on the soundness of the physical assets deposited with agreements of members, the seller judges the buyer's credit by the personal production capacity and transaction history, and the range and the amount of circulation of security are thus determined by the seller's acceptance and trust in the buyer.

Pare's model is considered self-evidently "not strictly a *principle of equity*" (ibid.), as it intends the use of labor notes while leaving the decentralized nature of the market. The unorganized market assumed in Pare retains the dispersibility of the market and the unfinished nature of the transaction, so there is no need to pursue fairness strictly in exchange. Labor notes are merely means of circulation that allow exchange "based *on equivalents of labour or cost between individuals*." Additionally, in a range of regions where products are designated as standards of value, Pare sees it as unproblematic for different commodities to serve as the medium of circulation, i.e., corn in the Western United States and wheat along the Eastern Seaboard, etc. This contrasts with the model of labor notes Owen developed in *Crisis*, which required the exchange to deal with all transactions centrally to match total demand and supply, premised on a system responsible for reproduction on a social scale. In contrast, Pare based his model on the assumption of partiality and the division of the market economy, in which there is no need to match total demand and supply under the local transactions. For Pare this opened the possibility for producers to participate and withdraw at will and to build economic relationships based on self-responsibility and consent.

The Viewpoint of the Medium of Exchange, the Means of Payment and Hoarding

Pare's theory of labor notes was supported by three layers of money and market analysis. First, it pointed out the segmented nature of the market for social supply and demand and the locality of transactions. Second, it indicated the period of the transaction, i.e., the monetary function of the means of payment and the hoarding separates the transaction in time. Based on this understanding, it became clear that money divides the seller and the buyer spatially and temporally, while the market could be regarded as offering a fragmentary opportunity of decentralized local and intermittent trading. Such recognition of money and markets reveals a high degree of sophistication, especially compared with the view in *Crisis* that money in a community should be merely an intermediary to match supply and demand.

Based on such an understanding of money, it is possible to clarify a number of issues concerning the distinction between his and Owen's model of labor notes. First, compared with Owen, labor notes for Pare were closer to credit money in nature. Whereas labor notes under Owen were based on real assets, where a claim is made on deposited products, for Pare labor notes were a claim on the payer's labor capacity. It is possible to set up a credit-debt relationship for labor, if the labor ability is recognized, and it is considered to include an opportunity for future money, by considering how it is possible to purchase products and services even without having cash. Thus, in terms of labor notes as a form of security, Owen's view was retrospective and Pare's was prospective.

However, there are aspects of the Pare model of labor notes that retain the various adverse effects contained in the market and credit money.

Pare's theory of labor notes has been remarkably market-oriented as a reaction to the inability to resolve the valuation problem of complex labor and that of supply and demand adjustment in Owen's community. First, Pare's theory of labor notes emphasizes market dispersibility, and despite using labor notes, it has no mechanism to prevent advance speculative transactions because it puts off a solution to the demand–supply adjustment issue on a social scale. Although Pare, along with Warren, rejected planned allocation of labor in the community, efforts were still made in the Warren's method to stabilize the prices and quantities of products traded to a certain level through a central normalization apparatus such as Time Stores. However, Pare did not provide for such a mechanism or apparatus. The producers are completely free, microscopic, and anarchic. Therefore, there is no guarantee that the issued securities will be finally settled.

Although Pare had removed the grand goal of finding a consensus between total demand and supply, as per the Owen model, the understanding of Pare-style labor notes and his focus on labor notes as a medium for building local and partial relationships helped to pioneer ideas about modern local currencies. Pare's labor notes were issued and received based on the credit regarding each individual's labor ability and future availability of payment based on the premise of a face-to-face relationship, such as continuing local, conventional business relationships. Further, the cost portion of raw materials was traded in cash and only the labor added to the raw materials was evaluated in labor time. A full transaction through labor notes was not envisioned, so there was a low threshold for participation in business relationships by using labor notes. For Pare it was possible to have a dual system characterized by segmented micro-markets in which labor notes were used, that could sit within a macro-market based on money, where the former is based on an equitable (non-market) principle. Through duplicating product prices, it is possible to see in Pare's model a strategy to gradually substitute markets and money by adding equitable principles into the market principles and connecting them with modern local currencies, which can be used to partially compensate social reproduction.

Bibliography

Bailie, W. (1972/1906). *Josiah Warren: The first American anarchist, a sociological study*. Arno Press and The New York Times.

Donnachie, I. (2000). *Robert Owen, Owen of New Lanark and New Harmony*. Tuckwell Press.

Nakagawa, Y. (2002). *Kirisutokyō Shakaishugi to Kyōdōkumiai: E. V. Neale no Kyōdōkyojyūhukushiron* [Christian socialism and cooperatives: E. V. Neale's co-housing welfare]. Nihon Keizai Hyoronsha.

Nishizawa, T. (1994). *Itan no Economisuto Gunzō: 19 seiki Bāmingamu Gakuha no Keizai Shisō* [Ensembles on heterodox economists: The Birmingham School of economic policy thought in the 19th century]. Iwanami Shoten.

Noyes, J. H. (2002/1870). *History of American socialisms*. University Press of the Pacific.

Oliver, W. H. (1958). The labour exchange phase of the co-operative movement. *Oxford Economic Paper, 10*(3), 355–367.

Owen, R. (1993/1821). Report to the County of Lanark. In *Selected works of Robert Owen* (Vol. 1). William Pickering.

Pare, W. (1856, June). Equitable commerce as practised in the equity villages of the United States of North America. *Journal of the Statistical Society of London, XIX*, 127–143.

Podmore, F. (1923/1906). *Robert Owen: A biography*. George Alien & Unwin.

Schuster, E. M. (1970). *Native American anarchism: A study of left-wing American individualism*. Da Capo Press.

Warren, J. (1854). *Practical details in equitable commerce*. Fowlers and Wells.

Warren, J. (1967/1852). *Equitable commerce: A new development of principles as substitutes for laws and governments, for the harmonious adjustment and regulation of the pecuniary, intellectual, and moral intercourse of mankind*. Burt Franklin.

Wunderlich, R. (1992). *Low living and high thinking at Modern Times, New York*. Syracuse University Press.

Newspapers, Magazines, etc.

The Crisis, and National Co-operative Trades' Union Gazette (Vols. 1–4). New York: Greenwood Reprint. 1968/1832–1834.

New Harmony Gazette (Vols. 1–3). New York: Greenwood Reprint, 1969/1825–1828.

Proceedings of the Third Co-operative Congress, reported and edited by William Carpenter, London: William Strange, 1832.

CHAPTER 6

Comparative Study of Owen's Theory of Labor Notes and the Theories of Local Currency

Identification of Issues

In this chapter, we return to the discussion in Chapter 3 where Owen's theory of labor notes was compared with modern local currency theory. There we established that each of the systems of labor notes and local currencies had developed their own ideas regarding issuance, and that this was reflected in the overall structure of the systems being proposed. To illustrate the point, we selected Time Dollar and LETS (Local Exchange and Trading System), as they possessed many of the typical features of modern local currencies.

Time Dollar is a local currency founded by Edgar Cahn in 1980, and as of 2002, 70 communities in the UK, Japan, and the United States have registered with Time Dollar (Cahn 1999b: 15).[1] Basically, it is used to

[1] To check its current activities see the Time Banks website (http://timebanks.org/).

© The Author(s), under exclusive license to Springer Nature Switzerland AG 2021

T. Yuki, *Socialism, Markets, and the Critique of Money*, Marx, Engels, and Marxisms,
https://doi.org/10.1007/978-3-030-80408-4_6

promote volunteer activities in non-market areas. Labor time is used as a unit of measure for the exchange of goods and services among members.[2]

LETS is a local currency system that was started in 1983 by Michael Linton in the Comox region on the east coast of Vancouver Island, Canada, and the name for its currency is the Green Dollar. The value of the currency is set to 1 green dollar = 1 Canadian dollar. The purpose of LETS was to activate the monetary cycle in the region to lower the unemployment rate on Vancouver Island, which had reached 20%. Through the campaign by Linton, LETS spread rapidly to Canada, Australia, New Zealand, and, especially the UK in the 1990s. Since spreading to the, UK there has been an increasing tendency via LETS to link monetary value to labor time. According to Maruyama, those who try to create a new economic cycle in the region connect national currency with LETS, and those who aim to activate community activities connect labor time with LETS (Maruyama 1997: 1–4).

As we have seen, Owen's theory of labor notes was practiced in the New Harmony Community and the National Equitable Labour Exchange (1832–1834). The intention behind the introduction of labor notes was to overcome the inequalities of market exchanges by taking labor time as a unit of measure. Although some initiatives that used labor notes were similar to local currencies, in the sense that they remained in the local territory, Owen's theory of labor notes was intended to be developed comprehensively and had been devised as an alternative to the national currency. We must keep in mind that the intention was for labor notes to function as a set of "community-labor notes" that would replace "market-metal money." This in some ways varies from the function of local currencies in recent years, which are based on the local functioning of the currency, and the co-existence of potentially many local currencies

[2] It is worth noting that in Japan a local currency, which is similar to the Time Dollar, has been developed as a "time deposit system" using "Fureai Kippu" (Caring Relationship Tickets). Tanaka traces two genealogical strands concerning the origin of the "Fureai Kippu." One is the "Volunteer Labor Bank" established by Teruko Mizushima in 1973, the other one is the "Lifestyle Helpers Association" in 1981 and "Kobe Life Care Association" in 1982 (Tanaka 1996: 91–100). The "Residents Participation Home Welfare Services Associations" that currently adopt "Fureai Kippu" exceeds 200 (ibid., 105–106). The "time deposit system" is different from the Time Dollar, which aims at synchronic exchanges. The purpose is to help and pass on the mutual support between generations by depositing the contribution time for nursing care and welfare services in order to receive the necessary services when the contributor is old. It can be said that this idea was rarely seen in Owen's theory of labor notes.

operating in their region and being pegged against the relevant national currency.[3]

The basic reason for approaching the mutual comparison of labor notes and local currency is that they both try to promote interactions and transactions among members by issuing currency that circulates in the region. In other words, it is due to the formal similarity between them, since if we treat a currency as one that coexists with the national currency and circulates only within a certain area, then labor notes could be regarded as an historical precedent.[4] Secondly, the ideological analogy of associating currency units with labor time is a recurrent feature of recent local currencies. Thirdly, when the robustness of each monetary system is judged against its "lifetime," or duration, rather than scale or comprehensiveness, it becomes clear that labor notes of the Owen-type have been short-lived, with efforts lasting approximately two to three years. In contrast, modern local currencies have been around for a comparatively longer period of time, and can be seen as monetary systems that have maintained a degree of robustness and durability. In this regard, they can be seen as having constituted a relatively robust currency system.

6.1 Idea and Theory of Local Currency

Outline of the Idea of Time Dollars

According to Cahn, the founder of Time Dollar, the United States faces three closely related problems. The first is the expansion of social inequality due to globalization. With the global outsourcing of the US manufacturing in search of cheaper labor, workers have been forced to move to the service industry, making skills and proficiencies unnecessary, while replacing stable employment with casual employment. With the labor market increasingly exposed to global competition, workers have experienced depressed wages and greater periods of unemployment, not to mention an increasing tendency toward the polarization of the workforce between an increased number of low-wage workers and a few

[3] Owen, Gray, and Proudhon, the representative labor note theorists, believed that the use of labor notes would allow any product or service to be traded. For example, Gray envisions a "whole system of exchange" that uses labor money or labor notes (Gray 1873/1831: 66–67).

[4] Sugimoto (1995), Nishibe (2002), and Maruyama (2003) examine labor money and labor notes as historical precedents for local currency.

high-income earners. In addition, unemployed people are generally those who are willing and able to work but cannot get the opportunity to work. However, the current monetary system takes no account of their ability to work and focuses solely on hours worked as an employee. The second problem Cahn identified was the increase in social unrest that results from this basic economic condition, such as homelessness and crime. The impact is also felt in the sphere of social reproduction, where the local community is working behind the scenes to enable labor capacity to be available for the formal economy. Until now, labor such as childcare and nursing care that are mainly done at home have come to be seen as low-value labor due to the penetration of market-based monetary values. The current monetary system is ill-suited to address this issue because its sole criterion for evaluating acts of labor lies in market exchanges against other acts of labor. When used as a basis for rebuilding the communities affected by globalization, the net effect is to disrupt efforts, especially the human relationships required for effective social reproduction, which obey a different logic than the market. Third, Cahn identified the impact of these first two problems on public perceptions and social security. Until recently, social welfare such as childcare and nursing care had been guaranteed through the redistribution of income, but due to financial difficulties in the public sector, it is no longer possible for state institutions to fulfill these roles. Furthermore, due to the reliance on national assistance, the criticism of welfare recipients has further created an ideological pressure that neglects the increasing dependency of the recipients on national forms of support, because they have lost their economic independence. To address these issues, Cahn argued for the necessary to "rebuild family, neighborhood and community" (Cahn 1999a: 499–500) through an alternative monetary system based on the labor capacity of people who have been excluded from the formal market economy.

Behind Cahn's advocacy of the Time Dollar is a critical view of the current state of the national currency. Certainly, money can serve as an economically rational measure and medium, but this does not mean it is free from causing harm in other respects. In this sense, the convenience and social disruption caused by money could be viewed as two sides of the same coin (no pun intended).

What, then, are the difficulties associated with money? According to Cahn, first of all, money has "all-purpose buying power" (Cahn 1999b: 73) in that everything can be purchased as a commodity.

However, the "all-purpose buying power" of money is accompanied by the ethical neutrality between the individual items of merchandise that can be purchased. This means that money itself does not impose any restrictions on the ethics of choice, which is fine in one sense but also means that drugs, guns, and sex can be exchanged using the same system as other types of merchandise, which results in an absence of norms concerning which aspects of human relationships should be regulated by exchange. In part, Time Dollar can be seen as an attempt to impose community and ethical restrictions on the exchange process. Therefore, the purchasing power of Time Dollar was not based on a universal or generalized system of exchange.

Second, money is characterized by free "mobility" (ibid.), and its range of circulation does not impose any particular geographical restrictions. Therefore, if speculative financial transactions are activated due to further progress in economic globalization, this increases the opportunities for money flow out of the region in which the labor took place. The impact of this net outflow of money will create a local shortage of money, hindering the local economic cycle and forcing job seekers to move out in search of work. This is a direct corollary of the non-normative and free-flowing nature of money. For those who depend on the market for their lives, the acquisition of money must be uniquely pursued while the community members who rely on employment and labor must move to a place where money is paid. This could deprive the residents of the freedom to stay and live in the local community. In order to eliminate such negative effects and keep the circulation of money within the region, Time Dollar emphasizes currency manageability, and it does not use freely circulating paper notes. It is also expected that limiting the range of currency circulation can promote local human and economic exchange and increase the sense of belonging to the community.

Third, money has a price function, which enables consumers to select commodities with the lowest cost. This is an essential function from the perspective of economic rationality, but the measure does not include broader social values and normative perspectives. There is a conceptual and functional narrowness to the measure. Therefore, Time Dollar provides an additional measure of "time" for assessing unjustified labor in the market and drawing up needs.

Fourth, it is said that money makes itself into a commodity due to its capacity to function as "interest-bearing money." The commoditization of money activates speculation targeting money. As a result, it separates the money trade from the subsistence of labor production. On the other hand, Time Dollar has set rules that do not generate interest in the currency. Therefore, it is unrelated to inflation in which only the amount of money deviates from the substance of production and increases unilaterally. Time Dollar is a local currency that partially replaces the monetary function while remaining closely related to labor and production. Through transactions by Time Dollar, the concept of labor and production is not limited to labor in a capitalist process of production, in which labor is solely determined by its role in producing commodities for the market. Behind this lies the recognition of the importance of including the socially reproductive forms of labor that are required in support of formal production activities.

As its name implies, Time Dollar is a monetary medium that is characterized by selecting labor time as a measure/unit of currency. Cahn presents his view of humanity and labor as a summary of his critical thoughts on money. Generally, only market-evaluated labor is recognized as valuable labor, but labor in the Time Dollar domain must be evaluated on the basis of the needs of the community and the interdependence of its members, regardless of whether it is purchased in the market. Both labor in the market and non-market domain are indispensable labor for supporting and reproducing society. In that sense, no rank or weight can be attached to any labor. This is because even if the value of a specific act of labor is considered to be low, if the labor is not properly carried out, the cycle of social reproduction will be hindered. Therefore, as mentioned in Cahn's analysis of the monetary function, Time Dollar is designed to address the criterion of the ethical ends required by social reproduction. Not only does the measure/unit of labor time express the belief that there is equality in the labor between members, but it is also required as a measure/unit that does not have negative monetary functions.

To address these criticisms of money, Time Dollar does not issue a tangible monetary medium such as paper notes, but adopts a method of recording on a personal computer using the "Computerized Time Dollar accounting systems" (Cahn 1999a: 501).[5] It could be classified as an electronic money type in the sense of digitizing the monetary medium. The system operates by entering the member's transaction amount into the

[5] "Timekeeper" (http://www.timekeeper.org/) is the software package purposefully designed for Time Dollar. It can not only manage time on the computer, but also matches users between services providers and receivers on the Internet.

accounting system on the personal computer installed at the Time Dollar office, instead of issuing a Time Dollar. For example, a member who provides a service may inform the secretariat of the time contributed, and then the secretariat records this amount into the contributor's account, while deducting the time from the account of the member who received the service. Each member can receive further services from other members according to their account balance.

Time Dollar is money that has no material collateral or guarantee behind its issue. Instead, it is based on the fact that member A provided member B with a certain amount of time. Member A, who is the service provider does not need to receive the compensation immediately from member B and may receive the desired item from the services menu that is provided by other Time Dollar members (in other words member C, D etc.).[6] Unlike a standard exchange transaction, the service is provided without immediate compensation, because members expect and trust that in the future they will be able to draw on services based on the time they have contributed. This process of give and take is not based on the assets of the issuing organization or the materiality of reserves, but that the labor contribution of member A will be returned to A again in the future. Therefore, the basis is the expectation and trust that it will be returned in the form of the labor of another member (B, C, D, etc.). Generally, the promise of payment for monetary debt is called credit. However, in the context of local currency theory, the term trust is applied if the issuing organization does not prepare physical assets and the debt is not a monetary debt. In this book, the promise to pay debts is generally referred to as credit, so it does not necessarily rely on the terminology of local currency theory.[7] The concept of credit is understood as a promise of payment related to commodity economic wealth, regardless of whether it

[6] The Time Dollar reward is a combination of the internal reward of psychological satisfaction and the external reward of purchasing power for one hour (Cahn 1999b: 9).

[7] For a limit-case of the conceptual confusion of "trust" and "credit" in the local currency theory, see Toshiharu Kato's theory of eco-money. In my paper (Yuki 2011), I critically assess Kato's theory and call attention to the potential abuse of the notions of "trust" and "credit" in local currency theories. As described later in this chapter, Maruyama states that "Green Dollar is a kind of debt certificate issued by the recipient of services and goods" (Maruyama 2004: 173). And "Green Dollar at LETS is circulated on the ultimate basis of the future labor of the individual. Therefore, the circulation area is limited to the extent that the labor capacity of individuals who issue Green Dollar is trusted" (ibid.).

is monetary/non-monetary or physical/non-physical things, and is distinguished from acting as the representative of existing assets. Therefore, credit includes real debt and labor debt, but does not include uncredited notes and currencies such as narrow banking and gift vouchers. Trust is a concept related to the economy of gifts and should be used in the sense of personal trust in expectation of reciprocal gifts and obligations based on the recipient's feelings of debt.

Given the role of the Time Dollar issuing organization in recording the transactions of its members, the question naturally arises as to whose debt is being compensated by Time Dollar. It would be difficult to understand this as a debt of the secretariat without any reserves, so it must be understood as a collective debt that individual members owe to each other. When an individual member provides a service, the community as a group issues a Time Dollar, and although the issuer of money is formally the secretariat, in terms of content, it cannot be said belonging to the personality of such an intermediate group. Member A creates credits through labor contributions, while other members (B, C, D, etc.) must provide labor to repay collective debt individually. Alternatively, the fact that member A is creating credit through labors means that behind the scenes member A is paying debts to other member at the same time. Therefore, in order to maintain these debt and credit relationships, the creation and elimination of debt by contributing labor to the community will be repeated to some extent contemporaneously and on a similar scale, which may be one condition for meeting expectations and maintaining trust among members. Of course, here, for the purpose of explanation, the relationship between debts and credits is merely imitated and should not be understood as a synonym for monetary debt.

In this respect, its practical implications may become clearer when compared to the Warren-Pare type of labor notes. In the Warren-Pare type, the acceptance or non-acceptance of labor notes was dictated by the credit power or creditworthiness of the product buyer. However, this imposes limits on the scope to offer credit, especially for the individual member. It also limits the range of circulation to the sphere of each buyers' acquaintances—as it will only be by knowing someone, that it would be possible to make a judgment concerning their creditworthiness. Under these restrictions, the exchanges tend to be short-term and limited in terms of amounts of hours being credited.[8] For Time Dollar, on the other hand, the requester (buyer) is not in a position to be investigated the creditworthiness by negotiating member, but rather is in a position to receive another member's time, because the creditworthiness of the requester is substituted by the NPO, which is issuing Time Dollar. This means that the scope for Time Dollar's operations is broadened beyond concrete individuals with direct relationships to encompass more abstract notions of membership that takes into account intermediary organizations. Therefore, the provider can provide the service with peace of mind by trusting the management and coordination of the intermediate group rather than having to rely on their knowledge of the individual with whom they are transacting an exchange. Meanwhile, the buyer who receives credit has no obligation to repay the debt, and will only have an ethical obligation (trust) to service the Time Dollar community in the future. This can obscure individual liability for payment promises. Moreover, as a consequence, the creditworthiness of the issuing organization may be put at risk.

Theoretical Survey of LETS

LETS is similar to Time Dollar in that it develops on the basis of a critical recognition of the national currency, but there are significant differences. In the following, we will provide an outline of the theoretical characteristics of LETS based on Nishibe (2001).

According to Nishibe, LETS starts out from the premise that standard monetary systems are based on the principle of "right to buy," where the possessor of money can decide to spend it indiscriminately. However, as a matter of course, the ownership of money itself is not guaranteed to all citizens. Given those premises, if the possession of money were to be used

[8] A local currency called a bond type such as a WAT ticket has a similar issue to the Warren-Pare type labor notes in the issuing mechanism (Murayama 2002: 134–146). WAT tickets are issued as promises of future payments, similar to the Warren-Pare type, but the notes can be endorsed and recirculated by the recipient. Even if it is limited to circulation among individuals, the endorsement is designed to enhance the creditworthiness of notes. However, the promised payment content is a fixed amount in the currency of the WAT ticket and may be less specific. Rather, like the Warren-Pare type, the promise may become concrete and the notes may be more easily credited by clearly specifying the kind and amount of labor to be paid, while using the commensurable counter of labor time as a standard.

as a legitimate claim for the right to live, then the ownership of money would have to be guaranteed to all members of the nation. In existing monetary systems, this is clearly not the case, as the individual possession of money is dictated by market forces. For LETS, however, the source of the problem lies in the personal separation of the issuer of money from the owner. If the right to issue money—and thus also the ownership of money—were to be enjoyed by every citizen, then the "right to buy" would need to be an unconditional guarantee, and that this is something LETS seeks to achieve for all its members. This is based on the recognition that the "right to buy" is an essential right for life within an exchange economy. The right to purchase is an essential right that constitutes the right to life or the right to live. Also, in LETS, granting monetary issuance rights to each member means that the authority to issue money is partially transferred from the hands of the state to individual LETS members. It has the effect of easing the centralized monopoly on the management and operation of currencies. If currencies are centrally managed and operated, the right to issue currencies will not belong to each member. By seeking to devolve these powers, LETS members would have to take responsibility for issuing and operating money.

The question of money interest is a second problem that LETS seeks to address. Currently, the charging of interest plays the role of a trigger, in that it enables the self-valorization process, whereby money is lent with the aim of accumulating further money at a future date; this injects a combination of endless consumer desires to keep an artificially high level of monetary circulation, and the potential for hoarding to accumulate money for its own sake. Furthermore, the discounted present value of future monetary value under a positive interest rate will be evaluated as low, and investment tends to be short-term (Lietaer 2013/1999). LETS enhances future valuation by setting zero or negative interest rates, in the hope of facilitating longer-term and more sustainable investment projects. In addition, the negative interest rate will reduce the motivation for money hoarding whereby "money bears money."

LETS finally seeks to address a third problem that was also found in the case of Time Dollar. Just as with Cahn's assessment of the negative impacts of monetary pricing, LETS also warns of the impact of centralized pricing by way of money in that it tends to foster market-centric values. Yet, there is a significant difference between the two alternative systems in that LETS does not seek to introduce labor time as alternative unit of exchange. Rather, LETS seeks to solve the problem by tackling the pricing mechanism itself. LETS uses a system of pricing designed to add not only economic value, but also to factor in the diverse values of the participants. Specifically, mutual values and prices are settled through the process of bargaining on the basis of mutual negotiation. As a result, it is expected that the price level will not converge to one price but will be diversified into multi-price agreements. "Multi-priced" means that non-market value may or may not be factored into the finally agreed price. In this case, LETS does not always attach importance to connection with labor time but opts for a different mechanism that is not directly linked to the question of equivalence or commensurability. This is because labor time makes us aware of the equivalence of transactions using the labor process as the means of measurement. With LETS on the other hand, due to the negotiated nature of the exchange mechanism, there is a risk that the local currency, which should form a lending and borrowing relationship mediated by the community, ends up reverting to a more directly coercive relationship between individuals based on the traditional relationship of debtor and creditor (Nishibe 2001: 37–39). We shall see below how LETS seeks to address this potential risk.

LETS is an account book method that uses each member's account book without issuing paper notes. An account book is distributed to each member and transactions are bilateral. The buyer writes in the account book minus the purchased commodity price, and the seller writes in the account book plus the sold commodity price. Through this procedure, it seeks to replace money issuance altogether. The important point here is that the deficit recorded in the buyer's account book does not constitute a direct liability to the seller (the trading partner). This deficit means a responsibility or promise to pay back in the future to the integrity of the community organized by LETS members. The debt in LETS is there referred to as a "commitment" (ibid., 39) because it is an indicator of the depth of engagement with the LETS community. Such a LETS community is one founded upon the mutual agreement of the following four principles. First, joining and withdrawing from LETS is free with the consent of the individual. Second, the accounts held by LETS participants do not bear interest. Third, the operating costs must be shared by the participants. Fourth, all the transactions of the participants are open to the public (ibid., 35).

Moreover, due to its "zero-sum principle," the total of all individual trading accounts is zero in both the deficit and the surplus sides of the ledger. Not only does the account balance bear no interest, but it is also not possible for individuals to make loans. Trading at LETS does not create a debtor and creditor relationship between negotiating members, and commitments represent unpaid future payment liability with no fixed date and promises to participants. Therefore, LETS can be described as "trust money" (ibid., 41) established under the relationship by which each member mutually trusts the other's commitment to future repayment. In light of the consideration of Time Dollar in the previous section, this can be referred to as "gentle trust money."

LETS also seeks to evade the materiality of money, because the issuing agency does not have physical collateral and is not empowered to issue paper notes. Yet, this raises the question of why the materiality of money matters so much in LETS. The reason lies in the recognition that money in the form of paper notes is a representative of precious metals, which causes the mystery of money. By replacing money as a symbol of material wealth with a system that is based on the symbol of human trust in the community, LETS aims to reduce the illusion that money itself has inherent value, thus seeking to undermine the fetishism of money.[9]

Furthermore, LETS operates with the principle of information disclosure, by which the transactional history of the participants in terms of what they need and what they can provide is made available to all participants. By relying on this form of information disclosure, it is possible to judge whether there is an effective matching of supply and demand

[9] In this regard, Associate Professor Tsutomu Katsumura (Hokusei Gakuen University) made some useful points in personal communication. He pointed out that the local currency is supposed to use the fetishism of money rather than reduce it. Perhaps in local currency theory, there is a tendency to recognize money as physical money, which may be a problem related to its over-emphasis on the materiality of money. In other words, metal money and paper money (credit money) are subject to fetishism as long as they are associated material wealth. And, following the instrumental view of money since Smith, that originally money was simply a means of exchange, it is understood that money should not necessarily be joined to goods or tangible wealth. Therefore, since money itself is not wealth, the original pursuit of exchange is well served by the dematerialization and symbolization of money. However, my understanding is that the fetishism of local currency lies in the search for a symbol of trust in a totally worthless currency, and by making it into an alternative currency based on the principle of agreement between members, in which money serves as a symbol of trust.

This differs significantly from theories of labor notes, whereby the problem is not one of money as a representative wealth, backed by metals, but in the fact that it is an imperfect representative. If money or labor notes could be the perfect represent of wealth, then the desire for labor notes would indicate a desire for wealth itself. The question is whether this enables labor notes to evade the trap of fetishism.

and whether the trading partner is reliable or not, so that it is possible to suppress the moral hazard of the participants and the arbitrage dealings of merchants.

In contrast with Time Dollar, LETS does not rely on an intermediary group for issuing currency, leaving the members directly responsible as part of a community. In lieu of being a debtor, the member who has benefitted registers a commitment as a deficit that they must pay. In addition, it is the two parties directly involved in the transaction that determine the amount of constituted by that commitment, and the agreement between the two parties also establishes the position of individual transactions with the community. Therefore, despite the fact that the transaction was made between two parties at free pricing, the payee for the commitment is not the seller but the third-party member who may have different values. If the transaction with an unspecified third party is continued, transactions between members holding different measures (standards of value) will be repeated. It is expected that the density of obligations produced by this measure will be corrected during a series of iterations. If such an inference holds true, it is doubtful whether various measures can be included in a single LETS price only on the condition of negotiation (especially when factoring in the issue of spatiotemporal dispersion). Perhaps the very fact that markets have an in-built process of correction enables it to function more effectively, albeit revealing the limitations of a system that does not fundamentally re-examine the way price should be.

Above, I have looked at the question of modern local currency from the perspective of the grounds and methods of issuance. In the following, we shall return to Owen's theory of labor notes, to see whether, in light of the foregoing examples, he was able to address the questions raised about the grounds and methods of issuance. After that, we shall consider how local currency has sought to overcome the problems of labor notes, and also in what respect labor notes retain a degree of validity today.

6.2 Robert Owen: Putting the Theory of Labor Notes into Practice

On Owen's Theory of the Labor Notes—Reprise

As we saw earlier, Owen developed an early form of underconsumption theory to explain the economic crisis of his time. This was based on four key points. First, with the end of the Napoleonic War, the market contracted with the drying up on military-related procurement. Second, merchants had been reliant upon this method to stockpile commodities and artificially raise prices—in the absence of social demand this continued to fuel inflation. As a result, overproduction appeared as a perverted instance of "poverty in abundance," where poverty is caused not by scarcity, but by the way markets are dictated by merchants. Third, with the increase in productive forces after the Industrial Revolution, there was an increase in demand for money which the Bank of England was unable to supply, because it was restricted by the policy of holding reserves for the payment of specie. The currency, which was restricted to gold reserves, did not reach the hands of workers and producers. It also restricted purchasing power, which promoted poverty and reduced the sales channels. Fourth, Owen thought that the total value of commodities in the market that could be represented by gold was limited by the amount of gold available, as gold money has a unique value as a commodity. In other words, the amount of value obtained by the value of gold multiplied by the amount of gold constitutes the total amount of social wealth that gold can represent. If the total value of various commodities increases rapidly, it will deviate from the total value of gold in circulation. If so, gold would represent only a fraction of the commodity value of the market. In order to eliminate the "lack of money" caused by this, it would be necessary simultaneously to satisfy the two requirements of (a) creating purchasing power for the working class and (b) securing sufficient sales channels. According to Owen's analysis, a crisis and depression could be avoided through the introduction of a labor notes system that would simultaneously and proportionally create purchasing power and sales channels.

It would require some explanation to discuss the fourth reason. In order to explain gold's unsuitability as a material of money, Owen states that the quantity theory of money is based on an implicit theoretical assumption that connects a certain level of the value of gold to the value of commodities, of productivity,[10] and of the velocity of the circulation

[10] Owen emphasizes that the monetary system of the gold standard cannot cope with the increase in productive forces due to the Industrial Revolution, but the theory of labor note does not take into account the change in productivity. The theory only considers the case of expanding production quantitatively under the condition of constant productivity. Marx criticized his failure to factor in changes to productivity change, which led him to question the viability of labor notes (Marx 1986/1857–1858: 72–76). Owen might have thought that the productivity within a community could be treated as constant

of money.[11] Owen appeared to have developed his theory of labor notes based on such theoretical assumptions or ideal conditions. If so, labor notes would have to be an extremely rigid monetary system as set out in the above terms. In the labor notes system, once the value of a commodity and a note are determined, they do not fluctuate, and in terms of circulation, the velocity of the notes remains constant (it is worth noting that when Owen and Gray refer to money as gold, it does not indicate only gold coins, but it also includes banknotes under the gold standard—in which they could be redeemed for gold). Unlike gold money, labor notes are to be issued immediately upon production, which implies a completely different process for the issuing of money.

In addition, as mentioned in Chapter 4, Owen sought to base the setting of labor time as a standard within the ideological framework of "environmentally determinist" theory of "character formation," so that for "*Any general character, from the best to the worst, from the most ignorant to the most enlightened, may be given to any community, even to the world at large, by the application of proper means*" (Owen 1993a/1813–1814: 34), because "*the character man is, without a single exception, always formed for him*" by his social environment (ibid., 62). According to Owen, a major part of an individual's personality is passively formed by the social environment. Therefore, Owen's theory of character formation argues that an individual cannot be held responsible for the character formed, or for the actions taken based on their character. In the literature, this is sometimes referred to as "non-responsibility theory" (Hijikata 2003: 47). Social beliefs such as personal responsibility and free will provide a philosophical basis for approving competitive market economies and punishment/reward systems based on private ownership as factors

for a certain period of time, because the best technology was always adopted within the community and the unevenness of the technical level was eliminated within one community.

[11] If the velocity of circulation and the value of money are constant, and if the commodities must be sold out and the money must be used up over every cycle or period, the commodity owners would have no choice but to reduce prices and make losses as the value of their products increases. Under Gray's assumption, the supply of money (gold) cannot keep pace with the increase in production, so that unequal exchange is forced. If we continue to exchange for the equivalent, we will end up with an underconsumption type of crisis due to lack of money (Gray 1842: 101). Although it does not imply a direct influence, it is believed that Owen was implicitly making the same assumption as Gray.

that drive people to embrace selfish desires and, as such, to disrupt social harmony. "[T]he supposition that each individual man forms his own character, and that therefore he is accountable for all his sentiments and habits, and consequently merits reward for some and punishment for others," is "the true and sole origin of evil" (Owen 1993a/1813–1814: 61). Therefore, in order to get rid of the selfish character of each individual, it is essential to change the social environment. Human beings can be free, only when they become the ones who manage the environment, rather than being managed by the environment.

Owen's theory of character formation was also reflected in the idea of labor evaluation, where the difference in labor evaluation among individuals was mainly seen to be caused by the difference between occupation and skill. In other words, a person's family at birth and social environment largely determined what kind of occupation they will have, especially when the cost of education and training had to be met privately. If the environmental deficiencies that cause the disparity in labor evaluation are improved, the initial conditions made fair, and the education and training costs are publicly borne, it may be possible to eliminate the disparity caused by the environment. Moreover, if the community using labor notes guarantees "many times the amount of wealth that is necessary to support the individual in considerable comfort" (Owen 1993b/1821: 301), it would be expected that the selfish desire would disappear and that people would behave altruistically.

According to Bidet, Smith "defines value by the quantity of labour understood as 'a sacrifice of the same quantitative magnitude'," "Ricardo referring to the power that people *possess*," and "Marx referring to the power that they *expend*" (Bidet 2009/1985: 39, 43). Owen's view had much in common with Smith's and Ricardo's labor-embodied theory of value, in that labor is a power associated with human nature and should be considered separately from the results of the labor expended. In this view, all forms of labor are viewed as a kind of sacrifice humans are forced to pay for working, and this should be measured in terms of external time as a natural standard. The theory of labor notes, which sets the equivalent amount of labor exchange as the principle of fairness, tried to realize this principle by confronting the mutual temporal sacrifices occasioned by different acts of labor by comparing them with one another. However, Marx said that the value of labor cannot be determined through the prism of personal and psychological sacrifice, but rather through the market, in relation to others. Hijikata has sought to explain this in terms of Owen's position as a transitional thinker between the classical enlightenment which thought in terms of a "general consideration of human's 'nature'" and the later utilitarianism which had "a tendency to pay attention to the individual difference in the 'personality' of each person" (Hijikata 2003: 60). However, with the binary confrontation of "truth = nature" and "falsity = artificial" in mind, Owen's theory of labor notes, which confronted metal money as an "artificial standard" with labor as a "natural standard" may be considered to be more firmly rooted within the enlightenment.

Again, needless to say, Owen did not believe his theory of labor note would be swiftly accepted by public opinion and carried out on a large scale. Owen thought he needed to build miniatures of the ideal society and present the results in a visible way. Therefore, the actual labor notes will be issued only within the self-sufficient community through the following procedure. To begin with, when producers bring their labor products into the warehouse-bank complex of the community, the assessor of the warehouse-bank complex certifies the labor time objectified by the product, and the producer receives in exchange a labor note with the face value of the certified labor time for that product. Since each producer can obtain the labor notes by the same procedure, all the products produced in the community will be stored in the warehouse. The producers who obtain the labor notes become consumers, and can obtain the result of other people's labor from the warehouse as much as the labor time they have spent. One could think of such labor notes as banknotes issued with labor products as asset collateral, as they are called "community banknotes" by Owen himself. At that moment, the total amount of bank assets measured in labor time and the total amount of issued banknotes should match, so the reserve ratio of the warehouse-bank complex in the community will be 100%. The circulation channels of the labor notes as a representative are limited between the producer and the warehouse, and between the warehouse and the consumer. There cannot be free horizontal circulation between the producer and the consumer. Labor notes were an effort to create community-based currency from the bottom up as a way of demonstrating the possibility of an alternative to the national currency. But in this case, it also acknowledged the need for centralized currency management such as the warehouse-bank complex of the community.

The Theory of the Labor Note in Practice

As we know, it was not long before Owen's theory of Labor Notes was being put into practice in the New Harmony experimental community and the labor exchange. These experiences have highlighted the way in which the practical running of these schemes were affected by questions of ownership. In a previous paper (Yuki 2004a), I described the practical differences arising from the way they implemented labor notes, by classifying them into two types: the "cooperative society type" and "independent small producer type," by paying attention to the way each handled the question of ownership. For the purposes of this chapter, I would like to update the description by referring to the former as the "New Harmony type" and the latter the "labor exchange type." Since New Harmony was examined in Chapter 4, we will consider the labor exchange type in this section.

As we saw in Chapters 4 and 5, Owen, who returned to Britain after the dissolution of New Harmony, was unexpectedly welcomed by the labor and cooperative movement, which had gained momentum due to the penetration of Owenism among their circles. Owen, for his part, chose to embrace the cooperative movement, as it looked like a feasible model for practicing labor notes, especially given the scale of financial losses he incurred when New Harmony failed, which meant he lacked the capital to build his own community in Britain. In these circumstances, the labor exchange was ideally positioned to fund new community projects, but it also meant that Owen was dependent on the structure of the movement which was mainly composed of independent small producers such as craftsmen and cooperative small business.

Prior to the establishment of the labor exchange, Owen had set out his views on how the labor exchange should work, in an article published in *Crisis*. Here, he announced that the labor exchange will be established under the name of "**Equitable Banks of Exchange**." This Equitable Banks of Exchange would be set up as an "**association for removing ignorance and poverty by education and employment**," and would be based on the work of equal labors "to receive provisions, clothing, and other property, and services of every description, to be exchanged on the equitable principle of *labour*, for *equal value of labour*, through the medium of *Labour Notes*." In addition, the Equitable Banks of Exchange also was to serve as a convertible business that "exchange the *Labour Notes* for the currency of the country." Although the Equitable Banks of

Exchange is called a bank, it did not carry out any deposit/credit activities, and operations were limited to depositing labor products and issuing labor notes (*Crisis*, Vol.1, No.15 & 16, June 30, 1832, p. 59).

The article goes on to criticize merchants and brokers for obstructing the equivalence of labor exchange between producers. Under the commercial system, in order for producers to obtain what need, they must exchange their own products for money. However, in order to obtain money, the product has to be sold to the money owners represented by the merchants, and thus the producers are inevitably deprived of direct mutual access by the merchant in the middle. Therefore, the producer is forced to sell to the merchant at a price below the value of the product, while, on the other hand, they are required to purchase the commodities from the merchant at a price above value. In this way, *Crisis* accurately analyzed the asymmetrical nature of money and commodities, in the way that personal relationships between producers (commodity owners) are mediated by merchants (money owners). And if money divides the normal exchange of the market into the buying and selling activities of sellers and buyers of commodities, the commercial system and the monopolistic possession of money as capital must be removed (hence cutting off the power of the merchant to appropriate the labor of others). The Equitable Exchange Bank would thus intervene in the exchange process by serving as a so-called fair merchant/commercial institution, but "This system is not only applicable to individuals but to Societies" (ibid.). This meant that it would not be enough for the Equitable Exchange Bank to behave in a fair manner, and that the participants would also be expected to adopt a sociable and fraternal manner.

Another issue cropped up concerning consistency and structural integration. Although the total amount of labor notes issued by local Equitable Exchange Banks and the total amount of deposits are equal in quantity, it is hard to say that they are qualitatively consistent. Therefore, the local branch of the Equitable Banks of Exchange exchanges the necessary products with each other, so that it is devised to deal with the local situation of supply and demand. The remittance work associated with the exchange of products between the branches is carried out by transferring the book accounts of the branches, so that the total supply and demand becomes the same through the network between the bank branches. Moreover, this would open up the prospect of local branches acting as mediators for the exchange of products via a country-wide network. For that purpose, it would be necessary constantly to exchange information between bank branches in each region, and for there to be some kind of infrastructure or centralized organization that would oversee adjustments in supply and demand at a regional and national level. It must be clearly understood what and how much would needed in which region (ibid.). The prompt and transparent communication of information between banks, remained dependent on the attitude of participants, and the assumption that they would behave fairly, unselfishly, and fully willing to co-operate. However, adjusting supply and demand among bank branches would not be so easy. According to Yoshida, although the opportunity for producers to deposit commodities at the labor exchange resolves the problem of *salto mortale*, or trusting things to chance, this would not resolve the difficulty of selling or finding an effective buyer—in that there appears to be nothing to prevent a holder of money from parting with it. Yoshida points out that, at the time of receiving the commodities, according to the rules of the exchange, there would be no choice but to resort to "selective purchase" or "forced sale" to labor money holders (Yoshida 2002: 67–69).

In fact, on September 17, 1832, a store named the "National Equitable Labour Exchange" opened on Gray's Inn Road in London. What materialized fell somewhat short of the spectacular image of the Equitable Banks of Exchange as envisioned in the article for *Crisis*. Nonetheless, there was an attempt to retain the fairness principle of equivalent amount of labor exchange, which in Owen's philosophy, is where exchanges would be based on the "value of equal labor." A compromise emerged that brought the natural standard of value as labor closer to its market evaluation than would have otherwise been possible. This was achieved by fixing the ratio of labor time and wages at five shillings, which was the average wage of one working day (10 working hours) at that time. By adopting this standard, the standard wage per labor time was worked out at 6 pence. Using this value as a new standard, individual depositors were categorized by job category, and the wages were divided by 6 pence to convert into labor time. Moreover, not only the living labor directly bestowed, but also the prices of labor products were converted into labor time by the same method of calculation. Using this method, the price structure of the product would be calculated by converting the raw material cost and the wages of directly bestowed labor into labor time by the above-mentioned method. Commission would be added for maintaining a labor exchange (*Crisis*, Vol. 1, No. 15 & 16, June 30, 1832, p. 61). As can be seen, the procedure of dividing the price of a product by the average wage and converting it back into labor time reveals the system's limitations from the outset in that it cannot be realized unless the market price exists outside the labor exchange. It can be said that such a method of calculating labor time was adopted in consideration of the unfairness among the participants, which is caused by the uniform evaluation of different kinds of labor as experienced in New Harmony. While Warren praised differences in valuation over different kinds of labor as reflecting the individuality of each person, in the case of a labor exchange, it was apparently a step backwards from labor time as a natural standard. It can be seen that the beliefs about the attitude toward the market, and eventually the standard as labor time, were beginning to fluctuate. Despite the fact that labor exchange transactions were booming at the time of their opening, the transaction volume gradually decreased, and it closed after 2 years.[12]

Another feature worth noting in the practical workings of the labor exchanges lays beyond the immediate sphere of exchange, in terms of the way in which they brought together supporters of Owen's cooperative ideas and enabled them to carry out entertainment and cultural activities. It can be seen that even if they could not provide it, they actively participated in the cultural activities of the exchange. In that sense, the labor exchange that issued labor notes played a role of furnishing a cultural and ideological symbol that connected the participants. Furthermore, labor notes were used by surrounding merchants and theaters. It is said that there was a period when the circulation range was expanded, and it began to exhibit some of the characteristics of an active currency (Cole 1953: 182–184). Yet, this did little to counteract the threat posed by the circulation of labor notes to merchants and companies that have not deposited their products in labor exchanges to the principle of the balance of supply and demand, and the idea of equitable exchange. It may have been difficult to comply with these principles as the issuance of labor notes was based on the paper note method that can be circulated. Moreover, these principles weakened the monetary nature of labor notes. It is also impaired the ability of labor notes as money to penetrate into peripheral economic areas. Originally, labor notes were only given the role of going back and forth between producers and labor exchanges, so there

[12] See Maruyama for an overview of changes in the trading volume of labor exchanges (Maruyama 1997: 21–23).

would be no need to use paper notes in particular.[13] Yet, if the emphasis on the principle of the balance of supply and demand, it would be more appropriate to use a book method that prevents the possibility of freely circulating outside the labor exchange like paper money. The fact that the labor note was used in a store outside the labor exchange meant that it was circulated among people who were not eligible to participate in the labor exchange. Therefore, it cannot be denied that labor notes were exchanged for money by outside merchants.

Although the value of products handled in labor exchanges (displayed as labor time) was calculated based on the market price of products, the value of products in labor exchanges did not always match the market price of similar products. Therefore, whenever the evaluation value of the products displayed in the labor exchange turned out to be lower than the market price, it would be resold on the external market. Where it was the other way around, it would be brought to the labor exchange. As a result, there was a pile of unsold merchandise inventory at the labor exchange. Most likely this was due to the fact that the labor exchange was indifferent to consumer trends and accepted the products brought into them indefinitely. Besides, there was no attempt strictly to regulate qualification for participation. In addition, the demand problem also arose from another cause. In terms of the labor exchange system, the types of products that could be sold were limited by the occupational composition of the participants. As a result, craftsmen-based labor exchange would only supply handicraft products, making it difficult to supply daily necessities such as agricultural products. While labor exchanges have the positive side of being able to evaluate the labor of producers who do not receive sufficient consideration in the market, they have the limitation that they cannot provide a way to sell the labor notes paid as consideration. This was compounded by the fact that physically the structure of the labor exchange ended up acting as a storehouse for inventory, which posed limitations on the volume of commodities that could be deposited. This limit is not only one of geography, in that only people who live near the labor exchange can participate, but also included logistical restrictions in

[13] *Crisis* says, "This note should be formed of the toughest paper that can be made, in order that it may last for a long period in circulation" (*Crisis*, Vol. 1, No. 15 & 16, June 30, 1832, p. 61) and mentions the possibility of circulation of paper notes. There is a description in labor exchanges where it was thought that total supply and demand would be matched if only the amount of paper notes issued was managed.

terms of transportation (ibid.). Furthermore, the participation of wage laborers who could not own labor products, where their own labor was excluded, alongside the participation of non-producers such as merchants could not be discounted. Ironically, the labor exchange was only suitable for independent small producers who had a craftsman-like working style in which they could own their own products. Of course, it could be said that the system was theoretically suitable for farmers, but the model largely precluded rural communities due to its geographical restrictions. It should be noted that the article in *Crisis* failed to provide a concrete solution to the question of intangible labor, even though it was proclaimed to handle service labor.

Below, I will summarize the problems that have arisen at labor exchanges. First, labor exchanges could only handle tangible labor products. Therefore, it was impossible to handle labor that did not result in physical form. This may have contributed to the negative recognition of intangible labor as unproductive labor. Second, even the workers who are engaged in the production process were excluded because of the condition of participation that limited the types of jobs to which they could deposit the products of their labor unless they had control of the conditions of production that allowed them to own the results of their production. Third, since handicrafts were mainly provided according to the occupational composition of the participants, even if fair exchange of chairs and chests of drawers was possible, for example, it would be difficult to exchange chairs and wheat. Fourth, it was more uncertain whether the deposited product was actually sold at its value, even if it was said that the market price at the time of the deposit was taken into consideration, because the labor notes are issued when the product is brought to the labor exchange, and the value of the notes and the product are fixed by the market value. The labor exchange lacked a mechanism to appropriately draw up the demand of the participants and reflects the value in real time (which as a theoretical problem was at the heart of Marx's criticism of Proudhon). In addition to associating the value of the product with the market price, it would also have been necessary to try to adjust prices for the inventory of deposited products—especially where they were not clearing. For example, if the date, job title, producer name, etc., were written, such as Warren-Pare type note, it would have been possible to retroactively revise the face value of the notes.[14] Therefore, is it worth questioning whether the mechanism for forming a social agreed price was sufficient since it was ultimately a value-price issue? Fifth, the method of converting market prices into labor time on the basis of average wages did not function well. The reason for this was that it was unlikely that the market price at the time of reference would completely reflect the fluid supply and demand trend. Besides, the method of dividing the market price by the average wage was not sufficiently reflected in the supply and demand trend, although that too is as long as the market price was reflected in the value of the product. Therefore, it was conceivable that an overvalued product could pile up as inventory in the labor exchange, which could be manipulated by a merchant operating as a seller across different markets who could take advantage of the difference between the market price and the value of product. Labor notes, which used the paper note method, could not prevent it from being passed to the merchants, creating an inevitable leakage. Finally, it can be said that the method of dividing the market price of the product based on the average wage inherited by the wage gap between occupations under the market economy, which was fatal in terms of addressing the fundamental reasons for establishing the scheme in the first place.

6.3 Key Aspects Concerning the Basis for Issuing Money

The New Harmony and Labor Exchange Types Compared

A common feature that underlies most theories of labor notes lies in the critique of metal money in all its practical manifestations. Based on the recognition that the money supply is constrained by the Bank of England's policy of holding gold in reserve for the payment of specie, the theories of labor note emerged as way of maintaining a closer relationship with the substance of production. On the other hand, it was developed within the framework of Chartalist theories of money in that it is predicated on a political settlement that enables money to be liberated

[14] The face of the labor notes issued at the labor exchange says that "Equitable Bank of Exchange / The Price of Labour is Sixpence per Hour. / No. of the Note issued. Date. / Deliver to the Bearer on demand, Exchange Stores of the value of —— hours." etc., and these matters are guaranteed by the trustee. The notes must also be signed by depositors and trustees (*Crisis*, Vol. 1, No. 15 & 16, June 30, 1832, p. 61).

from its metallic basis. While theories of labor notes explained the necessity for the relinquishment of the basis of money in precious metals, it was expected that it would lose the credibility of money if it pushed into unreserved money, as was advocated by contemporaries like the Birmingham based banker Thomas Attwood (1783–1856). It was said that the labor notes should reflect a labor-based substance of production, instead of just acting as a symbolic token. Moreover, the shape of the market to be reconstructed by labor notes was imagined as one that would be extremely static. This was because it was largely born out of a need to address an acute crisis of underconsumption, and was therefore, was designed with a focus on creating purchasing power and the sales channel at the same time and establishing proportionality between participants based on the substance of their labor. As such, the model failed to grasp the inherent potential within the system for participants to hoard money due to the lack of any in-built mechanism for purchasing power to be immediately converted to demand. It may be because of the idea that it is only necessary to realize potential demand by creating purchasing power based on the recognition of an underconsumption crisis, that these problems arose. Yet, such a theoretical requirement meant that the generated purchasing power would need to correspond to the amount of nominal value produced, and that the circulation channels of labor notes and products would have to be limited to the transactional relationship between members and labor exchanges or community warehouses. The system became rigid because it could not immediately respond to changes in productivity. Nonetheless, there is no a priori reason why labor notes should be unable to free itself from these problems, since the non-normative nature of the market is due to the behavior of merchant capital in pursuit of profits, or because credit creation on a scale that exceeds financial reserves liberates money from the substance of production.

It is necessary to pay attention to the differences between New Harmony and the labor exchange trying them as operating according to two types of labor notes. The New Harmony type was based on a closed society which operated according to a self-sufficient, communal life based on common ownership of the means of production. In the case of a labor exchange, each participant had an independent family household and property, and the exchange served solely as a place where products could be provided in the hope of mutual exchange. Therefore, the degree to which the participants depended on the labor notes system for their subsistence varied. In the case of New Harmony, the aim was to organize society completely through the development of a single system of labor notes that would act in lieu of any national currency. The method of achieving this was to be quantitatively based on the progressive growth of the community, and on the spread of its community-based way of life. It is also worth noting that Owen's communitarianism was evident in the hope that it would one day spread to be able to ace as a national system. At the same time, the approach resulted in a dual system whereby labor notes existed alongside the national currency, and made no attempt at a macro level to address this duality or to address the fact that the wider market economy remained intact. Perhaps it would have been difficult to overcome the anarchy of production by the method of establishing island communities run by people who have voluntarily chosen to exit the market. This raises the questions that Marx used when charging that the system of labor notes did nothing to change the production process or system of ownership. However, in the context of Owenism, which differed markedly from the likes of those targeted by Marx such as Gray (who will be discussed in the next chapter), the idea of a state directed program for the management of supply and demand had yet to be born. The reality of a collaborative, practical economy has just begun to be explored, and it would be anachronistic to project back onto Owen what only became apparent at the time Marx was writing (largely through his own theoretical and political labors).

When compared to labor exchange, New Harmony attempted to provide a comprehensive view of what could be imagined at that point in time, and it is worth examining these differences. First, the labor exchange was not able to handle intangible labor because it took the form of individuals depositing their products. It also was unable to tackle the issues which prevented wage workers from participating. However, in New Harmony, intangible labor was handled because it replaced the issuance of labor notes by book method, regardless of whether the products were deposited. When issuing notes, it was not necessarily based on the physical collateral of the labor product, but on the basis of the labor itself that contributed to the community. On the second point, the distribution of surplus based on common ownership saved them from the problem of exploitation in the production process due to wage labor. Under a community-based labor notes system of the kind represented by New Harmony, it should be possible for various social security systems to be combined through the redistribution of social surpluses. The community-based labor notes system would, therefore, be better suited to the purpose of building cooperative social structures. By socially accommodating surplus products accumulated in the community, it should be possible to take into account the broad needs of each member. Third, the cooperative lifestyle in the community could be considered to be relatively independent of the market economy, so it would be possible to maintain a practically applicable idea of a measure of labor time that expresses non-market values. In a cooperative society in which the economic resources of the community are guaranteed for each member, and equal rights, obligations, and generous social security are combined, it should be easier to feel the homogeneity and equivalence of labor among the members realistically, and the degree to which labor productivity, skill and proficiency, and other individual differences are reflected by income inequality in a market system would be lowered. Of course, it will not be possible to achieve it without clearing the labor exchange, which would apply equally within a closed community where the total supply and demand inside the community would need to be matched at some point.

The Labor Note and the Time Dollar

Let us consider what the Time Dollar and labor notes have in common. First, Time Dollar is similar to labor notes in that labor time is used as a measure. Second, Time Dollar does not rely on physical assets at the time of money issuance, and the medium of money does not take a tangible form such as paper notes. It is similar to New Harmony's book method in that the currency is managed centrally on the secretariat's personal computer. The difference is that Time Dollar benefits from the use of modern information technology, thus reducing the complexity of book-keeping, which imposed a considerable administrative burden on New Harmony. Third, the measure of labor time is adopted in Time Dollar, on the basis that a person's ability to work and the social interdependence that human beings are seen as intrinsically more of value that marketized conceptions of value. This can be said to conform to a view of human beings that has much in common with Owen's theory of human nature. Furthermore, it honors the proposition that labor is a fundamentally necessary activity for the cyclical maintenance of human society. Which again is a view of social reproduction that has much in common with Owen.

On the other hand, there are many differences. First, Time Dollar is said to be a local currency, and it is not aimed at a complete replacement of the national currency. Rather, its goal is clarified to promote and activate mutually supportive interchanges in local communities. Regarding the national currency, Time Dollar hopes to restrict itself to non-market exchange of labors, leaving market exchange entirely to the national currency. In this way, Time Dollar finds itself avoiding any confrontation with the ambiguous character of money, seeking a way to circumvent the negative aspects of currencies (rather than directly aiming to eliminate them). However, if the realm of Time Dollar is not expanded to the cover the same geographic area as is marked out by markets, then it has no choice but to serve as a safety net to save people from the worst effects of the market—rather than eradicating them at source. As Cahn himself has recognized, the advantages and disadvantages of money are inextricably linked. While separating functions of money and eliminating only its disadvantages leaves the endogenous defects of the market intact. Second, due to the nature of Time Dollar, which is based on gifted volunteer activities, the amount of money issued does not have to be strictly controlled by associating it with the number of services provided. This is because the act of acquiring Time Dollar often leads to a feeling of psychological satisfaction that contributes to a sense of belonging to a community, and the imperative of demanding some kind of like-for-like compensation is uncommon among those who participate. Of course, it stands to reason that this kind of forgiveness may be a factor that keeps the Time Dollar alive.

Maruyama, through a case study of the labor exchange, noted that in order for labor notes and Time Dollar to succeed, "the minds of charities and volunteers must grow more than among those who participate in it." "It is necessary for people and society to be mature to accept and demonstrate this kind of mind [charity spirit]." "Thus, Owen's 'exchange' is also feasible if the times change and the shape is changed" (Maruyama 1997: 29). Certainly, there Owen believed in the prospect of equivalent labor exchange becoming universally possible once the spirit of whole people matures and the age of tolerance comes. However, excessive expectations of the spirit, aside, it enabled him to probe the practical possibilities entailed in an economic and social vision based on human trust and gifts. When all that is taken into account, it seems to result in a set of theories of labor notes and local currencies that deviate sharply from the original aims of establishing an alternative system of exchange, whose basis was labor as the substance of production and wealth.

The Labor Note and the LETS

It can be understood that LETS is a local currency that not only has a critical view of the actual state of the national currency, but also has a negative attitude toward the idea of labor notes. The reason can be explained as follows. First, in LETS, the measure and unit of labor time does not necessarily have to be related to the value of the LETS currency and labor time. Certainly, as Nishibe pointed out, when transactions are carried out using the measure and unit of labor time, the issue of whether the equivalence of labor between the exchange parties is secured becomes apparent. Yet in practice, it can hinder the regeneration of the community, first by tying exchange relations to a notion of an exchange of equivalents, and second because it can allow credit to be hoarded, if the buyer chooses not to purchase. Meanwhile, LETS, with its emphasis on a negotiated model of bilateral transactions, aims to raise the values of people who evaluate non-labor by incorporating these elements into its system of pricing. Second, labor notes and Time Dollar could not gain purchasing power without making some contribution to the community through labor. In this method, the power to issue money is concentrated in the labor exchange and the secretariat who are acting as intermediates between the exchanging groups. In a way, this merely repeats the problem ranged against the centralized nature of the national currency, but just at a different level. LETS cannot be exhausted if it finds itself simply transferring the issuance of money from the nation to the regional community and intermediate groups. Furthermore, it is returned to the individual level. The right to issue money can only be attributed to an individual, who is free to realize the ideas of individual freedom and independence.[15] Third, in LETS, it is possible to participate in the purchase as the money issuing right belongs to the individual. Labor notes and Time

[15] Owen's co-operative society was a plan to push the market out of the internal mechanism of social reproduction, but Proudhon denied any centralized authority and said it was the most ideal place for the market to restore its personal authority. The concept of anarchism is reflected in LETS, which devolves money issuance right to the individual level. Nishibe pays attention to the position to which the money issuance right belongs and categorizes local currency into "centralized issuance method" and "distributed issuance method" (Nishibe 2001: 29–32).

Dollar had the constraint that in order to purchase goods or services of some kind, they had to consider working in advance to obtain notes or currencies and to save a certain amount. However, in LETS, currency can be issued and acquired upon purchase. It is easy to respond quickly to the crisis and the depression caused by underconsumption and "lack of money" because the opportunity of demand for purchasing precedes the opportunity of supply such as labor and production. Furthermore, by issuing money through purchasing, the supply of money and the supply of products within LETS will be the same simultaneously, and their face value will necessarily coincide. Moreover, it may be said that an individual, qualitative demand problem is cleared because not only the total amount of supply and demand is matched, but the currency is not issued unless purchase-sale is completed. This ensures a qualitative coinciding of total supply and demand within LETS. Fourth, LETS can handle any kind of thing or service. It can be said that LETS has greater scope range than the labor exchange, where members could not receive the labor notes without depositing labor products.

However, the fact that the purchasing power created within LETS and the value supplied are consistent does not necessarily result in a content that would enable social reproduction. The economy inside LETS and the economy organized through the market may have some overlaps and some divergences. This depends largely on the extent to which participants LETS depend on LETS to procure what they need for subsistence, the extent to which market commodities can be incorporated into LETS, or the degree of regional self-sufficiency.

On the other hand, there is plenty of common ground between labor notes and LETS. The same can be said for Time Dollar, but for LETS there should be no merchant capital or "interest-bearing capital" in the market it seeks to construct, and the currency should reflect the substance of production to a certain extent, thus preventing the problem of over-issuance. Merchant capital and "interest-bearing capital" are understood as unfair factors that induce profit-seeking forms of trade, and the issuance of credit money is also deterred as empty money without sufficient support. For labor notes and local currencies, money should be a pure means of exchange and not an independently working subject that is driving the market exchange process. The fact that money hoarding is not assumed in theories of labor notes can be seen to derive from its belief in the neutrality of money. Since local currency is not the core currency in the commodity economic market, it seems unlikely that there will be an incentive to earn profits through resale or loan. But if they will try to handle commodities directly like labor notes, there will also be the question of how to deal with the intervention of merchants as experienced in labor exchange.

Summary: Unity and Divergence of Theory of Labor Notes

Based on the discussion in this chapter, I will summarize the above description by highlighting some of the key areas in which these ideas branch off in ways that will be explored in detail in Chapter 7 and beyond. Despite stumbling on some difficulties, we can safely demonstrate that labor note theories have disclosed two models regarding the basis and method of issuing money. It can be construed that the theories of local currency avoid the difficulties that cannot be overcome in the practice of labor notes by following a set of similar objectives, but at the expense of sidestepping the question of an exchange of equivalents.

First, the labor notes used at New Harmony were issued on the basis of labor undertaken by its members. Labor between members was understood to be of equal quality and, therefore equivalent, and the value of labor was measured by external duration, namely, time. The notion of labor time as a natural standard served as the theoretical pillar of Owen's theory of character formation, in which he believed that what prevented the universal adoption of equal exchange based on equal labors was the inequalities that had grown up within a society or environment that could be changed. Owen's concept of rationality, was one in which equality and a levelling of lifestyles and standards of living, was taken as a social norm. Based on Owen's concept of homogeneity, the problem of skill among the members could be ignored. In place of metal money, which Owen viewed as an "artificial standard," labor would be employed as the "natural standard." Although given his search for universality, it may be more opt to describe labor as a "universal" rather than a "natural" standard. On the basis of such universality of labor, labor notes were issued in response to the contribution of the labor of the members, which meant they had the flexibility of not requiring any physical guarantee. Also, if labor could become the "universal standard," it would then be possible to be applied to the question of social reproduction to the extent that it can be organized, because it can handle all kinds of labor and their outcomes. However, the "hour for hour" exchange completely homogenized the hourly labor evaluation among the members. It was not a "standard" that could be accepted by all New Harmony residents who were mentally and materially unprepared.

Local currencies have adopted the following methods in order to avoid dissatisfaction with the remuneration of "standard" labor time. On the one hand, although Time Dollar accepts the universality of labor and uses the measure of labor time, its scope is limited to the extent that participants accept the Time Dollar reward. On the other hand, LETS harbors doubts about the universality of labor itself and whether it can be used as a method of accepting values that are not attributable to diverse values and labor. When issuing money, local currencies do not require any physical collateral like the labor notes issued under New Harmony. In that case, labor is still one of the grounds for issuing money, but in contrast to the fact that labor notes emphasized past performance and contributions as proof of credit. Although the debt is loosened in the local currency, it still represents the promise of future payments.

Second, the labor notes of labor exchange were issued against the background of the real asset value of the labor products deposited by the participants. When labor products were deposited at a labor exchange, the value of the products was calculated by using the market price as a medium. With that, the products deposited at the exchange as collateral for the issuance of labor notes were considered to be sound assets with valuations immediately available for sale. As a response to a certain kind of dishonesty involving the act of ordinary banks issuing money in excess of the value of assets held, the ideological integrity of issuing a representative based on complete reserve assets may have been one of the criticisms of the gold standard. However, the interposing of the market price in the asset valuation only heightens the risk of obscuring the attitude of the labor exchange toward money and the market. In other words, there is a logical inconsistency in that the money price cannot be held constant while the market is held. The hope is that such inconsistencies will be avoided if the market and price are included as duals like LETS.

With labor products being deposited as collateral, the labor exchange was firstly able to issue labor notes, and secondly able to operate as a single store, so the credibility of the issued notes could not be secured sufficiently. Furthermore, it may have been thought that the homogeneity of labor among the participating members was not allowed, and there was a gap in the prices of labor products as a result of labor due to differences in the occupations and skill of the participants. Even based on Owen's theory of character formation, it is difficult to perceive the homogeneity and equivalence of each person when the personality and qualities of the individual are formed heterogeneously in a heterogeneous environment. In some cases, the value of labor must be measured by the result of the expenditure of labor rather than the homogeneity of labor, and it may have been done from the standpoint of present status.

Local currencies avoid the difficulties that have arisen at labor exchanges in the following ways. First, labor exchanges tried to derive individual agreements between supply and demand by calculating the value of deposited products and being careful not to trade at an amount that unreasonably deviated from production costs. Nevertheless, the deposit amount was never adjusted. This may be because it was considered in theories of labor note that any price could be sold at any time, but as explained in Chapter 2, "immediate realization at reasonable price" is not possible. However, the *Crisis* article does not fully understand the qualitative differences between commodities and money. Therefore, they may not have noticed the conceptual difference between "buying and selling" and "exchange." In the local currency, the products are accepted only after the needs of the participating members have been established, so money will not be issued endlessly to circulate unnecessary things for which there is no stipulated demand. Since there is no need for a store-type intermediary group, inventory issues will not occur. Second, Time Dollars do not compromise on the application of labor time as a unit of measure. What makes this possible is that only those who have approved the receipt of the Time Dollar are participating, and they are doing so, furthermore, only for labor that can be traded by the Time Dollar. If we do not want to build an Owen-type community and want the secure participation of free-floating individuals, we will have to accept such conditions. Third, the principle of information disclosure will be an important condition for building a relationship of trust among local currency participants. It could not be said that information was sufficiently disclosed at the labor exchange, which resulted in a degree of operational uncertainty. In addition, it may have made it difficult to see the relationship between the participants by not allowing free transactions between them and intervening between labor exchanges.

In general, local currencies are not developed with the aim of establishing a self-sufficient cooperative society, but rather as a steady effort that starts with what can be done through the participants in the scheme. It is supported by the awareness that participants are building the scheme from scratch. In that respect, labor notes tend to predominate in projects like those favored by Owen for their top-down character, whereas local currencies operate in less planned environments. While local currencies can be seen to provide an answer to the difficulties thrown up by labor notes, it does so largely by pursuing a strategy of avoidance, in that they sidestep the tricky issues thrown up by markets, currencies, and ownership. The search for a unit of exchange that would be founded on a substantial theory of wealth, rather than one based on convention and mutual agreement at least had the merit of trying to confront this problem—albeit within a transactional exchange system. Yet, the lessons from local currencies enable us to shed light on aspects of labor note theory which were unavailable to Owen and his contemporaries, notably, in terms of the way information disclosure and information technology can facilitate participation in alternative models of exchange.

Lastly, it is worth noting that labor notes and local currencies have consistently sought to ground themselves in an understanding of the causes of crisis and economic distress, and especially in explanations that view these problems in terms of underconsumption and a shortage of purchasing power. This leaves room to reconsider whether underconsumption provides the best explanation for the cause of the crisis in the early nineteenth century or the present age, or whether other explanations would work better. What is more important, however, is to investigate the ideological basis for the repeated assertion that the causes and solutions to poverty lie in the sphere of consumption (the sense of "poverty amidst abundance") rather than production. That is, to explore the ideology that seeks primarily to reform the sphere of circulation and distribution in the hope of creating purchasing power among the masses.

These issues are reflected in the contemporary discussion in the realms of media, politics, and academia in response to the notable increase in economic crises that have marked the past decade and especially since my earliest draft of this chapter (Yuki 2004b). For example, there is now an entire discourse that focuses on the working poor or the precariat, in which the phenomena of unstable employment is captured from various angles. Considering such discourse, it is doubtful that the "excessive-wealth theory" (Baba, 1997), which argues that living standards in the advanced nations are rising uniformly, is capable of grasping precarity and similar phenomena. Even if people in precarious jobs live in a developed country, they are, nonetheless, fully exposed to the full effects of relative poverty—that is the cost of living in a highly commodified economy where housing, energy, transport, and child care can eat into people's earnings and result in higher levels of debt. Looking at the examples of New Harmony and the labor exchanges, even though their main theoretical focus centered on the problem of finding a universal equivalent that could replace money (i.e., labor), it should never be forgotten that this was to address the real suffering its members were experiencing within a market economy, not to mention the levels of unhappiness this created, which prompted the search for a better life for all. Often it is difficult to visualize the forms of poverty that people may be suffering in foreign countries far away or during distant historical periods, compared to the forms of poverty that are likely to imprint themselves on people's minds when they look around their immediate community. This can often prevent people from forming a global level of consciousness, and enables ideologies to seep in that focus on aspirations, social mobility, competition, and lifestyles that seek to emulate the rich or to gain social status. It also creates an ideological space where awareness of global poverty is overshadowed by racism and anti-immigrant views. This fear of being outsmarted, or seeking to belong to a superior group is something that leads to a race to the bottom, which in many ways was something that people promoting labor notes were aware of, as they sought to counteract the likes of Thomas Malthus and others who sought to explain poverty in naturalistic terms.

Considering the theoretical, ideological, and practical difficulties facing those who sought to find a standard for fair disparities in wages and labor evaluation, I am certainly struck by what is socially possible when we start to think in a way that seeks to emancipate us by recognizing that the freedom of one person can only exist when it is compared with another by way of a system that is absolute and grounded in a standard that ensures their equality. This forms the basic conditions for a true realization of individual freedom. So long as social production is grounded in market competition between owners of capital who are seeking to make a profit, there will always be relative poverty, despite any increases in the forces of production or technological development. While we have to reject the naive communalist egalitarianism that Proudhon, Warren, Pare, and Gesell could not accept, we also have to acknowledge that the question of evaluating labor disparities and developing a system which can fairly compensate people for performing complex forms of labor is one that remains unanswered.

Thus far, the discussions in Chapters 3 to 6 have demonstrated the way in which local currency theory, while refining the vision of money and the market, remains rooted in the same set of problems that confronted the pioneers of labor notes. In Chapters 7 to 8, we move from the exploration of labor note theories in the context of local currency theory, to look at the role that they have played in relation to traditional socialist theory. This will enable us to see how the same issues which emerged in the previous chapters reappear, such as—namely—the debates over comprehensive money reform, the consideration of whether a more egalitarian model of exchange can overcome the lack of stimulus, the persistence of patriarchal philanthropism, and the question of whether a fairer system of distribution is possible within a market framework.

Bibliography

Baba, K. (1997). *Shin Shihonshugiron: Shikakutenkan no Keizaigaku* [New Capitalism: The Economics of Changing Perspectives]. The University of Nagoya Press.

Bidet, J. (2009/1985). *Exploring Marx's capital: Philosophical, economic and political dimensions*. Haymarket Books.

Cahn, E. S. (1999a). Time dollars, work and community: From 'why' to 'why not?' *Futures, 31*(5), 499–509.

Cahn, E. S. (1999b). *No more throw-away people: The co-production imperative*. Essential Books.

Cole, M. (1953). *Robert owen of new lanark*. The Batchworth Press.

Gray, J. (1842). *An efficient remedy for the distress of nations*. Adam and Charles Black.

Gray, J. (1873/1831). *The social system*. Augustus M. Kelley.

Hijikata, N. (2003). *Robāto Ōen* [Robert Owen]. Kenkyusha.

Lietaer, B. A. (2013/1999). *The future of money: Creating new wealth, work and a wiser world*. Cornerstone Digital.

Maruyama, T. (1997). Ōen to Zenkoku Kōseirōdōkōkanjo [Robert owen and the national equitable labour exchange]. *Oitadaigaku Keizaironshū* [Oita University Economic Review], *49*(3–4), 1–32.

Maruyama, T. (2003). Chiikitsūka to Ōen no Rōdōshōken [Local currencies and Robert Owen's labour notes]. *Robert Owen Kyōkainenpō* [The Annual Report of the Robert Owen Association], *27*, 39–57.

Maruyama, M. (2004). Shihon ni tenka shinai "Kahei": Chiikitsūka. In M. Maruyama & R. Uchida (Eds.), *"Shihon" kara Ningen no Keizai he: 20 seiki wo kangaeru* (III) [From "capital" to human economy]. Shinseisha.

Marx, K. (1986/1857–1858). Economic manuscripts of 1857–58. *Marx & Engels collected works* (Vol. 28). Lawrence & Wishart.

Murayama, J. (2002). Chiikitsūka, Samazamana Jissen [Local currencies, various practices]. In R. Sakamoto & K. Kawamura (Eds.), *Ende no Keishō: Chiikitsūka no Kibō to Ginkō no Mirai* [Ende's warning to the future]. NHK Publishing.

Nishibe, M. (2001). LETS ron [On LETS]. *Hihyōkūkan* [Critical space], *3*(1), 27–52.

Nishibe, M. (2002). Shakai Kigyōka Owen [Social entrepreneur owen]. *Jūryoku 01* [Gravity 01], 256–293.

Owen, R. (1993a/1813–1814). A new view of society; or, essays on the principle of the formation of the human character. In G. Claeys (Ed.), *Selected works of Robert Owen* (Vol. 1). William Pickering.

Owen, R. (1993b/1821). Report to the county of Lanark. In *Selected works of Robert Owen* (Vol. 1). William Pickering.

Sugimoto, T. (1995). Jikanyotakusei to Rōdōkōkanjo: Ōen-ha Rōdōkōkan undō no Isan to Kyōkun [Time deposit system and labour exchange: Legacies and lessons of owenites' movement of labour exchange]. *Sēkatsukyōdōkumiai Kenkyū* [Consumer Co-operative Research], *234*, 35–42.

Tanaka, N. (1996). *Shiminshakai no Borantia: "Fureikippu" no Mirai* [Volunteers of civil society: The future of "Fureai ticket"]. Maruzen.

Yoshida, K. (2002). Shijōkeizai to Ekomanē [Market economy and eco-money]. *Robert Owen Kyōkai Nenpō* [The annual report of the Robert Owen association], *26*, 59–73.

Yuki, T. (2004a). Ōen no Rōdōkaheiron no saikentō [Reconsideration of Robert Owen's Labour Money Theory]. *Keizaigakukenkyū* [The Journal of Economic Studies], *46*, 13–24.

Yuki, T. (2004b). Chiikitsūka to Robāto Ōen no Rōdōkahei no Hikaku Kentō: Kahei no Hakkōkonkyo Hōshiki wo Shijiku toshite [A comparative study of local currency and Robert Owen's labor money: From the perspective on the grounds and methods of issuance of money]. *Hikaku Keizai Taisei Kenkyū* [The Jounral of Comparative Economic Studies], *11*, 80–96.

Yuki, T. (2011). Chiikitsūkaron wo meguru Mondai jōkyō: Shinraisetsu wo chūshin toshite [Theoretical problems on local currencies: A focus on the trust theory]. *Kikan Kojin Kinyū* [Quaterly of Personal Finance], *5*(4), 56–68.

Newspapers, Magazines, etc.

The Crisis, and National Co-operative Trades' Union Gazette. Vol. 1–4. New York: Greenwood Reprint 1968 [1832–1834].

CHAPTER 7

John Gray's Theory of Labor Notes and Its Relevance to Money and Labor

7.1 John Gray: Key Issues to Consider

Reception and Evaluation of John Gray's in the Literature to Date

John Gray (1799–1883) was one of the leading economic thinkers among the group known as the Ricardian socialists who were active in the nineteenth century. He was a multi-faceted thinker, whose ideas have been subject to varying interpretations that have prevented a clear evaluation of his place in the history of socialist economic thought. In this chapter, we consider Gray's most representative works (Gray 1873/1831, 1842, 1848) with the aim of reaching a more systematic understanding of his doctrine.[1] I hope to demonstrate the way in which his theory of labor notes ran as a red thread through his writings, and by following this we can come to a better understanding of his ideas. In the meantime, in this section, I will clarify a preliminary set of issues concerning Gray that can be summarized as follows: first, whether Gray is a consistent labor money theorist; second, whether he was a socialist or not; and third, if he was, what kind of socialism did he represent.

Marx played a significant role in framing the way we look at the first issue. In his *A Contribution to the Critique of Political Economy*

[1] In this book, among Gray's works, Gray (1997/1825) is divided into the early period, Gray (1873/1831, 1842) in the mid-period, and Gray (1847, 1848) in the late period.

© The Author(s), under exclusive license to Springer Nature Switzerland AG 2021

T. Yuki, *Socialism, Markets, and the Critique of Money*, Marx, Engels, and Marxisms,
https://doi.org/10.1007/978-3-030-80408-4_7

(1987/1859), Marx identified Gray as a theorist of petit-bourgeois money reform. In this reading, Gray pursued an idealistic theory of labor money, in which it would be possible for equal exchange to be established on the quantity of labor bestowed on a product, with labor money acting as a unit that would adequately reflect the ratio of labor to labor. In such a view, labor money would honor the actual expenditure of labor time and that each participant would be able to claim on the entire produce of their labor. For Marx, the account given by Gray, notably in *The Social System* (1873/1831) and *Lectures on the Nature and Use of Money* (1848; abbreviated as *Lectures on Money*), reflects a consistent theoretical position: "*John Gray* was the first to set forth the theory that labour time is the direct measure of money in a systematic way," and Gray's theory of money reform is called "labour money" (Marx 1987/1859: 320, 322). Marx's assessment of Gray, as a consistent labor money theorist, has become something of an orthodoxy when it comes to Gray's writings after 1831.

However, as Kubo (2002) has recently shown, while that view may hold for Gray's writings from 1831 to 1842, it is questionable regarding his later writings. Rather, it appears that during the period between 1842 and 1848, there was something of an ideological break. Kubo has pointed out that in the 1848 lectures, "fiat money issued by 'The Standard Bank' referred to in the *Lectures on Money* has almost no character, as it appears in the so-called 'labor money theory'—the theory that labour time is the direct measure of money" (Kubo 2002: 150). Furthermore, in *Lectures on Money*, the idea of each party to an exchange possessing the right to the whole produce of labor disappeared, and "there are almost no features that can be called 'socialism'" (ibid., 152–153). If we take Kubo's research seriously, the whole image of Gray begins to change, and we have to rethink our approach by starting with ideological break and questioning the systemic nature of Gray's writings prior to 1848.

Second, there is controversy over whether Marx was right to label Gray a petty-bourgeois socialist, and whether this is based more on Marx and Engels' definition of scientific socialism and their ideological attempt to banish various strands of socialism that sought to base themselves on markets and independent small producers.[2]

In the context of Marx's criteria, it is important to ask whether Gray's proposed vision of socialism refers to the organization of production,

[2] For example, Lowenthal says, "he [Gray] repudiated any connection with socialism" (Lowenthal 1911: 60).

and the need for a change of the relations of production. As Marx put it: "Gray merely wants 'to reform' the money evolved by commodity exchange," and "Gray seeks timidly to present his labour money as a purely bourgeois reform," (Marx 1987/1859: 322), but the problem is its logical consequence. This is because in Gray's social system, which appears to be that by using labor money in units of labor time, there is no built-in adjustment mechanism that uses price as an indicator. For Marx money existed precisely because labor time could not be directly represented, because value was not based on private or concrete labor time expended, but upon the average socially necessary labor time, which is an abstraction that only money could measure. This flatly contradicted Gray's assumption of a social system in which the price mechanism could be abolished and money replaced with labor time as an economic unit of measure.

According to Marx, Gray was unaware of the social role of labor time as a unit of measure and the problem of allocating total labor time to society: "Although Gray merely wants 'to reform' the money evolved by commodity exchange, he is compelled by the intrinsic logic of the subject-matter to repudiate one condition of bourgeois production after another. Thus he turns capital into national capital, and land into national property and if his bank is examined carefully it will be seen that it not only receives commodities with one hand and issues certificates for labour supplied with the other, but that it directs production itself" (ibid.). Marx points out that Gray in the end was led by the logic of his own argument to contradictory conclusions.

In addition, Marx drew on a passage from *Lectures on Money* to confirm that Gray's proposal was for an "**organization of exchange**" rather than a "**organization of labour**" (ibid., 320). In other words, if Gray's logic was followed, it would reveal that his proposals concerning a reform of money using labor money could never be realized within a market society and could only be achieved if the means of production were socialized.

For the purposes of this analysis, we shall refer to Marx's interpretation as "the production fallacy" to emphasize the fallacy he saw in theorists who sought to reform the economy solely in the sphere of exchange and circulation. However, even if Gray's vision fell short of Marx's criteria for the socialization of production, that does not disqualify Gray from being a socialist who sought to manage and control of market through the transformation of money. Kishi puts the point as follows: "evaluations of Gray vary widely among different commentators. However, these arguments may have lost sight of what was 'socialism' in Gray," "his actual demand may have been the allocation of social labor through the organization of exchanges" (Kishi 1978: 57). Nonetheless, this did not prevent Kishi's from remarking that *An Efficient Remedy for the Distress of Nations* (1842; abbreviated as *Remedy*), "assumes that allocation of social labor is planned!" (Kishi 1978: 71). This perhaps can be understood if the remark is meant to indicate that Gray was seeking to reorganize production through the reorganization of exchange.[3] Whatever once's interpretation, it is clear from these debates that the Gray's doctrine must be considered in the relevance to the production system as well as the issues of defining socialism.

Assuming Gray was a socialist based on these debates, this raises the issue of what kind of socialism he was propounding. In the early works on Ricardian socialism, most especially Foxwell (1899), which relied on the work of Menger (1886), Gray was regarded as a Ricardian socialist, because of his views on the worker retaining the produce of their labor.[4]

The publication of a seven-volume series entitled *The Ricardian Socialists* (1997), edited by T. A. Kenyon, has provided a more up to date and comprehensive collation of most historical materials and includes Gray's *A Lecture on Human Happiness* (1825) appears in the second volume of this series. So, whatever one's interpretation of Gray and whether there is such a thing as Ricardian socialism to begin with, there is no doubt about Gray's place in the debates relevant to this book and his influence on modern scholarship.

Despite recent attempts to evaluate his legacy, Gray remains an ambiguous figure who appears to defer any easy labels. As will be shown the topic is best approached diachronically, by looking at his successive treatments of money and labor over the course of his publications.

[3] Claeys states that he "design[s] the most complete system of centralized economic control," and credits Gray as a forerunner of planned economics (Claeys 1987: 129).

[4] "Since the name Ricardian socialism is one tendentious name, it is somewhat difficult to pick out documents that clearly belong to this school and determine the scope of them" (Tamanoi 1977: 178–179).

On the Relevance of Money and Labor

Marx was the first to consolidate our understanding of Gray's views on the questions we are exploring in this chapter. It was also Marx who noticed that Gray's focus on the money problem had resulted in the production fallacy, and that his critique continues to provide the frame through which we have to approach Gray's theory of money.

Gray's theory of money can be seen as one that sought to develop a proposal for socialist money while assuming the existence of a capitalist market economy. His proposals for socialist money reform can be seen as an attempt to associate money with the labor that has been alienated by capitalism. In this chapter, we must reconsider controversial issues, including the definition of labor money theory, from the perspective of the relationship between money and labor, in order to respond to the issues of the Gray's doctrine.

First, the concept of "labor" in Gray's theory of labor money must be questioned. As mentioned earlier, the theory of labor money is "the theory that labour time is the direct measure of money." In light of this definition, the first issue is whether or not the content of discussions in Gray's writings can be called labor money theory. And it was already mentioned that the main issue was whether this labor money theory is consistently developed. While many previous studies support the interpretation of his consistency, Kubo has a unique view. On *The Social System*, he states that "this is 'labor money' itself," but in *Lectures on Money*, "fiat money issued by 'The Standard Bank' referred to in the *Lectures on Money* has almost no character, as it appears in the so-called 'theory of labor money' —the theory that labour time is the direct measure of money."

However, it is doubtful whether Kubo's view of "the theory that labour time is the direct measure of money" sheds any light on Gray. This is because in many of his key writings, for instance *The Social System*, Gray never said that "labour time is the direct measure of money." As explained later, Gray cannot be considered a labor money theorist by the definition of a theory that uses labor time as a measure of money. Therefore, the meaning and content of Marx's definition in this respect remains to be determined.

The standard by which Gray believed "the direct measure of money" should be adopted is precisely "average wage" (1831, 1842) or "minimum wage" (1848). Gray's theory of labor money was, therefore, "labor" money in the sense that the monetary value is pegged to wages in some way. However, it does not mean that labor times themselves are a direct measure of money. Even if it states that the monetary value is regulated by a certain wage level, it is not labor money in which the labor times themselves are the unit of money. Gray consistently used nominal prices based on monetary values pegged to a certain wage level, such as the case where a central authority set an average weekly wage of one pound as a policy. There is a difference in whether the wage level adopted is "average" or "minimum," but the monetary value is aligned closely to a certain wage level, and the price is given in proportion to the wage level. It can thus be said in Gray's theory that the wage is proportional to price. The question then is, what social and theoretical conditions can make "labour time is the direct measure of money" and, how Gray sought to maintain a proportional relationship between wages and prices. As described below, despite Gray's assumption of the quantity of labor commanded as the measure of fairness, it should be pointed out that there was a problem of processing complicated labor. If wages are used to evaluate exchanges, then it says nothing about labor time but much about the complexity, skill, and scarcity of the labor being exchanged.

Therefore, Gray's theory of labor money should be understood as follows: Labor money is the theory that a certain wage level is the direct measure of money. At any given time, all labor times are indirectly understood as price/wage ($Lt = p/w$). In that respect, it can be said that "Pound, shilling, etc., the names of account of money [gold], are said to be names representing definite quantities of labour time." (Marx 1987/1859: 320). However, this definition alone is still insufficient, as it fails to furnish the conception of money on which his theory of labor time was based.

According to Marx's interpretation, Gray intended to abolish money, but in fact developed a system that would preserve money. For Marx, this was due to its dependence on commodity production. It is a criticism based on the logic of Marx's theory of the value form that relations in a commodity economy always generate money if commodity production remains. Marx's criticism of the contradiction between Gray intentions and the logical consequence was severe. A detailed breakdown of Marx's criticism reveals that it consists of two different issues. First, if a commodity economy exists money will be necessary to ensure the circulation of commodities. Second, the basis of money generation cannot be nullified unless the production of commodities is abolished by socializing the means of production. For Marx, the issue was binary: commodity economy and money as a necessary corollary or socialized production and the abolition of money. What was less resolved was the question of how money might function if it was possible to have a mixed economy of commodity production (and monetary circulation) alongside socialized production.

There is a subtle difference to be made in deciding whether the price mechanism of money operates the same way in a free-market economy as it would in a co-operative, and this plays a significant role in determining whether Gray envisaged a socialist society. In his socialist society where private ownership is partially permitted, labor money would only partially fulfill its function as money under the conditions that free entry and exit from the market was not allowed, and transactions were centrally managed and controlled by banks that issue labor money or labor notes. In the socialist society envisioned by Gray, private ownership of the means of production was partially allowed and commodity production retained, but prices were not free. The value of money was to be pegged to the wage level, and the price proportional to the wage. At the same time, the market was not free, but centrally managed and controlled by the centralized bank. Toward that end, the banks would have a firm control of the market for the means of production, but when we reflect on Marx's criticism, it appears that Gray's theory allowed for the existence of money in a partially socialized system.[5]

This helps us to situate Gray, especially in terms of the contemporary reception of his writings. First of all, it raises the question of what Gray meant by treating labor as a measure of money, and the relation between labor and money that this implied. Second, despite the fact that Gray tried to make the relationship between the two closer, due to the difficulty of measuring labor time, he ended up with a formula by which the amount of labor time that could act as a measure of value was determined by the wages the labor could be commanded in the market. Therefore, the problem of complex or skilled labor remained unresolved. Third, Gray's explanation of the social conditions for a money price to become a nominal expression of labor time remains problematic. In the

[5] Marx's criterion for judging whether the banknote presented by Gray is labor money or non-monetary labor notes is whether commodity production is assumed as the basis of social reproduction (Marx 1996/1867: 104).

next section, we will examine these points by focusing on some of the writings from the mid- to the late-period of his career.

7.2 The Basic Structure of Gray's Theory of Labor Notes

It has already been mentioned that Gray has a reputation among scholars of being a consistent labor money theorist. Concerning his proposals for the National Bank as set out in *The Social System*, Hirao states that "the 'receipt' is a kind of 'labor money'" and that in *Lectures on Money* he presents a "concrete plan of reform, in which the aspect of mutual cooperation has receded, and the attitude of entrusting everything to the National Bank and labor money has become prominent" (Hirao 1975: 84, 88). Kamata states that the "certificate" of the National Bank as presented in *The Social System* can be viewed as "a kind of labor note" as a "mere measure of value with a nature as circulating money." On the other hand, it is also called "labor money" because of its role in facilitating the circulation process (Kamata 1968: 300–301). In addition, Kamata notes that "the content of *Lectures on Money* is not beyond the points of labor paper currency theory, which has been repeated in previous books." Based on these observations it is easy to assume that Gray has settled the matter and was a lifelong advocate of labor currencies (Kamata 2000: 394–395). While uncontroversial for the period in which he wrote *Lectures on Money*, it is less clear with regard to his later works.

Then, how is the reality of labor money theory understood in the previous studies? For instance, Kamata says, "Gray gives the status as a certificate directly showing general labor itself on banknotes" in order for Gray to insist on gold scrap and to pass valueless things as a measure of value. He adds that "it is safe to say that Gray believes to reduce the amount of labor included in various commodities into social labor and directly measure it" (Kamata 1968: 305–306). Hirao also sought to base his claims about calling it labor money by stating that "the characteristic of Gray is that he was 'the first to set forth the theory that labour time is the direct measure of money in a systematic way'" (Hirao 1975: 96). However, the argument that Gray's labor notes functioned as a medium that directly display labor times, and thus were an adequate expression of "general labor" or "social labor," may have overlooked other aspects of Gray's ideas by focusing on the labor-bestowed theory of value. According to Ricardo and Marx's theoretical tradition, Gray should not be read only from the viewpoint of the labor-bestowed theory of value, but rather, should be understood as a hybrid thinker whose ideas also included the labor-commanded theory of value, in line with Smith. Without taking this argument into account, it is impossible to arrive at an accurate understanding of Gray's theory.

The Relevance of Money and Labor in Gray's Middle Period

Having reviewed scholarship on Gray, it is worth focusing more on his proposals concerning labor notes to clarify the changes his view underwent during the middle-period following the publication of *Lectures on Money*. According to Gray, it is not possible to understand the importance of labor notes without first grasping the difficulties for any gold-based currency to perform the monetary functions as a measure of value and as a means of exchange. This can be seen, first of all, in terms of the function as a measure of value, if one assumes that the value of money is basically decided by the cost of producing gold as a monetary material. However, any value attributed to money fluctuates over the long term due to the supply demand relationship in the market, and the value of banknotes based on gold conversion will change accordingly. Given this, Gray stated in *The Social System* that the fluctuation in monetary value has an impact on debt relations; in other words, a debtor may benefit by repaying a debt at a cheaper pound rate than the rate at which it was borrowed. In addition, creditors will benefit if the debt is repaid at a higher pound rate than the rate at which they loaned the money. Thus, the debt relationship becomes unfair due to the difference of the monetary value between the loan period and the repayment period.

This issue has given rise to debates over whether a debtor should repay a nominal amount of 100 pounds for a 100-pound debt, or a monetary amount with the same purchasing power.[6] For Gray, this could only be resolved if the purchasing power of money remains constant according to the amount of labor commanded because: "if the national creditor should be repaid in money of more value than that which was borrowed of him, then is the debt itself increased; that is, if the money he receives back will

[6] Marx noted that the "quarrel about the ideal standard of money, which began in 1819" continued between Attwood and Peel by 1845, on the debate whether the nominal amount of £3 17s. 10.5d. at that time represents "an *ounce of gold*," or "its *value*?" (Marx 1987/1859: 319).

buy the labour of two men for a week, whilst that which he lent bought only the labour of one, the debt is in effect doubled" (Gray 1873/1831: 99). Comparing different points in time based on the labor commanded, it becomes clear that the amount of money of the same name commands different labor quantities. Therefore, Gray says "the various values of a pound sterling *in wages*" undermine the fairness of the contract, but if the pound is pegged to labor, "on an average of a whole period, a pound sterling, or whatever sum it proves to be, would have purchased an *average* week's labour of a mechanic or labourer, *that sum*, be it whatever it may, ought to be the price now fixed as the average wages of labour, in paper money" (ibid., 97–98). The view is that keeping the amount of labor that can be purchased unchanged is necessary to avoid "fraud" resulting from fluctuations in monetary value and to maintain the fairness of contracts. Since, the issue of fixing the value of money is critical for the fairness of the contract, the "average price of labour, therefore, should be a subject of mutual consultation and agreement between the government and the Chamber of Commerce; and being once settled on equitable principles, *it never be altered*" (ibid., 99). In addition, the average price of fixed labor is "*an immutable standard of value*," and "a pound note from that time forth would be just another name for a *week* of reasonable exertion" (Gray 1873/1831: 99–100).

Similarly, even in *Remedy*, Gray says that "a *true* standard of value can never fluctuate" (Gray 1842: 6), based on the rationale that value is given by "*an average price of labour*." In other words, the "*immutable* character of the standard note, takes its rise from this circumstance—*an average price of labour* ... is to be fixed upon by the trade commissioners, with the consent and approval of the government" (ibid., 9–10). Then, "if the average price of labour per week be, for example, one pound, and the average weekly labour to be exacted from the operatives sixty hours, a pound note from that time forth would be just another name for sixty hours of the labour of a *good workman*" (ibid., 10). Furthermore, with respect to changes in monetary value over time, he writes that, "I conceive him to be justly repaid if he receive an equal sum of money, of whatever kind, provided it will give him the like command over the labour of an equal number of good workmen for a year, employed under the like circumstances, and aided by the best skill and machinery *now* existing" (ibid., 19). The value of money was, therefore, defined by the amount of labor that can be commanded by the given sum of money. We might also argue that for Gray, any invariance was to be maintained by the invariance of the quantity of labor commanded. Thus, Gray believed he had resolved the question of the variability of money as a measure of value by basing it on labor directly rather than a commodity such as gold or specie. This forms the first basis on which he developed his theory of labor notes.[7]

Next, let us examine Gray's analysis of the inadequacies of gold money as a means of exchange. For Gray overproduction and unequal exchange was a "demon of commercial error" stemming from flaws of money based on gold and specie (Gray 1873/1831: 58). He added that "as we cannot, with any degree of convenience, make direct exchanges of produce for produce, an instrument of exchange as a measure of value, becomes an indispensable requisite in every commercial society; and a fit and proper instrument of this description has never yet been used by any nation upon the earth" (ibid.).

Given his concerns about gold, this raises the question of what would constitute an appropriate alternative instrument of exchange. According to Gray, the "legitimate use of money is precisely the same as that of scales and weights and measures" (ibid.). In other words, money is an immutable measure of value, like the scale of a ruler. Such a view is simply obscured when money takes the form of gold or any other substance characterized by its scarcity, Gray argued. Therefore, money should take the form of a substance characterized by social necessity and an ordinary role in life. In other words, it "ought to be as cheap, as common, and as attainable" as anything one encounters in everyday life (ibid., 58–59). Gray continued, "Gold coin is totally unfit for this purpose, because it is ever used upon the principle of being itself equal in value to that which it represents; and as in, at least, ninety-nine cases out of every hundred, the thing it represents is capable of being far more easily increased than gold, every increase of other produce habitually takes place at the imminent risk of being sold at a reduced money price" (ibid., 59). In this statement, we have the crux of Gray's view of gold currency. As an industrially produced commodity, gold remains scarce, especially in comparison

[7] Kubo refers to *Lectures on Money* as an argument for the reformed "money that has neither deflationary nor inflationary tendency" (Kubo 2002: 144). However, Gray has consistently been interested in the issue of monetary value stability since around 1831, and it was something he was deeply concerned to achieve.

with other products, and cannot expand in proportion to the volume or productivity of labor in society.[8]

For Gray, gold foreclosed equality of exchange, because the total value of gold as a purchasing power cannot match the total value of products available at any given point in time. The logical conclusion Gray sought to draw was that the product must be equivalent to the total goods being exchanged, and that this was to be based on the production cost if it is to be a fair exchange. To put this concretely, we can consider how the price would move if a product of 100 dollars was in a market where the purchasing power of gold was 5,000 dollars.[9] If the price of 100 dollars per piece held constant, this would result in the sale of 50 units, but according to Gray, this is not the case. Gray implicitly assumed that if the velocity of circulation was the same, the price of the product supplied to the market will fall to the point where it is sold out, such as selling 100 units when the market price falls to 50 dollars. Therefore, selling the product for gold money with scarce purchasing power means that the sale of the value of 100 dollars cannot be achieved, and the seller yields a net loss instead of a profit, and the supply always exceeds the demand. In other words, this would contravene the classical notion that supply is the cause of demand. To set this argument in context, it is worth reminding ourselves of Gray's normative notion of money and its role:

> [The] desideratum in money is, that it may enable any man, at any time, to exchange any article, of any value, for an equal value of whatever marketable commodity he pleases to have in its stead, with the least possible expense of time, of labour, and of anxiety. (ibid., 62)

[8] Gray says that the amount of labor needed to collect seawater will not change from the first gallon to the last, however, when collecting water from a specific well where special water is coming, "*a constantly diminishing quantity* in proportion to the demands," for the last gallon of water, it must require "a greatly increased quantity of labour, waiting, and watchfulness" than the first gallon of water. Therefore, their monetary value also differs greatly. Gray states that the gold industry has the same properties as this well, explaining it using logic that should be called a crude marginal principle (Gray 1848: 79–80).

[9] Of course, if a product of 100 dollars was supplied to the 100-unit market, and there is 100 dollars worth of gold as a purchasing power, it is possible to exchange equivalents at a "fair price" (Gray 1842: 101).

> Money of no intrinsic value, can; and it is only by the adoption of an immutable standard of value that goods, continuing to cost the same labour in their production, can continue to maintain the same price in the market. (ibid., 85)

In order to reform these monetary flaws, Gray proposed the introduction of labor notes because "Money should be merely a *receipt*, an evidence that the holder of it has either contributed a certain value to the national stock of wealth, or that he has acquired a right to the said value from someone who has contributed it" (ibid., 63). As noted, gold money is quantitatively restricted due to the characteristics of the industry and its scarcity, so that it hinders the exchange of equivalents. This renders gold unsuitable both as a measure of value and a means of exchange. To avoid these pitfalls, "money should not be intrinsically valuable" and "money should be nothing more or less than portable, transferable, divisible, and inimitable evidences of the existence of wealth in store" (ibid., 63–64). For the most valuable and essential quality of money lies in its "*intrinsic inutility*" (ibid., 75). Or, "money should be the transferable representative of wealth, increasing and diminishing in quantity *in exact and invariable proportion* to the increase and diminution of that which it represents" (Gray 1842: 5–6). Expressed this way, the substance of money has only a representational role, that is to display the intrinsic value of the corresponding wealth. Furthermore, money comes to be based on a theory that stresses the immutable measure of value, in which the value of the substance of money must be measured by labor as "an immutable standard of value."

For Gray, the value of goods being exchanged is determined by the production cost as the amount of labor bestowed, and money is simply a medium that does not interfere with the exchange of products. It becomes clear that any claims to fairness or equal exchange are based on a real market able to fulfill these ideal conditions—in which exchange takes place at value. Such ideal conditions also assume an equilibrium between total supply and demand in order to realize individual equal exchange. Moreover, money is posited not as a means for explaining economic phenomena by the demand principle, but as a means of adhering to the classical proposition that supply creates demand. In order to eliminate the inadequacy of money as a means of exchange, it becomes necessary to match supply and demand, and for that to happen the substance of money must be worthless and not a value thing such as gold. This is the second basis for labor note theory.

From the above viewpoint, we can see how Gray sought to ground the principle of fair exchange by keeping the quantity of labor commanded by money constant and to develop a theory of value from the perspective of labor commanded. He hoped that this would realize equality of exchange based on the agreement between the total value of the goods produced and the purchasing power in the market, at least in terms of the quantity theory of money. The assumption here is based on the simple formula for the circulation of commodities in which commodity 1 is exchanged for a sum of money which is used to buy commodity 2: C_1–M–C_2. Yet, whenever the sale of C_1–M is hampered by the scarcity of money so that the commodity must be sold below its value, the purchase which takes place in terms of M–C_2 can no longer reflect the same quantity of labor as the quantity of own labor bestowed. The recognition that equal exchange between C_1–C_2 is blocked by money can only be resolved if the substance of money takes a neutral form through the issuance of labor notes. Only by this mechanism would it be possible to exchange an equal quantity of labor for an equal quantity of labor—that is, an exchange that fulfills the criteria of C_1–M–C_2, in which the quantity of labor bestowed is equal to the quantity of labor commanded. However, this raised two potential problems. First, even if the value of money is pegged to the quantity of labor commanded, what is that quantity of labor measured by? If it is measured by the "value of labor," which was considered to be represented by wages, it cannot be constant from time to time as pointed out by Ricardo (Ricardo 1951/1817: 15). Since, the "value of labor" is defined by the amount of daily necessities that depend on the standard of living in society, if the standard of living or the technology of the industrial sector that produces necessities changes, its value will also changes. Second, the reality of equal exchange, which is said to be achieved by money as a representative for "the least possible expense of time, of labour, and of anxiety," will be a problem. Gray said in his *The Social System* that a banknote with an average wage of one pound would be "just another name for a *week* of reasonable exertion," and in *Remedy* that a pound note representing the average wage would be "the average weekly labour to be exacted from the operatives sixty hours" or "sixty hours of the labour of a *good workman.*" If this average wage of a pound is a reasonable duration of time for "reasonable exertion" or "labour," which is called "labor expenditure," that expenditure will form the total value of the product. Gray here based his analysis on the assumptions of simple commodity circulation, in which the parties are two-skilled workers exchanging products they own, rather than their labor-power, placing out of consideration such factors as one of the parties not owning the commodity they produce or the influence of constant capital. If such argument holds, it can be said that Gray was a Ricardian Socialist during his middle period, in that he based his arguments on workers having a right to claim the whole produce of their labor. However, in the circulation theory that discusses money, despite the assumption that products will be exchanged based on the quantity of labor bestowed, Gray's value theory was subjected to revisions when it comes to the system of production. Therefore, Gray's value theory must be discussed in terms of the theory of production or the productive system.

Gray's adoption of labor commanded as a fair standard rather than labor time was based on resolving the technical issue how to measure labor time in a way that could factor in skills, proficiencies, and the impact of the division of labor. There was also the question of the ratio of living labor that goes into a commodity's production versus dead labor, i.e., past labor that has gone into building tools, machines, etc. that are used in the production process. Gray could not find a way to distinguish and factor these into a price mechanism. This made it unclear how it might be possible to determine the hours of labor that are actually are transferred to the product. Therefore, he hoped to find a way to add profit to wages for the laborer and the cost of materials in the hope of developing a value structure that reflected the amount of labor commanded in the production of a commodity.

On the Disposal of Complex Labor

In contrast to Owen's egalitarian approach to distribution, Gray was of the view that free competition was required in labor markets to ensure the elimination of overproduction and create an equilibrium between supply and demand, explaining that: "The average price of wages, then, as fixed by the Chamber of Commerce, upon the principle here defined, would be the price to be paid weekly for all the ordinary operations of the productive classes" (Gray 1873/1831: 102–103). This is "the price of common labor" (ibid., 105). However, Gray relied on Adam Smith to point out that inequalities with regard to up to five points will inevitably occur under such average wages. First, average wages create disagreements and discord among workers. Second, there are differences in the acquisition of labor skills, whether they are easy or difficult, or whether training costs are low or high. Third, there is a difference between regular employment and irregular employment. Fourth, there is a difference in the degree of trust among the workers. Fifth, there is the issue of whether a business is successful.

These considerations led Gray to conclude that there will always be a certain wage gap, and in his scheme, it would be important to ensure that salaries are paid to agents for the "direction and superintendence of labour" and these should be "fixed at a much higher rate than the wages of common labour, upon the grounds of responsibility, and the super qualifications required" (ibid., 104–106). "The average wages of the agents, therefore, that is, the wages of superintendence and of direction, should also be a fixed sum, having a proper relation to the price of common labour" (ibid., 105). Regarding salary, Gray thought that "liberal payment would also be a great incitement to good conduct" (ibid., 106). Furthermore, from a more utilitarian perspective, he argued that the "system of nature... be throughout a system of rewards and punishments" (ibid.), a view that notably varied from Owen's more utopian view of a perfectible human nature. Also, the work of the Chamber of Commerce, which coordinates the entire system, consists of many committees, but the committee members who are engaged in this task must be familiar with all professions. And, in proportion to the acquisition of talent, industry, patience and honesty, the reward must also increase. Furthermore, in the *Remedy*, he stated that, "whilst the average rate of wages would be fixed and immutable, the rate of individual wages would be as much open to competition as ever," recommending competition for wages (Gray 1842: 21). Of course, in order to maintain a fixed average wage rate, the fluctuation range of wages would also need to be kept within a certain range. That said, while it might be possible to establish a scale of wages for each type of labor, based on skills and market demand, etc., Gray allowed for a degree of negotiation between workers and managers when it came to rate setting.

The *Remedy* also promoted the introduction of competition into the commodity market. Gray stated that, "the disposal of the standard goods by retail would, in common with all others, be left to open competition; any and every person who should choose to deal in them, being at full liberty to do so; and to sell them at whatever profit he could obtain" (ibid., 8). Thus stated, the principle by which competition regulates profits becomes no different than in commercial societies. For Gray, it would be possible for a retail business to accumulate commercial profits on the production price, which adds official profit to cost. Yet, this creates a problem regarding commercial labor and whether it should be classed as productive labor. For even if discrepancies between supply and demand in the standard market are apparently resolved, thus permitting profit seeking and flexibility in the profit rate, this could be due to stock control, or accumulation of stocks, whose release on the market drives up or down the price.

On the Relevance to Money and the Production System in Gray's Middle Period

In his concept of the "social system," Gray was deeply aware of the need to create the right kind of social conditions that would turn his theory of labor notes into a real possibility. This is set out immediately in Chapter 2 of *The Social System*, in which he seeks to define the system, stating "*that it would be by no means difficult to place the commercial affairs of society upon such a footing, that production would become the uniform and never failing cause of demand; or, in other words, that to sell for money may be rendered, at all times, precisely as easy as it now is to buy with money*" (Gray 1873/1831: 16). In other words, the "social system" that Gray discusses here would be a system in which production produces exactly the same amount of demand; in other words, "what we chiefly want, is a controlling and directing power by which the various parts of our commercial system may be so fitted and adapted to each other as to produce a harmonious instead of an incongruous whole" (ibid., 5–6).

Gray drew on a number of illustrations to highlight the contrast between the principle of the "social system" with commercial society as it currently existed. In the "current system," all social members are depicted as individuals who are individually separated by the division of labor. And because everyone wants money and "want[s] to sell," but lacks adequate means of exchange, a shortage of money occurs, and everyone's money needs cannot be met. Under this system, since "*demand [is] the cause of production*," there is always an excess supply of goods in relation to money. All that remains is universal dissatisfaction. Gray states that in a commercial society where inappropriate currencies are used, there is an inevitable crisis due to the production of excess commodities and general underconsumption. On the other hand, under the "social system" proposed by Gray, "***production [would be] the cause of demand***," and all the members of society would be included by the system that produces wealth. Money here would serve as a way channel public stock from the worker to the consumer. Individual members could then provide goods and services that would contribute to the public wealth and receive as much from it in return. Here, since the producer's contribution to public wealth (supply) and the distribution that people receive from public wealth (demand) match, and there would be no excess supply due to lack of money. In this way, Gray directly grasped the notion that the amount of money supplied to the market as demand should be equal to the purchasing power of society as a whole (ibid., 29).

In a market economy based on private ownership and a division of labor, competition between private companies is endogenous. Each company supplies goods continues to produce without considering the size of the goods market or the conditions of other markets, which tends to result in overproduction and bankruptcy. Therefore, it is necessary to adjust the market in order not to hinder the effect of increased production due to division of labor. According to Gray, if producer A and producer B continue to compete in a market that supplies goods, and production continues to increase, the supply of products will continue until the size of the market reaches its limit. Then, when the market is saturated, the more efficient "A" remains while "B" is forced to exit. In that case, the only hope for the latter to survive lies adjusting the product to enter other markets where demand is not met. Gray believed that the market provided no such automatic adjustment mechanism, and that this would have to be artificial guided with conscious policy instruments. This was firmly in contradistinction to those like John Stuart Mill, who held to the theory of automatically adjusting markets. For Gray policies were required to ensure that "the kind of produce brought into the market might change from necessary to luxury, and from luxury to profusion" (ibid., 69).[10] The classical proposition that supply produces equal demand can only be achieved by providing an appropriate adjustment mechanism from the outside, not by the open market.

[10] Gray understands the problem of resource allocation as "the rational appropriation of the inexhaustible resources with which nature has supplied us" (Gray 1873/1831: 7). Therefore, the only scarce resource in origin is labor, and the social allocation of labor will be the standard for production adjustment.

In addition, we can see that Gray was interested in the question of establishing a balance of production between industrial sectors, and that without this, even full employment would create crises of disproportionality alongside those of underconsumption. To address this Gray was not opposing the market as such, but rather advocating policies that could provide guidance to markets to ensure a smooth transfer of resources between sectors that have saturated demand and those with a problem of oversupply. As will be shown later, Gray recognized the significance of free competition as an inducement to productivity and promoted market liberalization. However, this did not prevent him from pointing out the link between free competition and the overproduction of goods. Gray emphasized that a free and competitive market must be maintained within the "social system" in order to incorporate what he described as "the incitement to industry."

For Gray, this meant the creation of a "National Chamber of Commerce" (1873/1831: 31), which could act as an institution to coordinate production among various branches of industry. The Chamber of Commerce would be "but one controlling and directing power, but one judge of what it is prudent and proper to bring into the market" (ibid., 45). And a "master manufacturer... should be an agent" of the Chamber of Commerce (ibid., 46). He believed that this would enable factory owners and managers to respond quickly to signals from the Chamber of Commerce by adjusting production volumes to ensure a match of demand and supply. The Chamber of Commerce was to be founded on the basis that "all persons possessed of land, or capital, be invited to join this association" (ibid., 32) and these investors would receive a certain annual dividend in response to their investment. Therefore, the association centered on the Chamber of Commerce would take the form of a co-operative enterprise with joint investment.[11] This joint investment method would be similar to stock companies such as the East India company, but the purpose would be different. In other words, while for corporations "*private* advantage is the ultimate object of the whole affair," for the Chamber of Commerce, the "specific object of the proposed commercial association ... is to make production the infallible cause of demand, and to give the greatest possible effect to labour

[11] Gray states that he will establish a "National Commercial Association" (ibid., 36) with the aim of converting collateral property into cooperative property by paying off the advanced principal, which addresses the transition problem of the forms of ownership.

and capital … by means of a thoroughly organized plan of production, exchange, distribution, and accumulation" (ibid., 38). In the *Remedy*, Gray viewed this as a way to establish "a modification of the plan developed in *The Social System*, as may be both easily and quickly brought into operation" (Gray 1842: xi). This represented a shift from the low expectations he previously held toward voluntary combinations and a greater emphasis on the need to petition the government to establish a national banking-cum-enterprise complex which could initiate a large-scale free loan and investment program. Each national organization established by the government would be given the word "standard," and collectively they would be referred to as the "standard system." This was to distinguish them from the external private market economy (ibid., 16–17).

In *The Social System*, Gray developed the notion of a "National Bank" whose role would be to support the coordinating function of the Chamber of Commerce. In this way, the "social system" would take the form of an organic set of institutions made up the National Bank, the National Chamber of Commerce, and a set of "national warehouses." The National Bank would have two main functions, namely, the issuing of money and the management of the "national books" to adjust the supply across the system. The National Bank would "possess... the sole power of manufacturing paper money" and cannot be issued by other banks. This meant that for money to be issued, an "agent" of each association delegated to the Chamber of Commerce be required to consent (Gray 1873/1831: 64–65).

This raises the question of how the balancing of the national books would work. First, all the goods produced were to be transported from the producers to the national warehouse. At that point in time, the Chamber of Commerce would fix a price based on two components, the "direct cost" consisting of raw material costs and wages, and an element for "profit" (ibid., 64).[12] Then, a receipt equivalent to the price delivered to the National Warehouse would be issued by the National Bank and handed to the producer. This National Warehouse would have a retail store as a subordinate organization for selling deposited goods, and the books of the retail store would be tallied and reconciled with the

[12] Gray provided a breakdown of what should be counted in the profit side of the ledger, which should "pay the various expenses of rent, interest of capital, management, salaries, depreciation of stock, incidents, and all national charges." (ibid., 64).

National Bank. Having received a receipt for their goods, the producer in turn becomes a consumer and uses the receipt to purchase goods from a retail store linked to the National Warehouse. At this point, the receipt would be returned to the National Bank through the National Warehouse. Therefore, on the one hand, the value of the goods deposited by the producer and the amount of the receipt issued by the National Bank are the same. On the other hand, the amount of the goods purchased from the National Warehouse and the amount of the receipt returned to the National Bank are the same. As a result, the same amount of money would be issued according to the production amount, and the same amount of money returned according to the purchase amount. Therefore, "*Upon this plan it will be evident, that, as the nominal or money price of all the property in stock would be entirely made up of the money issued by the Bank to the respective members of the social community, the quantity of money in circulation would at all times be exactly equivalent to the nominal or money value of the property in store. Money, therefore, would increase as produce should be increased; money would decrease as produce should be redemanded or consumed, and demand would ever keep pace with production*" (ibid., 66). In this way, the "whole system of exchange" is formed (ibid., 67).

The National Bank in the system would keep an account book of the National Warehouse, in which the production output of goods is written, and the National bank would issue money according to the requested amount. By means of this process, the output of goods in the country and the amount of money issued should always match. However, the National Bank would also contain a "*counting-house*" (ibid., 68) to check for possible fraud and mistakes. On top of that, the agent appointed by the Chamber of Commerce would be responsible for each production organization, so "it is evident that a most effectual check would be kept upon the honesty of the agents" (ibid., 71).[13] Above all, "though every agent should deal with every other, the whole transactions of the association might be rendered perfectly clear and intelligible, and as strong a security be had for fair dealing between man and man, as any now in existence" (ibid., 68–69). That is, according to Gray, in the system of the National Bank, the National Warehouse, the Chamber of Commerce, the producer and the production manager each exist as an agent helping

[13] All members of society are "one body of commercial partners" (Claeys 1987: 121).

to run the system. Besides, each of them would be encouraged to act responsibly for their operations.[14]

It should be noted that profit was to be added to the price of goods in the warehouse-market managed by the National Bank. In of 7.2, Gray had stated that price should be determined by the production cost. Here, it is said that when the goods are deposited in the warehouse, profit should added to the cost and this would have to be reflected in the price as an additional component; thus, the price would deviate from the production cost. Meanwhile, the amount paid to the depositor should consist of the parts of labor wage and raw material cost. Although profit can be broken down to cover various items including rent and capital interest, there appears to be change in Gray's underlying theory of value, and especially over the question of whether land produces rent and capital produces interest. This further raises questions about how those elements can be factored into the price. It is not clear what Gray's views were on the matter and whether he ever deviated from his prior commitment to Smithian theory of value in which "labour is the only source of wealth" (ibid., 40). Of course, if we assume a cooperative production system constructed by turning advanced land and capital into its own capital, and if the investor is an independent small producer, profit will eventually be returned to the investors. According to Gray, "the *natural* rate of wages" that the classical school envisioned was set at the minimum level necessary to maintain a livelihood within a commercial society. His recommendation was for "the natural rate of wages to be *the whole that is produced* by labour, subject only to the above defined deduction" (ibid., 249). The "deduction" should be the "smallest possible deduction for the support of unproductive labour" from the total product of productive labor, which would be a "direct tax" (ibid., 237, 248) on the productive class. If this was the case, it could be understood that the bank association would adjudicate the distribution ratio between productive class and the unproductive class in a policy exogenously determined; in other words, as political rather than a market decision. As a result, the "direct costs" would be added to "profit" (profit here is probably an official and equal profit rate). Gray intended the public system to be governed politically, with its leading institutions acting strategically and using instruments such

[14] For the sound operation of the bank, "an annual balance sheet be published, exhibiting its whole receipts, expenditure, and the state of finances" (Gray 1873/1831: 36).

as nationalization and price setting. In the *Remedy*, the aim was to devise a system that would result in a fair distribution of the profit through the official profit rate and the official price set by the national and the standard bank. In this way, he hoped to reaffirm and modify the underlying labor theory of value that underpinned his theory of labor notes.

7.3 Metamorphosis and Conclusion of the Theory of Labor Notes

As we saw in Sect. 7.2, Gray sought to reconcile the question of profit and labor costs, and this was consistent with his Ricardian socialism. However, the basic structure was altered, by the time, we come to his *Lectures on Money* in 1848, the basic structure begins to alter as he increasingly sought to distance himself from socialism, while preserving aspects of the labor note theory he had developed. Commenting on Gray's tendency to distance himself from socialism during his middle period, Kubo notes: "What characterizes Gray's idea, however, can be said to be the consistent pursuit of the organization of production, as well as the organization of exchange," "in that sense, it is fully possible to call Gray up to this time a 'socialist'" (Kubo 2002: 135). However, in *Lectures on Money*, "Gray's views the harmful effects of competition, and the long-cherished idea of organizing production has disappeared without a trace. It has been proved that the emphasis on the utility of competition" has led to "disruption in his thought" (ibid., 135–136). In addition, the *Lectures* could be interpreted as a departure from the labor money theory by "exchange according to the quantity of labor bestowed" and contains "almost no idea of the right to whole produce of labor" (ibid., 151–152).

Certainly, during his middle period, Gray understands the profit as a deduction from the total product of the productive class to support the unproductive class while undergoing a revision of value structure theory, basically, he aims for the right to whole produce of labor. However, Gray's value theory is developed as a mixture of the labor-commanded theory of value and the labor-bestowed theory of value, which remains unarranged in the late term. However, I cannot help feeling the strong interest in Gray's theory of value, which tries to make the relationship between money and labor close.

Gray also seeks his definition of socialism in the system, not in ideology.[15] From a standpoint opposed to Owenism, Gray acknowledged the effect of the market competition and was trying to introduce it from an early stage. Even though it has been interpreted as trying to organize production, the fact was an ex-post adjustment to the production which was considered not to impair the freedom of the market. Rearranging the concepts of organization of exchange and organization of production presented by Marx from its theoretical implications, Marx calls the correction of the situation where anarchical production activity is coordinated *ex post facto* by the market, an organization of exchange; to carry out production activities based on advance planning instead of ex-post adjustment of the market is called an organization of production.

If so, what Gray intended was to organize exchanges in Marx's terminology, and in Gray's own words, it was still an "organization of exchange." The proposed change of the ownership in the mid-period can be said to be a material base for planned production, and it only constitutes the necessary condition for the organization of production. We have already mentioned some hypothetical conclusions. Based on the reorganization of middle term works in this book, how should the facts of Gray's theory and thought in the late term be understood?

Relevance of Money and Labor in Gray's Later Works

The works of Gray later period drew more criticism than those we have been examining so far. Criticisms were diverse ranging from the Owenites, classical economists, and thinkers like Attwood from the Birmingham School. The crux of these debates concerned the question of gold as a measure of value, which Gray caustically summarized as follows: "there is at present a great deal of discussion going on between the golden philosophers and those of paper" (Gray 1848: 8–9). While the paper philosophers contented that money was a mere good without inherent substance and value, this still raised questions concerning the existence of an appropriate scale or unit of measure because they could not find "a clear and explicit

[15] Gray argues that *The Social System* was misunderstood as a book of socialism, and that the "social system" had nothing to do with the aim of equal distribution which is the hallmark of those socialists. From early works like "*A Treatise of the Principle of Exchange*" Gray's prime concern lay in the economic system, rather than the distribution problem (Gray 1848: 283–284).

definition of the word *value*" (ibid.). For Gray, research on the question of money had developed since the days in which he wrote *The Social System*, and he hoped to draw on the latest research to demonstrate that labor notes could resolve the debated between the gold and the paper philosophers. At the time, debates over Gold Standard were raging, with classical economists insisting on its continuation and the Birmingham School calling for it to be abolished. Behind these debates lay the question of whether there was such a thing as immutable value (something Gray held to in his middle period) and how this relates to price variability. For those defending the gold standard, the equation of prices and money to the quantity of gold sought to resolve the tension, while the Birmingham School sought to resolve it through inter-sectoral balancing—a theory Gray advocated in his *Lectures on Money* with its focus on the "social system" and the "standard system." The Birmingham School had a more sophisticated grasp on questions of overproduction and underconsumption than their classical opponents. Indeed, according to Gray, the challenge of stabilizing prices could not be achieved by money reform alone, and that adjustments to inter-sectorial imbalances were crucial to currency management policy.

Classical economists such as Mill and proponents of the gold standard assumed that "production *is* the *natural* cause of demand, ad infinitum, without reference to any monetary system or systems whatsoever." It relies on the "mere theoretical dogma of a school of error" which excludes money from consideration (ibid., 55–56). Under such a theoretical assumption, the classical school assumed that the total supply never becomes excessive, and it is possible for an imbalance between sectors to occur. Moreover, the imbalance would be resolved naturally by the movement of capital through the price mechanism "till profits [rate] are equalized" (ibid., 51). For Gray, the classical sought was essentially stuck at the barter stage, "leaving the thing called *money* out of the question" (ibid., 52). Concluding emphatically that: "I deny that production *is at present* the cause of demand" (ibid.). By making this statement, Gray sought to point out that the classical school overlooked the extent to which overproduction can be caused not only by the inter-sectorial imbalances but also by the lack of money.

In response to the classical school's view of the theoretical dogma that production produces equal demand, paper philosophers were more than ready to accept the lack of money as a driver for underconsumption. Members of the Anti-Gold-Law League shared Gray's concern that gold was just a good and could not be a "true measure of value" (ibid., 120). However, their inability to find an immutable measure of value raised further difficulties. To address these, Gray examined a set of ideas that can be described as banknote theory. In this view, government notes or "Government bank-notes" (ibid., 121) secured by government tax revenues, and land-backed notes issued as land collateral could serve as vectors of value. He looked at the example the "Birmingham Monetary Reformers" and work by George Frederick Muntz (1794–1857) (ibid., 139). The question he was trying to solve lay in addressing whether say 50 million pounds of government notes can solve a lack of purchasing power when the total national revenue runs to 500 million pounds. Assuming that banknotes are not considered in circulation, the government notes as a representative for 50 million pounds of revenue cannot be a means of exchange that covers the entire circulation process of a nation. This would merely restate the problems with gold, as that latter cannot keep pace with an increase in national production and hence national revenue. In such a situation, deflation would set in resulting in a huge loss of profit. When land is considered, the same problems are encountered as are to be found with gold and government notes. This is because its amount of value is quantitatively limited, and any increase in the total quantity of goods for sale would result in deflation and profit loss. The Muntz plans as reported in *The Times* sought to address these challenges and can be summarized in four points. First, cash payments should be suspended. Second, the Bank of England should be completely separated from the government. Third, currency control and issuing authority should be transferred from the Bank of England to a new National Bank managed by a committee appointed by Parliament. Fourth, the committee should maintain a reasonable price level for a basket of goods made of gold, silver, wheat, etc., while taking measures to gradually raise prices. What these four measures shared with Gray's thinking were their common concern of identifying the problem as arresting the deflation caused by the lack of money and unshackling the money supply from the limits imposed by gold.

In setting out a vision of freedom, Gray declared: "*It is our right and province to create demand, instead of being created by it*. This, and this *only*, is true commercial freedom: this, and this only, *is the criterion* by which every monetary system must be tested" (ibid., 141). However, "the Anti-Gold-Law League party have not taken cognizance of the absolute necessity of preserving a precise balance between production and demand" (ibid., 134–135). In other words, Muntz was aware that the money supply had to be extended in order to release productive forces. But he overlooked the need to balance supply and demand to maintain an immutable measure of value. For Gray, the ideal monetary system should provide additional money without excess or deficiency with an increase in production, in order to stop prices from falling due to lack of money and the accompanying inequal exchange, and to maintain prices stably and to promote equal exchange. At the same time, it was suggested that the kind of free exchange that comes about in realization of equal demand can only be achieved through the social and monetary system as presented by Gray. While this catered for the question of deflation, it appeared that the classical school was more focused on its opposite, inflation. The classical school heavily emphasized gold as a deterrent against inflation because of the technical constraints it imposed on the free flow of currency. Besides, while the Birmingham School promoted the issuance of banknotes with little warning of inflation, thus laying themselves open to the classical economists, Gray sought to outwit both by envisioning a monetary system in which price changes would have nothing to do with monetary factors.[16]

According to Gray, both the classical and Birmingham schools understood only one side of the two factors of overproduction, so they could only provide an inadequate solution. Also, from the perspective of price stability, it was emphasized that money must be an immutable measure of value that would have no effect on the exchange ratio of goods. Yet, this raises the question of how can the value of money as a measure of value (i.e., as pure system of measurement like the scales on a ruler) be maintained? To answer this Gray suggested that: "[T]he everlasting blunder of the bullionists... consists in the supposition—*That a paper-currency, unconvertible on demand into any fixed weight of gold or silver, must necessarily be a depreciated currency!*" (ibid., 160) but they criticize paper money theorists, like Muntz, who also acknowledges that unconvertible banknotes will always cause a "'*depreciation*' *which must necessarily*

[16] Hawtrey criticized Attwood by noting, "the policy of always avoiding a fall of prices involves a progressive depreciation of the currency, unless it is accompanied by the policy of always preventing a *rise* of prices. Here is the true dividing line between inflationism and sound currency." Although Attwood had to present "some stabilising principle of its own" to replace the gold standard, he was not able to present an effective deterrent measure, which was understood as currency expansionism (Hawtrey 1928: 79–80).

be consequent" (ibid., 167). Gray added, "this supposition, however, is mere delusion; for *the value* of a one pound note unconvertible into *any fixed quantity* of gold, silver, or anything else, *may quite easily be fixed by law with mathematical precision and certainty*" (ibid., 160). What is presented here is concept of a value that is not defined by gold weight or physical relationships. Put differently, Gray was attempting to develop a theory of commensurability between commodities that would have no reliance on the commodity theory of money, in which the use value of the commodity being used for exchange can distort values and effect prices.

As a disciple of Smithian economics, Gray stressed that the value of goods is given directly by labor. In other words, "*human labour* is at once the source, the standard, and the *only possible measure of value*," "*Labour, therefore, is the real measure of the exchangeable value of all commodities*" (ibid., 155). In this way, according to Smith's version of the labor theory of value, labor was specified as the source of value and its measure. In this way, Smith believed it was possible to define the quantity of value and set wage levels appropriately around the notion of an average wage that is commensurate with an average amount of labor over a given span of time.

Gray adopted Smith's concept of the average wage, but he corrected by including a minimum wage too, to factor in the technical range of different kinds of labor that might be producing the same commodity. By doing this, Gray hoped it would encourage competition. "We shall suppose, then, the *minimum* rate of wages in a given employment to be *now* twenty shillings a-week... because it is the *unit* of our monetary denominative, namely, a pound sterling," he said, adding that the standard is only the level of minimum wage, which may be called 20 shillings or even 10 shillings in nominal terms.[17] He added: "If, then, a man be *at present* able to obtain a pound sterling in exchange for his week's labour, it is clear *that the produce of his labour*—be that produce whatever it may—must now be worth *one golden coin* ycleped a sovereign, *because* he is actually in the habitual receipt either *of that coin itself* in exchange for his labour, or else of a pound note which will instantly exchange for one" (ibid., 166). In this passage, Gray stated that the amount of nominal wages was just a convenient moniker for the amount set by the central authority. On top of that, when a weekly labor of an artisan receives a

[17] Gray says it is desirable to move the British monetary unit to the 10-decimal system by this measure. (Gray 1848: 251).

minimum wage of one pound, the price of the labor product will also be one pound. And whether a pound is represented by a banknote or a gold coin, there would be no change in the relationship the value buys back. The product, therefore, which is objectified in a standard week of labor would receive the minimum wage. Again, Gray envisioned this in terms of the artisan having the right to the whole value of the produce he or she has produced, and that this would be the wage they receive. However, when it came to the stage of envisioning a concrete production system, he had also to find a way to factor in profits and to add those to the production costs. He did this as well by setting an average distribution rate over a given timespan.

Moreover, the value of each good is not measured by the quantity of gold and silver, but rather, the value of gold and silver must be assessed by the wages spent on its production. In other words, the value of each good is measured by money that has a minimum wage as one pound, and the value of money is linked to the volume of employment of simple workers based on the minimum wage. That is, monetary value is nothing more than a nominal expression of labor. This idea of maintaining a constant relationship between monetary value and the quantities of labor-commanded through wages was something Gray had already arrived at in his middle period and was retained in his later writings.

Based on the above considerations, it may be possible to summarize Gray's approach to fair exchange by making the following two points. First, Gray was trying to measure the quantity of labor spending through wages, and second, he could have tried to measure the quantity of available labor through wages. In other words, it should be said that while considering the exchange between independent small producers in simple circulation as the starting point for consideration, the exchange was aimed at the point where the quantity of labor-bestowed and the quantity of labor commanded were the same. To understand these problems more fully, we must turn to the question of complex or skilled labor.

On the Question of Complex or Skilled Labor

In his later works, Gray followed the principle of the measure of value described by Smith, stating, "*that I see no practical difficulty whatever in accurately measuring value of any kind by labour*" (ibid., 158). To which he added, "*By what process is it possible to measure labour itself*? Equal quantities of labour—of hour's work" (ibid.). Such arguments can easily overlook the time invested in acquiring the requisite skills—i.e., apprenticeship periods, prior education, etc. For this reason, Gray acknowledged that skill and proficiency had to be taken into account, because "in the case of professional men, as for example, advocates, physicians, &c., the value of one man's hour is frequently greater than that of another man's day, or even week" (ibid., 158–159). This meant taking due account of skills to the point, "wherein he [the participant in exchange] may no longer be able to ascertain *the value* of his own time as compared with that of others, by the one and only true test of all comparative value, which is—*The precise sum of money for which, by free mutual contract, any labour, service, or commodity, can be sold?*" (ibid., 159) In other words, the function of the market is to set values to labor that correctly matched the nature of the labor, in which labor time is mediated by skills. Therefore, the "value of labor" will be given the nominal expression by the actual wages contracted in the market. According to Gray, there are three reason ways the wages differ: by skill and proficiency, by "trust and responsibility" (ibid., 162), and according to the supply demand relationship of labor. "*That the principle of free and unrestricted competition between man and man* throughout every occupation in life, be it professional, mercantile, mechanical, or labourious, *is in perfect accordance* with the natural measure of value—*labour*" (ibid., 159). And as long as it is regulated by free competition, it will also be possible to exchange for value, "*so long as every man shall be at perfect liberty to Name the value of his own labour, and to Obtain it if he can*" (ibid., 160). The minimum wage guaranteed by law is "a *mere staring point* in the race of competition" (ibid., 161), which guarantees equality of opportunity; however, it has nothing to do with equality of results. This is because the "co-operation, communities of property, and other bee-hive systems" involved in "the equality of the organization," must be rejected – hence the critique of Owenism (ibid., 40–41). The indivisible principle of division of labor and "individual competition" was, therefore, essential to provide motivation and stimulation to the acquisition of proficiency and skill.

Gray believed that wages were determined in a competitive labor market because he assumed the labor market was associated with the movement of capital that is allocated to each production sector as the goods market is subject to the business cycle of boom and bust. Since, the stability of the labor market will be supported by that of the goods market, the problem of inter-sectoral imbalance must be solved as an adjustment problem in the goods market.

So how should we understand the two issues outlined at the end of the previous section? In other words, how do we measure the quantity of complicated labor spending and the quantity of labor acquired through wages? Gray pointed to three main reasons for variations of the wage gap from time to time: the cost of training for skill formation, compensation for the supervision of labor that requires "trust and responsibility," and the labor market's supply and demand problem. The problem is understood as a disparity in the "value of labor," as it is said that the value of one working day of a professional man "is frequently greater than that of another man's day." As Smith pointed out, if labor is a measure of value, it should be able to measure the ratio of the quantity of labor-bestowed by "equal quantity of labor" or "equal quantity of labor time," but such commensurability is impaired because the "value of labor" is different from each other when it comes to complex labor.

According to Gray, the "value of labor" is unequal and cannot be used as a quantitative standard like the scale of the ruler. Gray had come to depend on market valuations because it was not possible to find the ideal form of value itself or the absolute level of the value in the way that would have been possible if one could construct a foolproof scale. The "value of labor," therefore, has elements such as skills and proficiency that cannot be clearly reduced to the quantity of labor. This fed Gray's skepticism concerning any Owenite visions of a non-market economy, because he recognized the importance of skills that are formed endogenously from the division of labor, as Smith had argued. For the time being, if "value of labor" is grasped as the amount of daily necessities including the cost for the skill formation, the cost of complex labor might be valued as a multiple of the wages paid for the simple labor expenditures required to guarantee the wages that can be used to compensate the workers' skills. In that case, the quantity of labor-bestowed and the quantity of labor-commanded would not match. These provisions for complex labor were not consistent with Ricardo-Marx's theory of value, in which the relative independence of the value of the labor power and its use value remained the key to theories such surplus value.

Concerning Money and the Production System in Gray's Later Works

Despite apparent similarities, nowhere is the change between Gray's middle period and his later works greater than when it came to the question of production. In these later works, the market for goods was to be regulated through a "great national banking association" consisting of "*Standard* merchants or manufacturers" and "Standard banks" (ibid., 111–112).[18] The specific mechanism of this association was to be as follows. First, when a standard manufacturer produced some goods, it was to deposit the goods in a standard bank. The standard bank would then calculate the value of the goods and would then sit in the creditor side of the manufacturer's ledger or "**cash-account**" as set by the bank. At the same time, the goods were to be stored in the bank's warehouse and the value owed to the creditor is written down in the manufacturer's "**stock-account**" (ibid., 115). Meanwhile, the "estimated value" (ibid., 114) of the goods estimated by the bank would be the expected price, which is the cost including labor wages and raw material costs plus the expected profit. The bank could then use the deposited goods as collateral and lend to the manufacturer "standard bank-notes" (ibid., 117) with the maximum expected price of the goods as the upper limit. This advanced loan would allow the manufacturer to obtain money and stock from the standard warehouse before the goods produced by the manufacturer were sold. Meanwhile, the price of the goods drawn from the standard warehouse would written in the debtor side of the stock account's ledger, and the same amount of money used for the purchase would debited to the cash account, and settled between the bank accounts. However, the value of the goods estimated by the bank would yield a price that would include the expected profit, and the bank will sell at that price. Thus, the price would be subject to variation around a mean, and that times it will exceed value, while at other times undershooting it. In that case, the asset value recorded in the stock account was to be reevaluated to match the "*actual*" value. Through this process, Gray hoped "that production [would] ever be equalled by demand" (ibid.). In addition, given that the supply and demand would not always be the same, a degree of temporary money hoarding was permitted to occur due to the accumulation

[18] Gray said that "a standard merchant and manufacturer" are "members of a great national banking association," it is "without, however, strictly speaking, associating at all," denying that the standard system is an Owenite socialist association (ibid., 112).

of stocks. However, in a standard banking system in which money was always abundant, it is not necessary to hoard money more than necessary, so there would be no reason for monetary interest to be generated.[19]

It should be noted that Gray identified several types of goods that were unsuitable for being handled by the standard banks. The first was perishable foodstuffs, the second, fashion-related goods such as clothing, the third, goods imported for special purposes and custom-made goods, and the fourth was dangerous goods and munitions that are difficult to store in warehouses. Finally, there were products, works, and services by artists and similar experts. When review this list of exclusions, it is clear that perishability is not the common denominator. After all, most of the means of consumption, including goods that are consumed daily and luxury goods, could be regarded as unsuitable for storage for longer period. Therefore, it is probably better to think about Gray had in mind as a stock account, rather than a standard goods account. During the writings of his middle period, this tendency toward the liberalization of goods was limited to the retail business based on the public ownership of themeans of production. For instance, in the *Lectures on Money,* Gray divided goods into a means of consumption and a means of production due to their nature. This was to be seen in the context where the standard banking system would become a mechanism for the handling of productive stocks—except for land (ibid., 110–111).[20] Due to such regulation of goods, Gray's standard banking system was based on a realistic assessment of the need to put in place measures to counteract crises of underconsumption, where there is insufficient purchasing power in the market, and producers can no longer exchange their goods at value. Gray saw underconsumption as a problem that arises from a lack of funds to purchase stocks, rather than the shortage of consumption demand due to the consumption expenditure from labor wages.

At this point, we can turn to the examination of the structure and functions of the standard banking system. First, as was the case in his earlier writings, Gray's vison of a banking system was based on the drive

[19] Kishi states that "'the only new feature' that was added to the current monetary system was nothing but the theory of free credit that made the acquisition of 'interest of money' unjust" (Kishi 1978: 65).

[20] Furthermore, Gray stated that "the wholesale department of the commercial interest would be annihilated" once the banks took on the management and facilitation of the goods market (Gray 1848: 117).

to achieve an immutable measure of value. Through the establishment of such an immutable measure of value, the relationship between the monetary value and the quantity of labor commanded would be strictly defined, so that the monetary value would remain invariant over time, with price fluctuations due to monetary factors abolished. A corollary to this was the maintenance of a constant ratio between the amount of money promised to be paid and the quantity of labor commanded, and a commensurate system of long-term debts and credit relations. Gray believed this would result in a fair distribution among the productive class, on the basis of equivalent exchange under an expanded economic system. Then, based on the immutable measure of value, Gray presented several specific solutions for underconsumption and inter-sectoral imbalances through the banking system. Pointing to the problem of inter-sectoral imbalance, Gray noted that in empirical markets, the allocation and movement of productive stocks tend not to be carried out smoothly. Therefore, in order to facilitate the allocation of stocks, the inter-account settlement mechanism and the standard warehouse centralize the stock market, with the bank supplying funds to each producer experiencing a lack of funds for purchasing materials, thereby eliminating underconsumption. Underconsumption and inter-sectoral imbalances were, therefore, not to be treated as separate issues, because they were effectively framed as crises of overproduction. Thus, the classical and Birmingham schools, who tried to solve the problem by focusing on one or the other, were criticized as false.

So how was the pricing mechanism in the standard banking system intended to work? The price of the standard goods or the stocks handled in the standard bank were to be given by standard bank estimates. The individual producers were not involved in the pricing because the cost of the standard goods and the added profit were given by the bank. In the sense that prices were not individually presented by decentralized economic agents, it is hard to say that prices in the stock market were free market prices. Moreover, the price of goods in the national bank system, as envisaged during the middle period of his writing, was to be composed of production costs and profits, and the supply and demand were to be met by adjusting the quantity under the guidance of the banks. This was to prevent the price from falling and to maintain a fixed price to ensure a fair price exchange. However, in his later works, Gray made allowances for price fluctuations depending to cope with incorrect market valuations that arise from the bank making an incorrect forecast of the level of demand. Gray said that if a stock was sold at a price above its estimated price, the surplus would belong to the producer, and contrarily the loss would belong to the producer. Nonetheless, it remains questionable whether the producer can be held responsible for whether a sale results in a surplus or a loss in a centrally managed system of production for the market. Producers can only get money within the estimated price as set by the bank, because they rely entirely on banks for funding. Therefore, if the sale below the estimated price is repeated, will the producer's cashflow be adversely affected? Will it result in producers in the industrial sector to exiting the market, because prices are below the level at which they can sustain reproduction. Or, would the same mechanism merely encourage producers to enter the market until the surplus becomes zero? If so, the bank's adjustment function for the market has been greatly reduced in these later writings. By this stage, Gray seems to have accepted the automatic adjustment function of the market by the price mechanism, he believes that the market will operate smoothly if it supplies abundant money and neutralizes it. Paradoxically, he implicitly appears to have come round to accepting the classical "theoretical dogma" and to rely too much on the neutrality of market competition.[21]

In the standard banking system, what kind of effect results from centralization, which is promoted from the two aspects of account concentration and geographical concentration? First, it reduces the need for money hoarding, which requires the sale of some goods prior the purchase of stocks. This was because the producer could temporarily deposit the goods in a bank and obtain money at an estimated value expected to be sold, before actually selling the goods and obtaining cash. Producers could secure funds for the purchase of stocks simply by depositing the produced goods in a bank. The narrow limits of commercial credit have been removed by receiving in advance the fund they would have gained in the future from the sale of goods. The bank here plays a role as an intermediary business, which proactively lends future funds free of charge. Moreover, since the total amount of goods deposited in the bank and the total amount of loanable money were always to be the same, the total supply and total demand of the stock market would also balance. Second, the geographical concentration or transaction concentration itself must, by necessity, impair the dispersibility and independence of

[21] Gray supposed that the standard banking system was a "*no-monetary system*" close to bartering (Gray 1848: 198, 250).

stock transactions. In a market where producers are monitored by banks and their products are centrally managed, the conditions under which prices tend to fluctuate, such as when goods are traded in a decentralized manner, are reduced and tend to converge on one price for one item. In a market where the trading of stocks is not done in a free or decentralized manner, profit would be given as the official profit rate evaluated by public banks that provide free credit in pursuit of the stability of the system. If the level of production cost is regulated by the minimum wage, the price of the means of consumption produced using that stock would also be determined by the cost plus the official profit. Basically, the prices of all goods would tend to settle at a certain level. If the response to demand is entrusted to the capital movement of the standard manufacturer as the stock owner, it would, in the end, be impossible to assume an equalization of the profit rate, as the classical school postulated—a marked contrast with Gray's middle period. Overall, Gray sought to overcome the classical market vision, by gathering total demand and total supply in one station. It can be argued that he continued to be trapped in the classical market vision in that his solutions failed to solve the problem of total supply and demand, as well as the mismatching of individual supply and demand.

Finally, it is unclear whether Gray was craftily skirting questions of ownership in his late writings, or whether it was simply an oversight. All that is clear is that most stocks were to be traded through standard banks. From this, it can be inferred that his previous commitment to the public ownership of the means of production has been abandoned, due to his acceptance of the existence of a trading system for stocks (with the exception of land). However, it remained unclear whether the "great national banking association" for the trading of stocks was to be based on private property. Furthermore, this left open the whole question of the relation between the price of stocks, which are not freely set, and the role of landowners whose means of living was based on something that could not be incorporated into the system. What is clear in all this is that Gray was not thinking along socialist lines, as the means of production were clearly no longer to be publicly owned. Instead, as Kishi has pointed out, the social system sought by Gray is better described as a system of organized or planned exchange. It is a system in which the current *ex-post facto* market exchanges would be replaced by a system in which banks can play a more directing role. Gray's social system might, therefore, qualify as an early version of what has come to be known as market socialism, where the banks intervene actively in the market for the means of production.

Bibliography

Claeys, G. (1987). *Machinery, money and millennium: From moral economy to socialism, 1815–60*. Princeton University Press.

Foxwell, H. S. (1899). Introduction. In *The right to the whole produce of labour* (by A. Menger). Macmillan.

Gray, J. (1842). *An efficient remedy for the distress of nations*. Adam and Charles Black.

Gray, J. (1847). *The currency question*. A. and C. Black.

Gray, J. (1848). *Lectures on the nature and use of money*. Adam and Charles Black.

Gray, J. (1873/1831). *The social system*. Augustus M. Kelley.

Gray, J. (1997/1825). A lecture on human happiness. In *The Ricardian socialists* (Vol. 2). Routledge/Thoemmes Press.

Hawtrey, R. G. (1928). *Trade and credit*. Longmans, Green.

Hirao, S. (1975). *Ricādo-ha Shakaishugi no Kenkyū* [A study of Ricardian socialism]. Minervashobo.

Kamata, T. (1968). *Kotenha Keizaigaku to Shoki Shakaishugi* [Classical political economy and early socialism]. Mirai-sha.

Kamata, T. (2000). *Shijōkeizai to Kyōdōshisō: Igirisu Shihonshugi-hihan no Shisōtekigenryū* [Market economy and cooperative social thought: The ideological origins of the critique of British capitalism]. Mirai-sha.

Kenyon, T. A. (1997). Introduction. In *The Ricardian socialists* (Vol. 1). Routledge/ Thoemmes Press.

Kishi, T. (1978). Jon Gurei no Kōkan Ginkōron [On the John Gray's exchange bank]. *Keizai-ronsō* [The Economic Review], *122*(3–4), 175–194.

Kubo, S. (2002). Jon Gurei no Kaheiron: Sono "Kahei no Honshitsu to sono Yūyōsei ni kansuru Kōgi" wo chūshin nishite [John Gray's money theory: Focusing on *Lectures on the nature and use of money*]. T. Otomo, Y. Ikeda, & Y. Sato (Eds.), *Keizaishisō nimiru Kahei to Kinyū* [Money and finance in economic thought]. Sanreishobo.

Lowenthal, E. (1911). *The Ricardian socialists*. Columbia University.

Marx, K. (1987/1859). A contribution to the critique of political economy. In *Marx & Engels collected works* (Vol. 29). Lawrence & Wishart.

Marx, K. (1996/1867). Capital, Vol. I. *Marx & Engels collected works* (Vol. 35). Lawrence & Wishart.

Menger, A. (1899/1886). *The right to the whole produce of labour*. Macmillan.

Ricardo, D. (1951/1817). On the principles of political economy, and taxation. In *The works and correspondence of David Ricardo* (Vol. 1). Cambridge University Press.

Tamanoi, Y. (1977). Ricādo-ha Shakaishugi no Gaiyō [Outline of Ricardian socialism]. In *Keizairironshi* [History of economic theory]. University of Tokyo Press.

CHAPTER 8

Reconsideration of Gesell's Critique of Marx's Theory of Capital

8.1 Background

This chapter focuses on Silvio Gesell (1862–1930) a little-known economic thinker from the early twentieth century whose ideas have come into prominence over the past 30 years. Gesell has increasingly been recognized for his contribution to the theory and practice of local currencies, and the emphasis he placed upon a reform of monetary systems focused on regional eco-cycles that protect local economies from the disturbance of exogenous financial transactions. His ideas first came into prominence following a series of global currency shocks during the 1990s, not least the 1997 Asian currency crisis, which occurred at the high point of globalization. Gesell has also been seen as a progenitor of several other ideas which have come into vogue, including the ethical critique of charging interest on borrowers, the role of rentiers in amassing unearned income, the importance of small government and the spirit of self-help. Some of the earliest local currencies were introduced in Austria and Germany soon after Gesell's death. Some examples of these currencies include the "labor certificates" (*Arbeitsbestätigungen*) used in the Tyrolian town of Wörgl and the *Wära* in the Bavarian town of Schwanenkirchen

© The Author(s), under exclusive license to Springer Nature Switzerland AG 2021

T. Yuki, *Socialism, Markets, and the Critique of Money*,
Marx, Engels, and Marxisms,
https://doi.org/10.1007/978-3-030-80408-4_8

(see Blanc 1998: 475).[1] These local currencies, nicknamed "dwindling money" (*Schwandgeld*) for their distinctive characteristic of decreasing in value over time. They were proven to offset some of the worst effects of the global depression in the 1920s and 1930s that had devastated the German and Austrian economies. Due to these practical examples, recent research has done much to promote and clarify Gesell's ideas.[2]

In the post-war era, Gesell's influence went into decline as steady economic growth powered by state intervention became the norm, but with the disturbances of neoliberalism he has proven in some quarters to be something of a "discovery" and a "forgotten thinker." According to Aida, the reception of Gesell's ideas has also been held back by a lack of French and English translations of his works, which meant that, apart from the German-speaking world, he was largely unknown across Europe and the US during the Cold War (Aida 2014: 31–32). Lastly, Gesell was an autodidact whose independence from the organized labor movement and academia meant that there was no steady body available to transmit his ideas.[3]

According to Preparata (2006), the resurgence of interest in Gesell was sparked by the resurgence of interest in anarchist thinking around the beginning of the new millennium, particularly in the context of a post-9–11 world. As Preparata states, anarchist thought contains "a few simple, yet penetrating analytical tools" for promoting a brand of "utopianism benevolently conceived as a normative socioeconomic blueprint" that has attracted "a growing number of radical economists away from the somewhat sterile games of Marxian transformation and into the yet uncharted theory of locally issued means of payment, especially those bearing the device of perishability" (Preparata 2006: 624). In addition, Gesell has proven to be an influence on anarchism as a strand of political thought

[1] *Wära* is a portmanteau term formed by a compound of *Ware* (commodity) and *Währung* (currency) (Blanc 1998: 481).

[2] Among economists, Gesell's works have perhaps been evaluated most by Irving Fisher, who dispatched an investigating committee to Wörgl and recommended Gesell's policies in the US (Barber 1997: 37–41).

[3] Another reason for Gesell's post-war neglect was due to the fact that several of his followers turned to fascism in the 1930s.

in Asia.[4] Many of the most successful applications of his ideas are to be found within non-Western settings.

An additional strand of the Gesell resurgence lay in its influence on Third Way politics at the turn of the millennium. Gesell's editor, Onken, has been keen to promote a vision of "a market economy without capitalism" (Onken 2000: 614), in which neither planning nor the market predominates, but rather a "third way." These ideas have resonated with those seeking to promote various forms of market socialism, anarcho-syndicalism and workers' co-operatives (Hodgson 1999: Sect. 2).[5] Such a viewpoint has sought positively to promote a market that fosters "competitive entrepreneurship" (Onken 2000: 609), while shedding some of the more defensive associations with market socialism that grew up during the 1980s in last days of the Eastern Bloc (and reconnecting them with a network of anarchist traditions).

The three abovementioned researchers commonly acknowledge the neglect of anarchism in mainstream accounts of economic theory.[6] Yet, when it comes to local currency theory, the contributions of thinkers such as Proudhon and Gesell, whose association with anarchism is undeniable, cannot be overlooked. However, as Aida has noted Gesell had much to say about local economies in the context of wider social reforms and

[4] Tosa points out that the intrinsic understanding of Asian society is possible through "reviewing the concept of the public sphere as dialectical processes that appear repeatedly in any society, and to train the concept of borderivity and liminoid" rather than regarding the way democratic consensus is formed as it is predominantly conceived in Western societies. Graeber also states that the desire for better social relations is called anarchism, and from these primitive desires, there are "consensus building processes" in any society. At the same time, he emphasizes the price a society that values consensus has to pay. This is because of the constant efforts expended upon the concealment of social violence, which hides internal violence, and the moral contradiction that results (Tosa 2007: 84). Anderson's argument points to the prevalence among Asian anarchism of processes of "accumulation of communication," in which the public sphere opens up the possibility of furthering social evolution in a Darwinian sense, by developing an international movement that has long been rooted in the nationalistic politics of each country (Umemori 2007).

[5] In addition, Zhiyuan points out that "Gesell's 'stamp scrip' proposal is a telling case of petty-bourgeois socialism's economic vision: instead of abolishing the market economy, we can create a market economy with more freedom and equal opportunity by reforming and bringing innovations into the monetary institutions" (Zhiyuan 2003: 61).

[6] Nishibe mentions that "local currency is an object of economics that, instead of 'has not been treated,' is rather 'untreatable'"; in addition, Nishibe introduces the economic doctrines of Owen and Thompson in the UK, and Proudhon in France, who expound views on local currency (Nishibe 2003: 5–6).

programs of nationalization (Aida 2014: 113). Hence, it is misleading to read Gesell's works simply through the lens of local currency theory.

Despite the neglect of his works in the post-war era, Gesell was referred to frequently before the war. Most significantly, Keynes mentioned Gesell in his *General Theory of Employment, Interest and Money* (1973/1936), when setting out the overall aims of the book:

> The purpose of the book as a whole may be described as the establishment of an anti-Marxian socialism, a reaction against *laissez-faire* built on theoretical foundations totally unlike those of Marx in being based on a repudiation instead of on an acceptance of the classical hypotheses, and on an unfettering of competition instead of its abolition. I believe that the future will learn more from the spirit of Gesell than from that of Marx. The preface to *The Natural Economic Order* will indicate to the reader, if he will refer to it, the moral quality of Gesell. The answer to Marxism is, I think, to be found along the lines of this preface. (Keynes 1973/1936: 355)

Thus, even if Gesell was "highly praised" as several researchers have noted (Aida 2014: 31; Morino 2000: 106), this is largely due to his status as an alternative to Marx as much as to any of his intrinsic merits.[7] Nonetheless, according to Preparata (2002), Keynes stole many of Gesell's ideas,[8] while ignoring Gesell's real intention, by diverting attention from wholescale social reform to amelioration of the existing system. He points out how Keynes translated several of Gesell's ideas to make them more compatible, including the concept of "basic interest," which he translated as "premium for liquidity" and "interest upon capital" which was rendered as "marginal efficiency of capital" (Preparata 2002). Ivanova points out "some striking similarities between Proudhon and Keynes, as acknowledged by Dillard, Wright and Mattick" (Ivanova 2011: 217), although Dillard states "There is no reason for doubting Keynes's statement that he

[7] Although Keynes evaluates Gesell's vision as "liberal socialism," the emphasis here is not on "socialism," but "liberal" (Darity 1995: 38–39). "Indeed, 'one of Keynes's main aims (as an enlightened conservative) was to save capitalism'" (Dowd in Preparata 2002: 246).

[8] "Though less exhaustive than his treatise on money, the land part of the *NEO* [*Natural Economic Order*], dismissed offhand by Keynes in the course of his idiosyncratic exploration of Gesell's main work as undeserving of notice on account of its lack of originality, is however, an integral component of the Gesellian vision" (Preparata & Elliot 2004: 924).

did not see the importance of Gesell's theory until he had independently worked out his own conclusions," and thus denies a direct influence of Gesell or Proudhon on Keynes (Dillard 1942: 64).

Gesell was born in 1862 in St. Vith, near Malmedy, in a part of the Rhineland that was to be included in the German Empire from 1871 and is today a part of Belgium. As a linguist, he traveled to Argentina in 1887 and was a successful businessman. However, despite Gesell's commercial success, the Argentine economy was repeatedly inflated and deflated by the government's meandering policy of joining and leaving the gold standard, which led to exchange rate turmoil and sudden capital-flight. These problems drew Gesell's attention toward monetary and financial problems in order to protect his own business interests. At this time, Gesell accurately identified price movements and amassed considerable assets but realized that the goal was less to shore up his private position than to search for measures that could eliminate financial instability and stabilize prices. This resulted in six books that he wrote in the 1890s prior to his return to Europe in 1900. While running a farm in Switzerland, Gesell became actively involved in the publication and editing of the magazine *The Physiocrat* (*Der Physiokrat*). In 1919, he became a member of the People's Committee of the Bavarian Soviet Republic, a revolutionary government after World War I, but he only worked there for seven days. However, Gesell's writing and publishing activities led him to pass on his ideas and theories to the Free Economy (*Freiwirtschaft*) movement and the Free Land Free Money Alliance (*Der Freiland-Freigeld-Bund*), which then led to the establishment of local currency schemes in the 1930s. More than almost any other contemporary associated with anarchism, Gesell can clearly be shown to have made an independent contribution to economic theory and practice.

While recently Gesell has been associated with local currencies, in his main works there is little reference to them, and his interests focused more on developing his view of "anarchist economics," with a focus on monetary and land reform, as well as his particular theory of capital which sought to distinguish itself from Classical, Marxian, and marginalist economic theories (Gesell 1958/1916; 2007b/1922).[9] What is striking in these texts is that despite much common ground and a shared commitment to human emancipation, Gesell sought to distinguish his ideas from

[9] This book refers to "anarchist economics" as economic doctrines in the line of Gesell and Proudhon.

those of prominent contemporary Marxists such as Karl Kautsky and Lenin. These differences will be explored further in this chapter to elucidate both the differences between anarchist and Marxist economics and to show how Gesell's theory of capital provided a framework for achieving his visions. Therefore, Gesell's criticism of Marx reflects his direct stance in terms of the critique of social reform and the creation of a society based on "Free-Land and Free-Money" (Gesell 1958/1916: 12).

The difference between Gesell's ideas and Marxism revolved around three key issues that will be explored: (1) a market-centered vision of society (2) an independent small producer model, and (3) a money–capital doctrine.

8.2 Market-Centered Socialism

As mentioned already, Gesell firmly sits within the anarchist tradition. Nowhere is this made more abundantly clear than in the following statement:

> The Natural Economic Order stands by itself and requires no legal enactments; it makes officials, the State itself and all other tutelage superfluous, and it respects the laws of natural selection to which we owe our being; it gives every man the possibility of fully developing his ego. Its ideal is the ideal of the personality responsible for itself alone and liberated from the control of others-the ideal of Schiller, Stirner, Nietzsche and Landauer. (Gesell 1958/1916: 23)

There are a number of defining features in this statement that sets out his particular variant of anarchism. First, the reference to the natural economic order respecting "the laws of natural selection to which we owe our being" indicates his application of Darwin's theory of evolution to the social sciences. Second, by situating this social Darwinianism within a lineage that includes Max Stirner, it is clear that Gesell is committed to an ego-based model of society in which "every man [is given] the possibility of fully developing his ego" in a natural economic order.[10] Additionally, Gesell states that "*the free-money theory answered*

[10] An egoist differs from a self-interested person in the ordinary meaning. Stirner (1995/1845) demonstrates the personal ego alienated by an ego of God in the processes of dialectic development in *The Ego and Its Own*, and reveals that the personal ego is

the questions that *Proudhon* left unsolved" (Gesell 2007b/1922: 373). By positioning himself as a critical successor to Proudhon's and his theory of free credit, Gesell could present himself as an anarchistic socialist whose theory of human freedom based on natural evolution served as a foundation for his particular theories of economic and land reform. However, it is worth pointing out that this also contraposed his variant of anarchism to the more social and communistic variants associated with Mikhail Bakunin and Prince Kropotkin, who rejected all forms of market society and oriented toward a non-market approach along the lines of Bakunin–Kropotkin "Communist anarchism" or "social anarchism" (Preparata 2006: 263). Rather, Gesell's anarchistic socialism is closer Proudhon's individualistic tradition since it tended to treat the market as the basic framework for society and emphasized that the goal shared by all anarchists could be achieved through market reforms that would create genuine social equality.[11] That is to say, the market was the economic mechanism that could unite disparate individuals into a social framework where they could exchange on an equal basis, whereas communistic economic systems that based themselves on the presupposition of a collectivist society impose their model of social interaction on the individual participants. In today's world, this rivalry within anarchism boils down to the question of how they envisage a post-capitalist society functioning, with who follow in the tradition of Proudhon and Gesell practicing what will be referred to in this book as "market-centered socialism" (MCS).[12]

Having situated Gesell within the field of anarchism, it is possible to expand on his relation to Marxism by showing how he sought to exploit inner tensions within Marxism, especially between those who were

even subject to thoughts of humanism since Feuerbach. Stirner describes egoists as persons who hold onto "ownness" as the master of themselves without being subject to any other people or thoughts.

[11] More correctly, we should call it "anocracy" instead of anarchy (Preparata 2006: 619). Gesell points out an error of terminology with "anarchy of production" being conflated with "anarchy." "Often, the wrong sense of the word *anarchy* is used to accuse the private sector with reference to its *plans*. When accusing private sector participants, an economy is considered to be perfectly led by plans and with the aid of statistics. However, this thought is too naïve" (Gesell 2007b/1922: 393).

[12] Although the term MCS is not generally used, this chapter defines it to avoid confusion between the "market socialism" current in China and other reforming socialist countries, and "marketism" in the neo-liberal meaning.

partially open to market-based conceptions of socialism. In the introduction to *Exploitation, its Causes and its Struggle* (*Die, ihre Ursachen und ihre Bekämpfung*), he included the following extract from Karl Kautsky's *The Dictatorship of the Proletariat* (1919):

> To be exact, however, Socialism as such is not our goal, which is the abolition of every kind of exploitation and oppression, be it directed against a class, a party, a sex, or a race ... If in this struggle we place the Socialist way of production as the goal, it is because in the technical and economic conditions which prevail today Socialistic production appears to be the sole means of attaining our object. Should it be proved to us that we are wrong in so doing, and that somehow the emancipation of the proletariat and of mankind could be achieved solely on the basis of private property, or could be most easily realised in the manner [indicated by Proudhon], then we would throw Socialism overboard, without in the least giving up our object, and even in the interests of this object. (Kautsky as cited in Gesell 2007b/1922: 352)

What is noteworthy here is that Kautsky entertained the possibility of a market-based transition to socialism, while Gesell openly advocated such a road. Within this distinction lay a fundamental set of economic premises that pointed in radically different directions.

For Marxists including Kautsky, the abolition of exploitation entailed the negation of private ownership of the means of production. The social and communistic implications of such a negation were firmly at odds with the egoistic nature of humanity as described by Darwin and Stirner (ibid., 354). As Gesell put it: "The economic order here discussed is a natural order only in the sense that it is adapted to the nature of man" (Gesell 1958/1916: 9), and "By the Natural Economic Order we mean, therefore, an order in which men compete on equal terms with the equipment given them by nature, an order in which, consequently, the leadership falls to the fittest, an order in which all privileges are abolished, in which the individual, obeying the impulse of egoism, goes straight for his, aim, undisturbed by scruples alien to economic life-scruples which he will have opportunities enough of obeying outside economic life" (ibid., 11–12). Gesell went on to point out the necessity of "justified egoism" and "equal equipment for the economic struggle" as conditions for reconstructing the economic order. "The prosperity of mankind, as of all living beings" would be achieved via the same "laws of natural selection" (ibid., 9–10,

12).[13] In addition, he stated that the "the proletariat can no longer pin their hopes on the Marxist description of Capital. This description leads inexorably towards the demand for a communistic form of economic organization. Either capitalism or communism, that is the sole conclusion which the Marxist theory of capital seeks to draw. This image fails to grasp the fact that the communist economic order fails because of the nature of man, that is, because of its very basis, since the days of Adam, only ever changes gradually, if at all" (Gesell 2007b/1922: 354). Thus, for Gesell, the Marxian view of human nature was flawed, in that it sought to achieve suddenly what can only be done gradually and relied on a communist notion of society as a way quickly to achieve a transition that ran contrary to human nature. This is not the same thing as stating that he did not believe that communism could not abolish exploitation—it was rather the feasibility of the claim in relation to human nature that bothered him. Due to this, he was convinced that even with the abolition of exploitation under a communist system, the question of oppression and coercion would remain unanswered. By forcibly negating the private ownership of the means of production, Marxism, in his view, was forced to embark on a program of state-directed nationalization: "The first [Marxian] theory demands the *abolition of private property*, and also of the private economy, of *self-responsibility* in logical application. The distribution of products is carried out by the *State*, which *directs the production*. The principles to which distribution should occur are regulated *by law*" (ibid., 358–359).[14]

According to Gesell, "However, *both* [Gesellian and Marxian] systems claim, to their strength, that the *main goal of socialism is to realise the elimination of exploitation completely*." Yet, revolution achieved in this manner in Russia had not only removed exploiters for the time being but caused the following: "[T]he Russians seem to have paid dearly [sacrificed] to achieve [the goal], such that some long for the happy times of capitalist exploiters again" (ibid., 359). Otherwise, revolution would simply replace

[13] The ideas of Stirner and Proudhon oriented his "wish for communal desire within a tempered regime of private property"; in other words, "a mixed system of property balanced by the redistributive action of the public hand" (Preparata 2006: 621–622).

[14] From the viewpoint of Gesell, although Kautsky (1919) was a critic of Bolshevism, he felt that the Kautsky-type of social democracy would result in a "planning state" as well as the Lenin-type of socialism of the Soviet Union. In addition, people did not accept the Soviet Union-type socialism, which was being shown by increasing immigration from the Soviet Union to Germany (Gesell 1958/1916: 49).

an old state of exploiters with a new power as a state for the sake of abolishing exploitation. Free from the world of eternal recurrence, a dramatic replacement of power holders is described in *Directions to Servants*, where "exploitation is, according to this theory, a product of violent interventions in the natural [order], by itself, which results in the regulation of the economy itself. [However, we should] eliminate these interventions to eradicate exploitation" when maintaining the conditions of the private economy (ibid., 359). At the same time, this would create a society of egoists composed of people with equal power under anocracy.

Gesell was thus laying the groundwork for his own alternative by denying Marxist conceptions of the market and private ownership, and by critiquing Soviet-type systems.

8.3 Independent Small Producer Model

By arguing for the abolition of exploitation while retaining private ownership, Gesell was aware of the Marxist criticism that this fails to consider exploitation at the point of production. To address this, Gesell put forward an alternative theory of exploitation.

While socialists of all stamps can be defined in terms of "*everyone involved in the fight against exploitation*," Gesell was clear that there was "still not a clear picture of the nature of exploitation power" among socialists. Even if it were possible to define exploitation on the basis of "*economic superiority*," there is no consistent view on what economic superiority is (Gesell 2007b/1922: 356). While for Marxists, the cause of exploitation lies in "*the private ownership of the means of production*," Gesell sought to shift the focus onto "*the results of our defective institutions for money and land*" (ibid., 358). For Gesell, the insistence on private ownership as the cause of exploitation, results inevitably in the nationalization of the means of production and the abolition of the market as an economic ground of freedom. To avoid this outcome, Gesell argued that socialists should seek to abolish exploitation by ensuring that "the *land and money should 'be socialised'*"; a formulation that highlights the influence of Proudhon (ibid., 359).[15]

[15] For instance, see Proudhon's "Fifth Study: Social Liquidation" in *General Idea of the Revolution in the Nineteenth Century* (2007/1851).

To support Gesell's abovementioned perspective, it must be proved that *the "positive evidence for a non-exploitative economy is fully compatible with private ownership and the private economy"* (ibid., 362). Gesell's thesis that the cause of exploitation lay in *"our defective institutions of money and land"* can be stated negatively in antithetical terms; namely, that the cause of exploitation is not *"the private ownership of the means of production."* Therefore, Gesell to set about demonstrating the flaws in the Marxian theory of exploitation, and in the following we look at whether he was successful, and whether he was able to furnish a viable alternative model of exploitation.[16]

For Gesell, Marx's theory of exploitation rested upon two misconceptions, the first was Marx's *thesis of the commodity of labor power*, and the second was his *thesis of equal exchange* in which ordinary money is nothing more than a medium of exchange because *"Money is a perfect equivalent in the exchange of obtained commodities"* (ibid., 360). By reading Marx through the prism of his critique of Proudhon, Gesell in turn criticized Marx using the same theoretical arguments—but in reverse.[17] For Proudhon, exploitation took place in circulation processes caused by the power of money, whereas Marx criticized any theory that sought to abolish exploitation by realizing equal exchange in circulation processes. Gesell re-critiqued Marx, by stressing that unequal exchange does not lie in the inequality between the cost of labor power and the value of the commodities it can be used to produce, but rather in the distorting

[16] In the preface, Gesell states his aim: "The abolition of unearned income, of so-called surplus-value also termed interest and rent, is the immediate economic aim of every socialistic movement." What is notable here is the attempt shift the terrain of exploitation from the extraction of surplus value at the point of production to a redefinition of the concept as any kind of unearned income that could include interest and rent (Gesell 1958/1916: 27).

[17] "If Karl Kautsky had started to summarise from the *whole* works, he would not have been confused by the sophistry of the work, he would have happened on the site in *Capital* Vol. III. In Vol. I, in what Marx confirmed so clearly and so unmistakeably himself through a lack of apprehensive words, that to clarify the possibility of exploitation existed before entrepreneurs existed, it is 'not necessary' to eliminate all exploitation because 'neither natural nor artificial monopolies have to falsify commodity-exchange in favour of buyers or sellers.' In that case Marx's whole struggle against *Proudhon*, who said the same things, thus Proudhon was attacked disgracefully by Marx, as well as the manner of Marx in III. By the way, this is the volume which Friedrich Engels also commented on in respect of the cause of capitalist exploitation: that by holding back from the medium of exchange, therefore by it is possible to store money" (Schwarz 2008: 27–28).

role played by money, which results in unequal exchange. By reframing the subject, Gesell sought to reignite the controversy between Marx and Proudhon.[18]

Before examining Marx's *thesis of commodity of labor power*, this chapter discusses Gesell's summary of Marx's theory of exploitation and capital.

> The entrepreneur buys the commodity of labor power for its full value, and therefore, without exploitation. However, he does not buy labor power because of its exchange value, thus not as a merchant. He buys it as a consumer in order to consume. However, the commodity of labor power has the peculiarity that its use value is bigger than its exchange value; in other words, the consumption of a product of the commodity of labor power as a product is bigger than the production cost of labor power, and therefore, bigger than the wage. *This difference is the surplus value*. This gives us capital theory. (ibid., 365)

This passage demonstrates that for Gesell, the owners of the means of production were not capitalists, but entrepreneurs. Furthermore, entrepreneurs do not buy the commodity of labor power as merchants, but as consumers in order to utilize labor power to produce their products. Clearly, this harks back to the influence of a model of commercial society based on independent small producers. In this model, the *dramatis personae* consist of entrepreneurs as owners of the means of production (functional capitalists), laborers as owners of the products of labor (independent small producers), and capitalists as owners of hording money (moneyed capitalists).

These three actors are defined at the start via a relationship between entrepreneurs and laborers in which the commodities bought by entrepreneurs are not laborers' labor power. Because Gesell did view labor power as a commodity, his position encounters two difficulties that would need to be addressed if he were to provide a successful repudiation of the Marxian theory of exploitation. First, labor *power* as the ability to work cannot be bought because only labor *products* can be bought. In order to purchase "*the will to work*" (ibid., 363), labor must be purchased as a product that is based on the worker's capacity to work. Second, it is difficult to define the value of labor power using the real wage (cost of

[18] However, we should pay attention to the fact that neither Gesell nor Marx noticed that "Proudhon was well aware that exploitation occurred at the point of production" (McKay 2011: 8).

reproduction) because labor power is not a labor product; therefore, it is also not possible to grasp the difference between the concepts of value and use value of labor power.[19] On the other hand, entrepreneurs do not pay wages to laborers in advance. Because, the "entrepreneur lends" the means of production to laborers, laborers sell or "provide" their products of labor for "remuneration" (interest of the means of products or interest of real capital) to entrepreneurs. This is the content of the contract of employment. Wages are paid from entrepreneurs to laborers as a selling price or "the *piece wage*" (Gesell 2007b/1922: 363–364).[20] By entrepreneurs offering wages to laborers, "the offer is demanded at the employment of the laborer by the entrepreneur according to the whole products that he expects from the laborer. In addition, the laborer demands his wage depends on his labor product" (ibid., 363). Laborers are contract producers, and entrepreneurs are merchants who sell commodities produced by entrustment.

The relationship between entrepreneurs and capitalists appears as a relationship between functional capitalists and moneyed capitalists, in which moneyed capitalists lend funds for business and functional capitalists borrow funds to buy the means of production. Furthermore, decision-making and investment actions by entrepreneurs are exposed to competition for borrowing funds, which is a factor of interest rates, and, on the other hand, a kind of two-sided competition to buy and lend the

[19] Gesell denies value theory completely to describe the abstraction of labor time as a substance of value of a commodity through the so-called method of distillation. In Chapter 1 Commodities in *Capital* Vol. I, "Marx's abstraction cannot be demonstrated in any crucible [manner]," "but the other investigators of value are no whit better." To demonstrate the irrationality of Marx's value theory, Gesell says "the theory of value is of fundamental importance in economic science. But a theory so important in economic science should be still more important in economic practice," because "In every other sphere of human activity science and life go hand in hand; in commerce alone nothing is known of the principal theory of the science with which it is connected. In commerce we find only prices, prices determined by demand and supply. A business man speaking of the value of a thing means the price that its owner would probably obtain under the given circumstances of time and place. Value is therefore an estimate which upon completion of a transaction is converted into a measured quantity of exchange products, that is, a price. Price can be measured to a nicety, value can only be estimated, that is the sole difference. A theory of price must therefore apply equally to price and to value" (Gesell 1958/1916: 151–153).

[20] "The *wage contract* is nothing more than a *sales contract about these commodities* made between the worker and entrepreneur. *In the case of the piece wage, this relationship will be clear*" (Gesell 2007b/1922: 363).

means of production, which is a factor of the interest rate of real capital. Competitive outcomes would then be decided by a standard correspondence between the money interest rate and the interest rate of real capital. In a money market, demand for borrowing funds increases insofar as the interest rate of money is below the interest rate of real capital, and vice versa. Regarding the purchase and lending of the means of production, the supply of commodities would rise in an industrial sector in which demand exceeds supply because the interest rate of real capital for this sector exceeds the general interest rate of real capital; however, supply again would plummet to the general interest rate of real capital relative to demand.

Entrepreneurs, as assumed by Gesell, not only own the means of production but also lend the means of production, even if they do not commit to production directly; thus, this kind of entrepreneur has no ability to control the processes of production. The content of the employment relationship can be described as a production contract in which laborers are no different from leasehold farmers who lack the conditions to sell the products of their labor. Laborers have to sell their products by reason of having no merchant talent, but if "the laborer were to have generally economical creditworthiness, the laborer could himself create entrepreneurial business, provided he also obtained the necessary knowledge [to do business] – *similar to what leasehold farmers do*" (ibid., 364). In summary, laborers are independent small producers but are not fully independent since they must borrow the means of production from entrepreneurs. If it is viable for them to become entrepreneurs through having "creditworthiness" and "knowledge," they can make the leap to fully independent small producers. The theoretical significance of the employment relationship described by Gesell does not amount to "buying and selling of labor *power*," but rather "buying and selling of labor *product*." Thus, the "independent small producer model" is entirely analytical.

In the three-actor model described above, moneyed capitalists can claim a money interest from entrepreneurs by reason of money's scarcity and the monopoly it engenders. By the same token, entrepreneurs can claim a real capital interest from laborers by reason of the scarcity of the means of production and its monopoly thereof. Both moneyed capitalists and entrepreneurs hold the power to claim interest based on the scarcity of resources. However, this is not primarily due to the scarcity of the means of production, but the scarcity of money. The scarcity of money prevents laborers from buying the means of production and, as a result, they must be reconciled to accepting the situation of paying dual interest for money and real capital.[21]

Interest earned as surplus value in the processes of circulation is obtained by "*economic superiority*" caused by primary scarcity and the monopoly of money. If that is the case, both the scarcity and possible monopoly of money would lose the property of abundant money supply. Furthermore, monetary interest might ultimately fall to zero. If the scarcity of the means of production were no longer a factor, because it could be bought with currency that does not bear interest, it would be possible that the interest of real capital would also fall to zero. With the "*economic superiority*" of money, in other words, the power of money to fall, monetary interest would also disappear. This was the context in which Gesell proposed the creation of "free money" to dismantle the power of money; anyone would be able to obtain money freely by supplying money abundantly. On the other hand, Gesell pointed out that Proudhon "is a dangerous fellow since there is no denying the truth of his contention that if the workers were allowed to remain at work without hindrance, disturbance or interruption, capital would soon be choked by an over-supply of capital (not to be confused with an over-production of goods)" (Gesell 1958/1916: 28), and describes this perspective as "a sea of capital flooded from the old marginal income. *The interest rate will drown in the sea of new capital*" (Gesell 2007b/1922: 377).[22]

[21] "Capitalism—An economic condition in which the demand for loan-money and real capital exceeds the supply and therefore gives rise to interest" (Gesell 1958/1916: 244).

[22] Gesell's term "marginal income of capital" was translated by Keynes' as the term "marginal efficiency of capital" (Keynes 1973/1936: 355). According to Gesell, to attack the power of capital, we should not organize industrial disputes, as Marxists claim, but rather create a situation in which moneyed capital cannot obtain interest by performing labor to create an over-supply of capital, which would further decrease the interest rate of real capital. Excess capital decreases interest and rent and, on the other hand, must raise the scarcity of laborers relative to increasing wages. Excess capital, in general, could produce a moment of crisis under capitalist production, in which a stationary situation occurs that clears away excess profits under a "free economy."

8.4 Theoretical and Conceptual Background of the Independent Small Producer Model

This chapter defines Gesell's economics as "the independent small producer model." However, how would this translate into an analytical model—especially considering the basic reality that laborers are propertyless, possessing only their labor power? For any model that seeks to base itself on the existence of independent small producers, addressing this theoretically is of the upmost importance.

Understanding this is a key issue for identifying "the economic subject" who would also be "the subject of human emancipation," in which social hierarchy and classes are abolished. Just as the Marxian school adopts a rigorous theoretical position by insisting that the independent small producers would ultimately be marginalized by the competitive nature of the capitalist market which results in the concentration and centralization of capital, anarchists tend to view this as reductionist.[23] Graeber states that "anarchists have never been much interested in the kinds of broad strategic or philosophical questions that have historically preoccupied Marxists" (Graeber 2004: 5–6). This is because, for the purpose of exploring "an ethical discourse" and "forms of practice," it is unproductive to have reservations about constructing "high theory" to address such questions as "Are the peasants a potentially revolutionary class?" or "What is the nature of the commodity form?" (ibid., 6–7). Nevertheless, Graeber comments that Bakunin "claimed that revolution should come not from the most alienated people in advanced capitalism, but from small farmers and artisans in Russia and Spain who maintained traditional autonomy. And, Bakunin was right" compared to "the traditional Marxist explanation that revolution would be realized by industrial workers in the UK and Germany, the most advanced industrial powers in those days"; Graeber then identifies "small farmers and artisans" as being "simultaneously the least alienated and the most oppressed people" (Graeber 2006: 11–12).[24] Indispensable propensities for anarchist economics include "a spirit of self-aid" and "a feeling of self-esteem" by autonomic subjects having the

[23] See Kautsky (1910/1892), Chapter 1: The Passing of Small Production.

[24] Graeber's review of Bakunin is to some extent unfair because Bakunin also focused on wage slavery.

ability to make decisions about their management.[25] However, they have not sufficient qualities to become historical subjects for self-emancipation, because "employed workers" have neither abilities to earn their own living nor the power to make decisions concerning their management as they have lost the indispensable propensity of self-esteem. The first condition shows not only that anarchist economics is an analytical theory but also that reductionist conditions from their vision must be included if economics is to have clear goals, such as "abolition of exploitation" and "realization of freedom."

The second condition is an assumption of a social foundation of unowned land and free land (Gesell 1958/1916: 52), which means laborers would not be propertyless. The dependence on uncultivated and unowned land around society opens the theoretical possibility of laborers dissatisfied with their returns in wages becoming self-managing farmers who cultivate their own land.

Gesell developed the concept of Free Land and classified it into three classes. "Free Land of the first class" is represented by "the vast tracts of uncultivated land in North and South America." This Free Land can be moved to freely and cultivated to own. "[F]ree Land of the second classes" are the wider fields of "America, Africa, Australia and Asia," which is not owned by anyone, "however, large areas that are not cultivated, but which by some abuse of State-power have become the private property of individuals living in some far-off place" (ibid., 52).

"The most important Free Land, however, and that which is also of greatest significance for the theory of rent and wages is Free Land of the third class" (ibid., 53). This is free land that can be created continuously by improving the way land is used, as in the case of Germany. In general, Gesell's "Freeland of third class" would create superior land from inferior land by improving agricultural techniques to increase harvest yields from the same plot of land. This example shows the creation of "Free Land" by improving the utilization of urban land. This could be considered as "the space above the stories already in existence, up to the clouds, as free building land" (ibid., 55). If stories were to be built toward outer space in this manner, the result would be that the rest of land "would form a

[25] "The work bears witness to this 'peace-dripping' spirit, which is ultimately the feeling of strength and security, and meets anyone who is aware of making himself this. However, this sense of security is a precondition for clear thinking and fair judgments" (Gesell 2007a/1920: 226).

surplus" with the effect of falling land rent (ibid., 53). Gesell presents a second example, a case in which expansion of inferior land disables differential rent. Furthermore, improved techniques make it possible to cultivate untouched land, which would create land profitability based on whether there was differential rent. Thus, "Free Land of the third class" is created by improvements in the way of using land, such that land would not secure differential rent (ibid., 54).

Therefore, it is theoretically possible for all land in Germany to be transformed into the "Free Land of the third class." In addition, "the farm-laborer may at any time take refuge on this Free Land if dissatisfied with his wages. The wages of farm-laborers cannot fall permanently below the proceeds of labor on such Free Land of the third class, any more than they can fall below the proceeds of labor on Free Land of the first class" (ibid., 55).[26] That is, the amount of minimum regulated income of laborers would be decided by "the proceeds of labor" in the "Free Land" and by the movement of labor in electing whether to receive wage employment or cultivate "Free Land."

Free Land has existed widely as already described, with excess profit on the superior land exploited as differential rent accruing to the existing landowner. It would be necessary to transform the differential rent into treasury revenue through nationalization of land in order to abolish the form of exploitation that is differential rent. This is Gesell's perspective on land reform. It appears similar to the Marxian school criticized by Gesell in the deployment of land nationalization but they are not the same, needless to say. Certainly, while the state also owns land in Gesell's proposition, it does not interfere with the way land is used. The right to usage would be lent for a certain period alongside the manner of use entrusted to private managers.[27] Further details on the plan are described hereafter. Specifically, in the following clauses:

> Clause 1. All countries which join the big league of peace replace completely the special ownership of land (private ownership). The land

[26] "Free Land of the first class" is not committed to forming standards for the proceeds of labor because it is always higher than non-rented "Free Land of the third class".

[27] Subjects who participate in public leases are not limited to individual and private management. Insofar as they agree with "Free Land," the institution includes "Also large tracts for communistic, anarchistic, social-democratic colonies, for co-operative societies, or religious communities" (Gesell 1958/1916: 89–90).

> is then the property of the people and the land is rented to private management which tendered the highest price in the public bidding system.
> Clause 2. Everyone can participate in the public leases....
> The rent money is distributed evenly and completely to women and children without distinction [to their origin]... (Gesell 2007a/1920: 68)

Clause 1 shows the policy is compatible with a free competitive market society. In the trade relationship of these countries, "agrarian specific interests" and "the horrible thoughts of closed trade state" will become extinct, bringing a freer market society (Gesell 2007a/1920: 69). In other words, it would clear away those who appropriate the rent of land, and who "attacks the class state at its source" (ibid.). Of course, the banishment of landowners should not be forced such that the "rent thus calculated is then capitalized (capitalization of rent refers to the sum of money which would yield interest equal to the rent) at the mortgage rate of interest, and this amount is paid to the landowners in interest-bearing state securities" (ibid., 73). These plans would be followed as a process of socialization of land as had been proposed by Proudhon. On the other hand, the free public bidding system declared in Clause 2 supports the freedom of movement of laborers, which is a condition for equitable competition. Laborers push up the price of land on expectations of higher proceeds of labor, which in turn pulls down the bidding price. The bidding system works as described above, and consequently the proceeds of labor are oriented toward social equalization. However, in this case, the motivation would not be lost to find a bigger difference between the expected proceeds of labor and the actual bidding amount, hence, the disparity is not solved from the difference of competencies as merchants of bidding entrepreneurs. Rather, this case recommends the transfer of excess profit over average profits to laborers in order to maintain their power to drive the economy. Lastly, rent as surplus value will be redistributed by the state to provide for women and children.[28]

Therefore, a land nationalization policy would no longer need to rely on the abolition of exploitation as a goal of socialism, replacing it with the maximization of the income of individuals as "the whole proceeds of

[28] "This economic strength and economic independence will of course change the whole relationship of man to man; manners, customs, speech and character will become freer and nobler" (ibid., 114).

labour" (ibid., 36). However, "the whole proceeds of labour" would not be an individual concept but rather the "right to the collective whole proceeds of labour" (ibid., 38). This collective category of income is Gesell's concept of class. Its content is to maximize the whole proceeds of the laboring class, by removing the income of the landowner's class.[29] However, maximizing the whole proceeds of the laboring class by nationalization of land would not involve equalization of individual income and would not even secure the minimum wage. Those with the competence to be merchants might obtain excess higher than the average for the same products, while professional occupations need to "some natural physical aptitude (such as singing, for example)" and "workers who perform the most highly qualified work are most securely withdrawn from the competition of the masses, and are therefore able to obtain the highest price for the product of their labour" (ibid.). In summary, the proceeds of labor will not be "determined arbitrarily, but by the conditions of the market" by demand and supply of the products of labor (ibid., 39).

8.5 Doctrine of Money–Capital

This takes us to the question of Marx's *thesis of equal exchange*. Gesell states that "the *free money theory* also researches the nature of Marx's formula of exchange of capital, M–C–M' (money–commodities–surplus money)" (Gesell 2007b/1922: 366). "However, it does not imply, as *Marx* does uncritically, that the money is a perfect equivalent of commodities" (ibid.). Marx narrowly defines money as the equivalent of commodities in his formula whereas the free money theory found in "Marx is formulated by general design of exchange for which there is evidence that money is more than an equivalent" (ibid.). Even though Marx, in *Capital*, states that profits will be produced incidentally by nothing less than the fraudulence of merchants, and that commodity and money are exchanged equitably in the processes of circulation, the free money theory understands that "Marx's formula M–C–M′ is *a proof that is right for them* that money is independent capital, and that M′ is not a product of eternally repeated fraudulence but *the result of superiority of the money owner over the owner of commodities, and thus, the product of an economic power factor*" (ibid.)

[29] In short, Gesell's use of the term "proceeds of labor" should be understood to mean real wages in kind.

The question of "*why money as capitalmay be against commodities*" has been answered to focus on "the nature of things" as money (ibid.). Under a production system involving division of labor, "commodities are their contractor and their owner is directly useless. To take advantage of them, commodities must be *replaced*" (ibid.). Then, from the standpoint of the owner of commodities, money would be claimed as a "*medium of exchange*," the owner of money would not have to respond to their claims in the order of the essential difference of "the nature of things" (i.e., commodity and money). This is because gold as money must not be exposed to a loss of things in any proceeding period. The owner of money loses only an opportunity to earn interest on money that is lent. To the contrary, commodities as things would incur various types of losses and natural depreciation over time that otherwise must maintain these qualities. In spite of there being few costs for keeping and carrying over money, there are substantial costs in relation to commodities. Commodities depreciate on a daily basis, and must be sold as soon as possible, whereas money is not forced to depreciate and there is no motivation to quickly exchange it for commodities. For this reason, money as a medium of exchange would result in hoarding money because of its superiority to the use value of materials, and furthermore, horded money would turn into capital. Material commodities cannot be hoarded because of their inferiority in respect of keeping value. The Marxian definition of capital stresses the materiality of means of production as a key aspect of its commodity status. But depreciating commodities have no capacity to become capital, and only money that is hoarded would be capital.

Gesell refers to the disparity of "the degradation rate of capital" between commodities and money that would occur from the difference of "the nature of things" as follows. "*It is so obvious that here is not full equivalence*, that the money owner rules the owner of commodities by a special compensation. This request can be waived by the owner of commodities carrying over trade to create a direct *loss of substance*" (ibid., 369). "*Money is debunked as independent capital. There is no perfect equivalence. Money is more. And this extra value creates surplus value*" (ibid., 370). In other words, the disparity of "the degradation rate of capital," through creating an asymmetric relationship of power between commodity and money, would create money interest or surplus value. Gesell defined the interest charged by the power of money as "basic interest" [Urzins] (Gesell 1958/1916: 371). According to Gesell, Marx was mistaken in his definition of money as a medium of exchange, because he overlooked the issue of hoarding money. Therefore, Marx had not noticed that money is capital and has wrongly defined real capital (the means of production), which is inferior in use value as capital. The use of gold as money would lead to the economic power of money due to its material superiority and scarcity, then, it must be close to ideal as a pure medium of exchange by depriving its position as money, alongside general commodities which are transformed into material things that cannot be hoarded.

Consequently, the mistake in Marx's capital theory results in a doctrine that turns material things into capital, which can appear in the form of the means of production, made logically identical to capital.

However, there is still the question of "basic interest" to resolve, in terms of the asymmetry that arises in any exchange relationship between a person who possesses a commodity she wants to sell and a possessor of money. The reason for this is explained by a contradiction in words in the following example. Suppose that 100 dollars of money does not equal to 100 dollars' worth of commodities. Money holds economic power, in the sense of obtaining "basic interest" through the purchase of a commodity. If an owner of money *A* buys a commodity equivalent to 105 dollars with 100 dollars of money, whenever *A* resells her commodity that is equivalent to 105 dollars, she has to pay "basic interest" to an owner of money *B* who holds economic power. Consequently, *A* cannot pocket the "basic interest." Likewise, it would not make sense to buy a commodity worth 105 dollars with money worth 100 dollars. What does this mean for the superiority or inferiority of the nature of use value and the effect of its depreciation on the equivalence of the commodity and money? It would not be unreasonable to suspect that price always shows an equivalence at the close of any successful transaction.

Furthermore, consider the following. Supposing that "basic interest" is collected based on differential rates of depreciation between commodities and money; when an owner of money worth 100 dollars and an owner of a commodity worth 100 dollars is exposed to a physical loss of 5 dollars a day in the moment of exchange, even if the 5 dollars difference of the depreciation rates can be collected, what processes would be required to ensure the collection of "basic interest"? Gesell explains the process of collecting the "basic interest" by an owner of money in terms of the "general formula of capital" as M–C–M′.

> Money claims interest for each time it is used, somewhat as a cab claims a fare. Interest is counted among the general expenses of commerce and

> collected with these-it is immaterial whether [it is] as a deduction from the price paid [to] the producer or as an addition to the price demanded from the consumer. As a rule the merchant can estimate by experience the price which he can obtain from the consumer. From this price he deducts the costs of commerce, wages for his own work (net profit of commerce), and interest. Interest is calculated by the average time, known to the merchant by experience, which elapses between the purchase and the sale of his merchandise. (Gesell 1958/1916: 384)

This passage appears to refer to an entrepreneur acting as a merchant who directly collects "basic interest." In Gesell's explanation, it is not clear whether the deduction of the cost added as "basic interest" to the primary cost of the sales price would be "net profit of commerce."[30] "Basic interest" deducted from the sales price would be paid by the entrepreneur to the moneyed capitalist as the lender of funds. The producer has nothing more than a means or ability to sell her products at any moment and must transfer commodities to the merchant. Furthermore, the economic superiority of money creates a disparity in that the possessor of money could choose not to exchange, while the producer would have no such option and would risk the deflation of the price they can command. To revisit the abovementioned example, the merchant with 100 dollars of money would be pressed to discount the commodity price that could be sold at 105 dollars to an equitable transaction at the price of 100 dollars. The sales price for the consumer would be 105 dollars, and the difference of 5 dollars would include both the "net profit of commerce" and "basic interest." That is, "the tribute is contained in the difference between them," which refers to the price of the consumer and the price of the producer. It has to be noticed that this is on condition that the "tribute can be levied only on the sale of wares, and requires the fulfilment of one essential condition: During the interval between buying and selling a product, its price must not fall" (ibid., 230).

This would explain why Gesell's market vision should be called a theory of "market conditions" (ibid., 168). As described, stable prices have to be shifted under certain terms to obtain "basic interest." However, such a stable situation does not occur commonly under the forceful actions of the owners of money. In the economy characterized by the division

[30] The quotation from Gesell makes it clear that the concept of profit is defined as the wage of the merchant and entrepreneur, which would be categorized as labor income.

of labor, the owner of a commodity has to exchange her commodity for money to purchase a commodity that she wants, using money exchanged to buy the commodity. Furthermore, although commodities have a natural propensity to age over time, money has a kind of immortality. Owners of material things take into account their asymmetrical natural property in the relationship of exchange, whereby the commodity owner considers avoiding depreciation by selling quickly; otherwise, the owner of money waits for a market situation in which she could buy favorably through the natural superiority of money. In the case in which an owner of a commodity wants to buy another commodity more quickly, a higher rate of "basic interest" would be claimed. Therefore, the "longer sale is delayed, the less favourable the market conditions" (ibid., 225). However, under the economy characterized by division of labor, this is an ordinary market situation for all participants. However, according to Gesell, "those of us who are unable to grasp this ghostly property of commodities called value, and who therefore regard the exchange of commodities as an action, and the commodities and state of the market as accessories of this action, will be able to discover no other motive for such action than the desire common to all owners of commodities, [which is] to give as little as possible and to receive as much as possible" (ibid., 163).

The "state of the market" is characterized by unpredictable incidents. This means that an owner of money waits for the chance to buy a commodity at a price reflecting its state of depreciation amid the general tendency of falling prices. Whenever there are falling prices, it is difficult to collect "basic interest," which leads the merchant to hold back on purchasing commodities. In this case, "a general opinion that prices will fall" spreads among merchants and owners of money would reduce their demand even further (ibid., 232). "But prices fall just because the supply of money is insufficient" (ibid., 231). In spite of declining prices in order to decrease demand, the decline of demand would be caused by falling prices. **"This, therefore, is the law of demand, that it disappears when it becomes insufficient"** (ibid., 235). "The equilibrating forces, of which so much is written, never come into play. The evil is intensified, not mitigated; there is no sign of any compensatory tendency" (ibid., 234). Money, as far as it includes the power to claim "basic interest," would tend toward a shortage of "the supply of money" to bring about a crisis of underconsumption (ibid., 231). In contrast, the owner of money threatens to present "nothing of the kind; they try to effect the sale by reducing their prices, they all try to attract money by lowering their claims" (ibid., 331). This applies to producers that forgo buying as a "strike of money" aimed at excluding "tribute" under unfavorable market conditions (Gesell 2007b/1922: 376). This occurs as the difference between price for consumers and prices of producers. By clarifying these processes of transaction, the law of demand could be explained by the exploitation of surplus value not relating to whether its existence is created by production processes.

However, at the same time, one should question what it means to produce a physical commodity that is equivalent to the "basic interest" that can be collected on it. In other words, does this theory exclude the logical possibility of creating surpluses in the processes of production? To revisit the earlier example, products equivalent to 5 dollars are transferred to the owner of money, which would otherwise be owned by the producer under a scenario in which money has no superiority. These products, certainly, have been exploited, but the debatable aspect is who they are owned by. Of course, by Gesell's claims, money forces producers to discount, and producers will always be the final payer of interest. This is certainly the case if we can prove that Gesell's capital theory concerning the possibility that exploitation of the processes of circulation do not relate to the production of surplus products that create surplus value under the processes of production.

On the other hand, in order for Gesell to concentrate on the concept of capital as money-capital, it is not possible to view material things completely; in other words, commodities could also be capital. Even if it is supposed that the means of production are not capital, it can be questioned whether commodity capital as stock and as a work-in-progress are excluded from the concept of capital. This issue relates to Gesell's theory of money reform. Gesell's theory of free money is a policy that involves the claimant levying a carry-over fee on money which is similar to the rate of the natural depreciation of material things. The theory does not take into account that the value of commodities can carry over; moreover, commodities might increase in order to define capital only as money. Therefore, Gesell had to furnish a supposition that would "require the fulfilment of one essential condition: During the interval between buying and selling a product, its price must not fall," however, it is not necessary to hold capital in a form of money in the period of raising prices to maintain and increase the value of capital in the form of commodities. In addition, Gesell made allowances in his concept of capital to compensate for concentrating money-capital as the concept of capital. On the other hand, it is too narrow to view the concept of decreasing value as physical wear and tear. This is because non-monetary financial and asset commodities could maintain their value without physical loss. Hence, for consistency with Gesell's theory of free money, as pointed out by Soddy, the object of levying would expand to all financial assets (Soddy in Seccareccia 1997: 133).

Although Gesell himself defines the doctrine of money as capital theory and criticizes the Marxian "doctrine of material things as capital theory," this would be a somewhat slipshod critique of *Capital*. According to Gesell, Engels correctly understood capital as hoarding money, as Engels explained the transformation of hoarding money into capital, described in *Anti-Dühring* as follows.[31]

> If Dühring wants to keep metallic money, he therefore cannot prevent some from setting aside a small money hoard, while others are unable to make ends meet on the wage paid to them...on the one hand to form a hoard, and on the other to run into debt.... And, *as the builder of the hoard is in a position to extort interest from people in need, usury is restored along with metallic money functioning as money*.... The usurers are transformed into dealers in the medium of circulation, bankers, controllers of the medium of circulation and of world money, and thus, into *controllers of production, and thus, into controllers of the means of production*. (Engels cited in Gesell 2007b/1922: 374; emphasis by Gesell)[32]

However, because Marx has also argued that money as capital has to be hoarded before discussing "the transformation of money into capital" in *Capital*, Marx's theory cannot be considered a theoretical antagonist to the "money as capital theory" and "material things as capital theory." It could be described rather in terms of the criteria for stipulating the value of money. In opposition to the "material things as capital theory" which stipulates the value of money as the production cost of materials, the logic of critiquing "material things as capital theory" was a precursor to the emerging doctrine of fiat money.

[31] Furthermore, Schwarz, in referring to the same description of Engels criticizing Marx, interprets material things as capital by pointing out that hoarded money is capital. Moreover, Engels' claims contradict even the value theory of labor (Schwarz 2008: 9).

[32] The sentence "If Dühring wants to keep metallic money" does not exist in the original text (Engels 1987/1878: 289).

We should understand that Engels' description was intended to criticize directly Dühring's theory of labor money. A summary of Gesell's earlier quotation is as follows. Dühring intended to realize "an exchange of 'equal labour for equal labour'" (Dühring in Engels 1987/1878: 286) by viewing metallic money (labor money) as the standard of value in labor time. However, Dühring overlooked the possibility of individual hoarding of money and was not aware of the possibility of circulating metallic money as world money outside of communities. If labor money with gold material as a standard value of labor time includes the opportunity to transform hoards of money by individual accumulation, it would translate to "*metallic money functioning as money*," and the possibility would remain of transforming it into capital through investment and management in a world market of metallic money. The standard value of labor time is not a sufficient condition to prevent labor money from functioning as money. Money hoarders appear to be moneyed capitalists in the beginning, turning "*into controllers of the means of production*" to be industrial capitalists. On the other hand, Owen's labor notes were designed in order to prevent the transformation of labor notes into capital, while Engels' criticism of Dühring did not concern the question of whether Marx viewed money as capital, or material things as capital, but rather it was a criticism of Dühring as a labor money theorist. Based on this reading of Engels' critique, it is possible to see how Gesell's free money theory might prevent the transformation free money into capital, and commodities (Gesell's material things) into capital whenever commodity production is undertaken.

Finally, we can look at Gesell's theory of fiat money as a criticism of the doctrine of commodity money. Commodity money theorists claim that precious metals equate to money offered at a value of money decided by the material value of commodities. To the contrary, Gesell proposed that if monetary value is decided by the material value of money, then the exchange of commodities and money would be nothing more than a kind of barter. If "the money is a perfect equivalent of the commodities," it seems that equity in both can be measured by their production cost, which is price. However, price is "the ratio of exchange between money and wares" (Gesell 1958/1916: 191). If it is assumed that equity is measured by their price, what price would be given? On this issue, Marx relied on the labor theory of value by introducing a third measure as the quantity of labor bestowed to avoid such self-contradiction (Obata 2005: 56). However, Gesell denied Marx's logical solution as overly abstract and designed at all costs to support his position that the value of a commodity is based on the quantity of labor bestowed.

Gesell's "money-capital theory" focused on two factors: first, the transformation of material things into capital, and second, the exchange of money and commodities as equivalents. The logic of money being equivalent to commodities conflicted with Gesell's claim that the material value of money is not money, and that money is essentially a medium of exchange which is unrelated to its material value and any assets it is backed by. Gesell conceptualized that the equitable exchange of money and commodities with regard to value theory is nothing more than barter and does not grasp the property of monetary exchange. In addition, owners of commodities do not take part in exchange relations for the purpose of the monetary or exchange value of the exchange, but because of the use values of the commodities, with money functioning as a medium of exchange. In other words, value is not money, but use value (medium of exchange) is money. Therefore, this supports the conceptualization of the quantity theory of money (index of prices); that the "quantity of money alone is of importance, for upon it, partly, depends the magnitude of the supply of money and the amount of commodities that we ca[n] buy for it" (Gesell 1958/1916: 176).[33]

From start to finish, Gesell's capital theory was developed with the Marxian doctrine in mind. Therefore, his doctrine should be contextualized in terms of how it sought to refract the general understanding of Marx's capital theory by pointing how that it relied upon a mixture of a commodity theory of money and "material things as capital theory."

Gesell's capital theory and social vision can be summarized as follows. His capital theory was that money can collect interest from material things that depreciate naturally. Therefore, any attempt to identify capital with

[33] Although Gesell is a fiat money theorist, the practical successes of his theories cannot also be said to have grounding in fiat money. This is because, with both *Wära* in Schwanenkirchen and *Arbeitsbestätigungen* in Wörgl, enterprises and local governments were issuers of local currency based on secured assets in terms of payment of the salaries of public officers and the costs of public works. Thus, there is an unclear route for supplying currency in terms of Gesell's theory of fiat money, as successful local currencies issued have been paid as an equivalent of labor and enterprise. This remains to be evaluated. Kanagawa prefecture in Japan, which has issued a local currency known as LOVES (Local Value Exchange System, 2002–2007), would otherwise make a remarkably similar mistake to the theory of fiat money as its local government has issued 10,000 units among roughly 90,000 residents.

material goods was incorrect. This was because the means of production as material things can be positioned directly against labor, which makes exploitation possible. The interest of real capital must essentially be explained from the interest function that money can perform. In addition, Gesell denied the view of class society as a base for "money-capital theory." For Marx, profit, which appears as surplus value originates in the proceeds of labor, and should be explained via the antagonism of social categories in which income divides a class that obtains the proceeds of labor and a class that obtains unearned income. Although this chapter could not survey all Gesell's policy claims, Gesell's money reform and land reform were deemed to make unearned income the national budget, and to maximize the amount of labor income through its redistribution. As argued in the first part of this chapter, Gesell's vision supports policies in which philosophical norms, such as nature, freedom, and labor, were interpreted through the prism of independent small producers, whose existence expressed these normative concepts collectively—and that this formed the social subject of his variant of anarchist economics. The essence of "market-centered socialism" would be concentrated on the creation of an economic order centered around the mechanism of a "non-exploitative market" or "non-capitalist market." Within this vision, the collective of independent small producers become analogous to Marx's proletariat, who would oversee the emancipation of humanity via an institutional reform of money and land.

Bibliography

Aida, S. (2014). *Sirubio Gezeru Kenkyū* [A study of Gesell: Silvio Gesell and the natural economic order]. Pal.

Barber, W. J. (Ed.). (1997). *Correspondence and other commentary on economic policy, 1930–47. The works of Irving Fisher.* (Vol. 14). Pickering & Chatto.

Blanc, J. (1998). Free money for social progress: Theory and practice of Gesell's accelerated money. *American Journal of Economics & Sociology, 57*(4), 469–483.

Darity, W., Jr. (1995). Keynes' political philosophy: The Gesell connection. *Eastern Economic Journal, 21*(1), 27–41.

Dillard, D. (1942). Keynes and proudhon. *Journal of Economic History, 2*(1), 63–76.

Engels, F. (1987/1878). Anti-Dühring. *Marx & Engels collected works*. Vol. 25. London: Lawrence & Wishart.

Gesell, S. (1958/1916). *The natural economic order*. London: Peter Owen.

Gesell, S. (2007a/1920). Einleitung. Freiland, die eherne Forderung des Friedens. Vortrag gehalten in Zürich am 5. Juli 1917 [Introduction: Free-Land, the Essential Condition of Peace. Lectures in Zurich 5 July 1917]. In Die natürliche Wirtschaftsordnung durch Freiland und Freigeld, 4 letztmalig vom Author überabeitete Auflage. *Silvio Gesell: Gesammelte Werke*. Bd. 11. Gauke: Berlin.

Gesell, S. (2007b/1922). Die Ausbeutung, ihre Ursachen und ihre Bekämpfung: Eine Gegenüberstellung meiner Kapitaltheorie und derjenigen von Karl Marx; Vortrag gehalten in der sozialistischen Vereinigung zur gegenseitigen Weiterbildung in Dresden, 8. Mai, 1922 [Exploitation, its causes and the struggle against it: A comparison of my theory of capital and that of Karl Marx; Lecture given at the socialist association for mutual education in Dresden, May 8]. *Silvio Gesell: Gesammelte Werke*. Bd. 13. Berlin: Gauke.

Graeber, D. (2004). *Fragments of an anarchist anthropology*. University of Chicago Press.

Graeber, D. (2006). Madaminu Nihon no Dokusha he [Preface to unseen Japanese Readers]. *Anarchist Jinruigaku no tameno Danshō* [Fragments of an anarchist anthropology]. Tokyo: Ibunsha.

Hodgson, G. M. (1999). *Economics and Utopia: Why the learning economy is not the end of history*. Routledge.

Ivanova, M. N. (2011). Can 'it' happen again: The limits of money artistry. *Critique, 39*(2), 211–232.

Kautsky, K. (1910/1892). *The class struggle* (Erfurt programme). Charles H. Kerr & Co.

Kautsky, K. (1919). *The dictatorship of the proletariat*. The National Labour Press.

Keynes, J. M. (1973/1936). The general theory of employment, interest and money. *The collected writings of John Maynard Keynes*. Vol. 7. London: Macmillan.

McKay, I. (Ed.). (2011). *Property is theft! A Pierre-Joseph Proudhon anthology*. AK Press.

Morino, E. (2000). Wasurerareta Shisōka Sirubio Gezeru: Rōka suru Okane no Riron to sono Jissen no Ayumi [The forgotten thinker Silvio Gesell: A development of the theory and practices of aging money]. *Ende no Yuigon: Kongen kara Okane wo Toukoto* [Testament of Ende: An original inquiry of money]. Tokyo: NHK Publishing.

Nishibe, M. (2003). *Chiikitsūka to Chihōjichi* [Local currency and local governance]. Tokyo: Kojinnotomosha.

Obata, M. (2005). Kaheizōka to Kachizōsyoku: Kahei no Shihon heno Tenkasetsu hihan [Increasing money and proliferating value: A critique of the transformation of money into capital]. *Keizaigaku Ronshū [the Journal of Economics], 71*(1), 48–77.

Onken, W. (2000). The political economy of Silvio Gesell: A century of activism. *American Journal of Economics and Sociology, 59*(4), 609–622.

Preparata, G. G. (2002). On the art of Innuendo: J. M. Keynes' plagiarism of Silvio Gesell's monetary economics. *Research in Political Economy, 20*, 217–253.

Preparata, G. G. (2006). Perishable money in a threefold commonwealth: Rudolf Steiner and the social economics of an anarchist Utopia. *Review of Radical Political Economics, 38*, 619–648.

Preparata, G. G., & Elliot, J. E. (2004). Free economics: The vision of reformer Silvio Gesell. *International Journal of Social Economics, 31*(10), 923–954.

Proudhon, P. J. (2007/1851). *General idea of the revolution in the nineteenth century*. New York: Cosimo.

Schwarz, F. (2008/1951). *Das Experiment von Wörgl: Ein Weg aus der Wirtschaftskrise* [The Wörgl experiment: A way out of the economic crisis]. Darmstadt: Synergia Verlag.

Seccareccia, M. (1997). Early twentieth-century Heterodox monetary thought. In A. J. Cohen, H. Hagemann & J. Smithin (Eds.), *Money, financial institutions and macroeconomics* (pp. 125–139). London: Kluwer Academic Publishers.

Stirner, M. (1995/1845). *The ego and its own*. Cambridge: Cambridge University Press.

Tosa, M. (2007). Kōkyōken no Gainen karamiru Ajiabunka [Asian culture seen from the concept of public sphere]. *Asia Japan Journal, 2*, 77–91.

Umemori, N. (2007). *Benedict Anderson Gurōbarizēshion wo kataru* [Benedict Anderson taking globalization]. Tokyo: Kobunsha.

Zhiyuan, C. (2003). "Xiaokang socialism": A petty-Bourgeois manifesto. *The Chinese Economy, 36*(3), 50–70.

CHAPTER 9

Concluding Reflections on Money and the Market: Possible Lines of Development for Labor Notes Theory

This book has considered the various historical phases of the development of theories of labor notes along with various debates over money and market that have been waged by representative thinkers. The reader by this stage can appreciate how the status of labor fluctuates at times while retaining its centrality to labor notes, and at other times seems fall out of the theory altogether. The lack of a clear understanding of what is meant by "labor" is a key feature in the history of labor note theories. This can be seen, for instance, in the way in which the concept was handled by Warren, Pare, and Gray, who viewed labor largely within the conceptual framework of Adam Smith's concept of labor as sacrifice, and how this enabled them to develop a model of labor notes that would be based on a comparative quantification of the degree of sacrifice that went into the production of various commodities. This raises questions about the way in which the social nature of labor is to be theorized and evaluated (or literally valued), most notably whether such theories position labor as the basis of social production. For labor note theories, labor acts as something of a pivot to ensure that money does not function as an autonomous force that floats free from the substance of production. This is why money is an abiding feature of all the labor note theories considered in this book. Common to most of the theories is a concern that money acts as a disturbing factor, disrupting the workings of the market,

© The Author(s), under exclusive license to Springer Nature Switzerland AG 2021
T. Yuki, *Socialism, Markets, and the Critique of Money*, Marx, Engels, and Marxisms,
https://doi.org/10.1007/978-3-030-80408-4_9

and this led theorists to deepen their understanding of the functions of money as a measure of value and a standard for comparison between the products of labor. They sought to redefine the relation between money and markets by questioning money's function as a measure of value. In contrast to the theoretical bluntness of orthodox economics, and its faith in the ability of money and markets to auto-correct and work toward an equilibrium, the labor note theorists sought to grasp the reality of the market as a structure that is open to distortion and disequilibrium due to the nature of money. This inevitably led to the close alignment between most of the labor note theories and various strands of socialism, while the failure of the orthodoxy is linked both to its imposition of an abstract notion of market society and a voluntaristic methodological individualism that only serves to perpetuate the capitalist market system.

The historical evolution of the development of labor note theories, not least when it comes to their relationship with money, took place over a sequence of phases. First, Chapter 2 clarified that the question of the market was at the heart of the controversy between Proudhon and Marx. The chapter revealed that these thinkers held opposite views of the market; whereas Proudhon pursued the ideal vision of a stable market through the establishment of an Exchange or People's Bank that would interest free credit, Marx pointed out that markets preserve the anarchy of production that inevitably gives rise to crises. The consequences of this debate between them revolved around Proudhon's purposiveness or desire to find an institutional solution to the existing market, and Marx's analytical critique. This resulting in conflicting views of money as to whether it should be viewed as a neutral medium that does not interfere with exchange in its purest or original sense or as being inseparable from the market and its distorting activity. This led to disputes over the question of whether money is a substance derived from the commodity itself or instead something that lacks a substance and serves in a purely symbolic function with regard to relations between individual producers. In many respects, Proudhon's vision of a reform of the market via monetary improvements and the establishment of a People's Bank did not survive the attack launched by Marx on the basis of his theory of value form. Yet, Proudhon retained a certain allure subsequently among those who were disenchanted with the Soviet experience and were seeking a non-Marxist alternative to economic orthodoxy. For these thinkers, the starting point was the retention of the market, and the idea that the Soviets had abolished the market without abolishing oppression and emancipating human beings. Reviving Proudhon was done in the hope of finding a way to usher in an ideal society in the form of a market based on truly free and equal exchange, whereby the labor of each individual would be adequately reflected in the means of payment. Yet, even if we accept the situation in which theory appears to have twisted around to make Proudhon appear more contemporary, it nonetheless does nothing to blunt the realism of Marx's critique of the market in terms of the social fragmentation that results from its operations. Moreover, the continuation of influence of Marx's realistic critique raises the question of whether it is possible both to critique the market and avoid the kind of top-down planned version of socialism implemented in the twentieth century.

By reviewing Marx's critical research on the theory of labor money and the theory of labor notes, it is possible to conclude that socialist monetary reform within a market would be an unrealistic proposal. Yet, as pointed out in Chapter 3, such reform might be feasible if labor money had a non-monetary form. Marx had criticized the theory of labor money as a fancy product dreamed up by petty-bourgeois thinkers that overlooked the problem of the anarchy of production. In contrast, thinkers like Proudhon focused their energy on the state in its role in foisting a metallic money on all the market participants, arguing that it was the workings of the state institution that was responsible for the economic damage suffered by the mass of the population, rather than the private ownership within the productive system that created commodities in the first place. But the problem does not end there. Labor money theorists found that the root of injustice lays in money's function as a measure of commodity value, which prevented a due evaluation of the actual labor time that had been expended upon the production of a commodity. Given their acceptance of the market as such, their task became finding a way to bring the substance of production into closer contact with the monetary sphere of the economy, so that the latter would lose its autonomy and serve as a reflection of the former. The problem, as Marx was acutely aware, is that within a market economy, there is no transparent way to equate labor time with the exchange value of a commodity, since there is a disjunction between the quantity of labor and the quality of as a substance.

The socialist perspective presented as a logical consequence of Marx's criticism of labor money theory is, of course, not the one developed by advocates of local currency theory. Rather, it is a sketch of a society that has overcome the anarchy of production. Robert Owen appears as something of a progenitor for this theory in the sense that he gave more space to the way in which heterogenous acts of production are co-ordinated forcefully within a market, and because the connection between the theory of the market and of money was central to his thinking and social experiments. Yet, what was not clear in Owen's thought was the basis of money itself. Marx argued against the monetary bias of labor money theory, which led him inevitably to a position that sought nothing less than the negation of the market—for only in a future society based on cooperation rather than market exchange was it possible to abolish money in the form of the metallic currencies of his day. Yet, given the fate of his own theories, it is worth considering whether there might have been something that Marx missed regarding his own theory of the market.

This raises the question of the similarities and differences between Marx and Owen. Unlike Marx, Owen did not carry out a detailed analysis of the commodity form, and certainly did not consider the private social character of labor, such as the conflict between the private labor and the social labor, which was key to Marx's handling of the whole question of labor time. Rather, Owen developed an early version of the under-consumption theory, according to which the interference of gold money resulted in an economic depression due to the insufficient purchasing power of the workers and the excess of supply over demand across the market. This coincided with certain aspects of Marx's theory of the anarchy of production in a market system, wherein insufficient demand was seen as a consequence rather than a cause. Although the analysis of the factors that cause the difference in total supply and demand is different at a fundamental level, Owen presented not only the quantitative problem of the purchasing power, but also the problem of the inter-sectoral organization of production corresponding to what was also presented as a community construction plan. Since the problem of inter-sectoral organization was grasped after recognizing the limit of quantitatively matching the total supply and demand through monetary reform, Owen, like Marx, later came to the conclusion that it is not enough to modify the monetary form to overcome the problem of money. To this extent, both agreed on the need for the sublimation of money and the consequent abandonment of the market. Nonetheless, although arriving at a similar conclusion, it did not stem from the same logical process. It is clear that Owen overlooked the qualitative problem of the market in particular. He thought that money deviated from its ideal form by being inhibited by gold being a scarce material commodity in its own right. Therefore, he sought to introduce labor notes as a means to stabilize the system through the use of valueless paper money by anchoring it with labor and separating the link between money and gold. Such a systematic approach to the management of banknotes was subsequently adopted in Gray's theory of labor notes, as examined in Chapter 7.

This raises the question of non-monetary forms of labor money, and whether they can be consistently held without abandoning the meaning of money altogether—an issue that is developed theoretically and practically in Chapter 6. By looking back on modern local currency movements from this theoretical perspective, it may be possible to evaluate more recent forms of local currency such as Time Dollar. As discussed, the circulation of the Time Dollar is limited to the non-market economic sphere, whereas Marx and the labor money theorists focused solely upon money movement within the market-productive sphere. By exploring the role of local currencies outside of the sphere of the market, a wider area is opened-up for discussions of the maintenance and reproduction of society. In the exchange process that takes place in the extended reproduction sphere, it is important to build a relationship that accepts inequality rather than pursuing equivalence and recognize that the sphere outside the market is not incidental to reproduction. LETS rejected this because it made the measure and unit of labor time aware of equivalence. But indefinite labor time eliminates differences between labor, such as simple or proficiency, different or complex, and its ability to understand the meaning of treating unequal labor equally is more important than inducing the conventional thought of weighing equivalence. The difference between LETS and Time Dollar's view of measure can be identified by the motivation of re-questioning the measure, although it results in different units of measure such as labor time and unique units of LETS currency. The equivalence of labor is conscious as long as it is requested for standardized labor through the production process of capital, and as long as it is measured in the eyes of the market couched by a productive sphere. If we can understand interdependent relationships among members of the same community and evaluate each person's labor from a broader social point of view, the extent to which we have to rely on the market for the measure will be low. It may no longer be a viewpoint of labor but an affirmation of existence.

At this point, it has to be admitted that the market vision, presented by Owen and partly by contemporary local currencies, is indeed idealistic. There is a doubt concerning the robustness of the cognitive base on which they rely, and a lack of realism that can leave people feeling vulnerable. Rather, it is important to base any attempt at developing a comprehensive understanding of the theory of local currencies from the starting point of the state of the currently existing world. At this point, it may worth venturing a few general remarks about the vision of labor note theories that emerges in Chapters 4 and 5 by reconfirming the criteria used in Chapter 4. There it was stated that four criteria are required: (1) the dominant model of ownership, (2) the evaluation and measurement of labor time bestowed on the product, (3) the form or method for issuing labor notes, and (4) the relationship between the evaluation value of the product measured by labor notes (labor quantity) and the market (money) price.

As already pointed out, Owen's theory of labor notes was based on the notion of an ideal market and monetary system, where the discrepancy between the total supply and demand caused by metal money would be overcome, resulting in a rational social allocation of labor and community-based labor notes under a common ownership system. In general, the New Harmony type labor notes implemented by Owen were based on four assumptions: (1) a common ownership system as the premise, (2) labor times bestowed in the product commensurate with the quantity of labor measured in natural time, (3) labor notes recorded at the time labor has been expended and reported by members under the supervision of others, and (4) the internal economy of the community strictly distinct from the external economy with no mechanism for referencing to market prices explicitly. Owen's labor note theory was a result of trying to realize the idea of "fair income" and "fair exchange" by building homogeneity and cooperation among members.

Josiah Warren, who critically inherited Owen's theory of labor notes was concerned that individual responsibility and independence would be buried in the collectiveness of the community and sought to rearrange the labor note theory as a system that could demonstrate the individual's free independence as much as possible.

Warren's theory of labor notes was based on the presupposition of a regional community where individuals are loosely connected. He was concerned to not deny the disparities that exist between individualities, skills, labor times, and types of labor that arise from many of the systems of labor notes. It was therefore pointed out that the labor times bestowed by heterogenous labor were unequal, and to acknowledge these differences between heterogenous labor and the exchange of "labor for labor" as it is really performed. This meant a revision of the Owenite vision of the exchange of equal labor times in favor of exchange consisting of "time for time." In Warren's system, labor notes are certificates issued at the responsibility of the individual and show promises of future payments. The Owen-style book-keeping method, which favored joint management of social labor allocation, was rejected by Warren because it exceeded the scope of individual responsibility and involvement. Unlike Owen, Warren did not envision a closed community, so the price of the product could be determined by reference to market prices outside the community.

Warren's theory of labor notes had been devised to bring out individual responsibility and spontaneity, based on his reflections on the failure of New Harmony. For example, it established the disparities in the evaluation of different types of labor and posited the issuer of notes as an individual. In addition, competition within the community was promoted. Warren's theory of labor notes tried to overcome the deficiencies of Owen's egalitarian labor note theory in this way, but his shift to a microscopic approach left out some issues such as ensuring fairness and cooperation from a social perspective as Owen sought to accomplish. It is also questionable whether tolerating labor inequality would result in a fair measurement of the sacrifice of labor itself. The New Harmony project was also a situation in which the contradiction between achieving individual responsibility, spontaneity, and economic incentivization on the one hand, and cooperation and equality across the community and society on the other was left unresolved, thus presenting an ongoing issue for labor note theories.

It is questionable whether Warren had truly grasped the nature of money and its basis in labor, leaving it to Pare, an undeniable Owenite, to try and inspire the cooperative movement to seek a synthesis between Warren's theory with Owenism, although it is doubtful how conscious Pare was of the fact.

Certainly, Pare was actively engaged in opening the Birmingham branch of the labor exchange, and he himself stipulated that the function of money was "a standard of value" and "a circulating medium." Pare's monetary vision did not look so different from that of Owen. However, it is observed that the currency, which should have been defined as "a standard of value" and "a circulating medium" by Pare, behaved in a way that deviated from the way it regulates the actual market. Pare detected the act of "each party giving and receiving an equivalent in labour or the product of labour," as a different opportunity both temporally and spatially, and emphasized the locality and incompleteness of market transactions. The reason why the opportunity of buying and selling of labor and labor products is divided in this way is because the exchange of the market is mediated by money, and money is carried over as a means of payment, settlement, and hoarding. The market does not always promise completeness of transactions, and the place and time of selling labor and labor products should be different from the place and time of buying for each transaction. Despite these obvious facts about actually functioning markets, they tend to be obscured when focusing solely on total supply and demand and labor allocation within the community.

If the carryover of money and the incompleteness of transactions are the normal state of the market, labor notes presented as the alternative should be initiated to alter the actual state of money. It may not be necessary to conceive of a product purely in terms of its dual functions as a "a standard of value" and "a circulating medium," which are ideally talked about. The labor notes, given their character of a substitute for money carried over for future payments, were already explained by Warren, and consolidated by Pare in his attempt to arrive an undistorted monetary system.

The theoretical contribution of Pare may be seen to go further. In particular, he raised three issues. The first lays in its attempt at introducing a method for comparing different types of labor with the aim of solving the problem of how to establish a fair system for the commensurate reduction of qualitatively distinct types of labor to a single quantitative system. On this question, Pare clearly stated that the labor evaluator must be the producer himself. If the evaluation criteria and judgments were extrinsic, the evaluation would often be less convincing for those who are evaluated. It is reasonable that the evaluation method understood by the evaluated person is nothing but self-evaluation. In addition, honest declarations and standard labor were set as the criteria for obtaining the sociality of one's own judgment. Although rules such as honest declarations can only be followed according to the conscience of the individual, application of standard labor as a standard is not a despotic rule that forces all labor to be put into the standard formwork. In other words, it is only a guideline for self-evaluation and a standard of reference. Therefore, it can be said that the legitimacy of self-evaluation depended on its acceptance among trading partners, rather than being enforced by an external body.

The second point regarding the feasibility of labor notes centers on the question of the issuer's creditworthiness. Owen considered the question to some extent when addressing the difficulty of circulating paper money, by requiring real asset collateral of the same value to be deposited whenever labor notes were issued. According to Owen's theory of labor notes, credit transactions obstructed the flow of supply and demand due to its temporal nature and was therefore to be regulated. The labor notes were nothing more than delivery certificates for deposited products. He was also aware that the issuance method for labor notes in no way served an institutional guarantee for the total equilibrium of supply and demand. In contrast, Pare abandoned such social-level attempts at controlling the ratio of supply to demand, preferring to focus on individual transactors and their mutual roles as producers and bankers. This meant that the question of creditworthiness was focused on the individual rather than the system. At the same time, considering the possibility of carrying over money, he stopped investing any hope in an achieving an ideal market vision in which all transactions were simultaneously completed with neither hoarding nor credit transactions. This meant he was approaching a view in which labor notes resembled credit money, insofar as "it combines the properties of a circulating medium, and a means of credit."

Owen's and Warren's observations of the economy from a macroscopic perspective reveal an ongoing commitment to address the significance of the question of social regulation. With Pare, such a social viewpoint is almost forgotten, but in doing so, he also abandoned the real macroscopic issues arising from the disruption to supply and demand that arises from the actions of short-sighted individuals who disturb social harmony by exercising profit-seeking behavior. Aware of potential criticisms, Pare's approach was to emphasize that the business of social change could only be started by each individual taking the initiative. In this, we can see that Pare was neither a utopian philanthropic entrepreneur in mold of Owen nor someone in search of a collective subject as was the case for Marx, but rather pinned his hopes that on utilizing labor notes as a means for individuals to trade independently of whatever disturbances were happening at the macroscopic level. In that sense, the microscopic nature of Pare's approach played an important role helping to define the question of social cooperation, and to highlight some of the contradictions among those socialists who thought that it was possible to introduce labor notes as a way to balance supply and demand.

Chapter 7 examined Gray's theory of labor notes. Gray, like other labor note theorists, grasped that money had two functions, serving as a measure of value and as a means of exchange. Although his understanding of money was almost identical to that of the classical economics, unlike them he stressed that the two functions only really held under ideal theoretical conditions and should not be assumed to exist in their full form in reality or be abstractly projected onto actually functioning markets. For Gray, the functions of money retained their ideal or theoretical purpose and could serve as a policy guideline. This enabled Gray to observe divergences between theory and reality and to build a "whole system of exchange" to bring money closer to the ideal vision.

Gray was motivated by two factors. The first lays in deficiencies around how to measure the value of money. Despite the fact that money functions as a means of measuring value, the fairness of market transactions cannot be confirmed due to variations in the absolute quantity and range of that measure. For example, in a money lending and borrowing relationship, even if interest is excluded, a fixed amount of debt may represent different purchasing power depending on the value of money at the time of borrowing or repayment, although the nominal amount is the same. Thus, a worker earning 100 dollars in a day, may find that if he or she borrowed a day's earnings, it would be worth two day's labor by the time it has to be repaid. Which raises the question of whether the debtor should pay back 100 or 200 dollars, as the question of their purchasing power has become obscured in the meantime. In the lending and borrowing relationship, the process of fluctuating monetary value therefore obscures the question of fairness—whether it is fair to loan and to repay at any given amount. Gray responded to the issue by stating that the purchasing power of money, measured by the quantity of labor-commanded, should be the standard. If the value of money fluctuates independently from production, the original relationship of exchange based on the quantity of labor bestowed in the production process will be overshadowed. It will not accurately reflect the quantity of labor bestowed in the production process. However, since the circulation process of the market is merely an auxiliary to production, money should simply mirror what is happening at the level of production. Money itself does not measure value, the actual measure is labor itself. The absolute scale that divides the quantity of labor is the substance of the "immutable measure of value." As Gray mentioned, "enjoyment of life is the common object of every human pursuit, and the original source of all the means of enjoyment is labour." This revealed his underlying view of labor-money as the "originally purchase-money" in which it is labor to buy and labor that is purchased.

The second factor for Gray was that money is defective as a means of exchange. Money, or to be more precise, the current gold money, does not fully function as a means of exchange, because the money itself has an inherent value as a commodity. Moreover, the production cost of gold gradually increases due to the characteristics of the gold-producing industry. This issue is closely related to the first factor, but since money itself, which is a monetary material, has a unique value, it is recognized that the change in value hinders equal exchange between products. If the monetary balance representing equal purchasing power was fair, the exchange of products would have to include equal quantities of labor. However, if the value of the money that mediates the exchange fluctuates, there is no way to expect an equal exchange between the products that appear at both ends of the currency transaction. In addition to that, the money supply becomes insufficient whenever there is a scarcity of gold, and the act of exchange itself becomes difficult.

Based on the above ideal monetary analysis, it was revealed that the market injustice caused by the obstruction of gold was normalized by the exclusion of gold from money, and Gray critically continued the view of the Birmingham school and shifted his attention to the issue of inconvertible paper money management in the event of a departure from gold. The Birmingham School pointed out that gold has an inherent value as a commodity, which disrupts the market and limits purchasing power, leading to an underconsumption crisis. Gray accepted this point of view by adopting a policy of creating purchasing power by making gold money into banknotes. But he takes issue with the Birmingham school, which recommended government notes, for being insufficiently vigilant against the possible adverse effects of the decline in monetary value due to the additional supply of currency. Moreover, even if the gold standard is not the best monetary system, it cannot cope with the criticism from the classical school that it undeniably keeps the expansion of the currency in check. On the other hand, while Gray participated in the controversy over currency management, he came up with a unique solution to labor notes that aimed to stabilize the currency value by aligning money to production, so currency management could not be done solely by managing currency. He clarified that the adjustment of the disequilibrium in the inter-sectorial balance of production must be done as a part of any currency management policy.

This takes the argument to the turn of the twentieth century and the ideas of Gesell, which are explored in Chapter 8. With Gesell, we see a return to the question of exploitation, which he tried to tackle head-on. He did this by recourse to Proudhon and attempted to link Proudhon's market vision to the question of exploitation, which Marxists had taken up as a political issue at the time. Gesell advocated a vision of a market not based on the real operations of the market, but on its ideal functions, in a society purified of distortions. In particular, this meant reviving Proudhon's view that the power of the use value of money as a commodity hinders the process of equal exchange in the market by increasing the value of money. By reviving these issues, he was also reviving the controversy between Proudhon and Marx. The root of Gesell's theory of exploitation lays in the qualitative problem of the physical property of money and whether its status as a commodity enhances the value of money. For Gesell, this problem was exacerbated whenever money appeared as interest.

A key issue for Gesell, which is of contemporary interest, was the question of how to realize economic security for those sections of the population who did not take part in wage labor, but whose lives were effected by market transactions and money—most especially women and children. By focusing on questions of circulation and land reform, he was trying to address the needs of these sections of the population who are more bound up with questions of social reproduction. Although not necessarily considered from the same perspective, there is evidence to show that Marx and Owen's shared this interest in social reproduction as set out in Chapters 3 and 4, in which the advantages of a community-based economic systems are considered in terms of acting as a fairer mechanism for redistribution. Which method should be followed today depends on the way we think about class income and value theory—and how this relates to value or values in terms of economics and social justice. The Warren-Pare type of labor note theory attempted positively to utilize the existing system of money and the market, by questioning where outside that sphere it might be possible to have an alternative system of exchange—and how that would relate back to the market and money. This raises a question for today and the future, in terms of whether labor note theory should function as a mechanism to ensure greater redistribution within the existing market system, or whether an ideal of the market purified of the distortions of money should be put forward as a serious political proposal, without appearing unrealistic or too utopian.[1]

Now, finally, I would like to touch on how local currencies crystallize the entire history of labor notes. Given the focus of local currencies on spatial units such as towns or regions, and the fact that they aim to act as citizens' currency with a degree of sovereignty for all citizens in that space, it is possible to see certain aspects of the Warren-Pare model being reflected. Even though this spatial aspect was rarely an explicit focus for labor note theorists, it is possible to connect their concerns about circulation with questions of sovereign space, territory, and citizenship, in which the creditworthy issuer of a labor note becomes a legitimate citizen—in the sense of being a member of the local currency system. The idea originally pursued in the Warren-Pare-type model was based on the restoration of the independence and dignity of labor, which led to a specific conception of sovereignty and citizenship that can be seen at work in local currency theories. In other words, it was based on the principles of active social participation and fair exchange. Furthermore, it sought to locate the sovereign not in the state or in an institution or company, but directly in the citizens in a way that had not been clarified properly in the history of labor note theories. Labor notes, from this perspective, should

[1] Marx and Owen suggest that if social surplus occurs, it can be used flexibly, and in that case, it is significant to use labor time as a unit of measure for the labor allocation and distribution. Their original point is to understand the economic quantity from the viewpoint of labor and labor time, and to present a future social vision with a strong awareness of the position of workers, but how and in what way it should be achieved remained open to question. Even in the communities Owen established, it cannot be said that the significance of elastically utilizing surplus products and labor to redistribute the social surplus was well understood. For the time being, it may be that we have to start with government taxation as the best-known current model of redistribution and work from there to where Marx and Owen may have ended up had they produced analyses of the state's fiscal activity. Not least in importance is whether this return to the state raises serious issues for anarchism as well as for Marxians and Owenites in terms of taxation as a measure of social control versus a measure of redistribution, and whether it can aid the emancipatory process. Of course, the same goes for Warren-Pare labor note theory. Under the economic calculation that combines the calculation of labor time, it will be consciously divided into the part where one's work supports one's life and the part that contributes to the maintenance and reproduction of society.

In Yuki (2009), I pointed out that the utilization of social surplus under the Warren-Pare type labor notes economy may, for the time being, be due to the voluntary donation of each producer. It would be a donation to others in a face-to-face relationship, but if we could go further and establish an association that pools the donations of each producer, it would have greater reach.

not be directed by governments or through major reforms to the banking systems, but directly within civil society. The confluence of labor notes and local currencies would have to be based on a realistic vision of the money and market—in terms of how they exist, rather than positing an ideal type of market and aiming to approximate it in practice. This takes us back to the question of reforming the system of production to overcome the anarchy of production as posed by Owen and Marx. Any such reform would be likely to result in an excessive demand for new theories of labor notes, along with a reconsideration of all the issues raised about money and market reforms discussed in this book. Of course, it is difficult to imagine trying to overcome the anarchy of production by partially utilizing the existing system, which is based on that very anarchy, whether it is through labor notes, local currencies, or any other alternative to current system of money and markets, although local currencies at least have provided an inkling of how such systems could potentially develop within the interstices of the current system. A specific issue which is perhaps more challenging for labor note theorists and local currencies is the question of long-term labor input planning and planned social allocation; not least of which is the question how it could be possible to envisage a range of production plans that are suitable for demand that will become aggregated once a local currency system is fully operational and handling the bulk of exchange activity.

It seems clear that any type of labor note that utilizes a local currency will need to be based on the Warren-Pare model. Local currencies should not be understood as efforts undertaken by government agencies or any abstract or institutional subject. This is because in practice, the individual should always be the subject. If this point is accepted, and if it becomes necessary to go beyond that and lift the limit of what can be done by individuals, it will be desirable for intermediate groups to be set up for the issuing and managing of certificates, and this should take the form of associations.

Participants in such a labor notes system will issue the certificate based on their individual creditworthiness, as in the Warren-Pare type. The reasons why it should be issued individually and the social conditions for making it possible are described below. The reason for having to be personally issued is directly derived from the historical lessons of labor notes. The first reason is that it is difficult to set up a customized system in which labor notes are familiar to participants because they are tailor-made to suit their individual needs—this would lead to multiple systems and models of labor-notes and a kind of "anarchy" of circulation—to borrow Marx's phrase. Even if the issue of the validity of labor evaluation arises when using labor notes, the validity and fairness of labor evaluation is unlikely to be satisfied by the supply and demand relationship of the labor market or by labor rating and examination agencies, etc., which is the second reason for considering the Warren-Pare model. In relation to this point, LETS emphasizes the freedom of pricing as the expression of individuals' intentions regarding the community to which they belong. Just as there is a LETS-like way of saying that it is important to express self-intention as a producer, rather than as a consumer, the local currency market can also be used as a place for self-evaluation and self-affirmation as reflected in the issuing of local currency in the form of a labor note type. The Time Dollar exemplifies the way in which the local currency market serves as a place where various types of labor that are not properly evaluated in the ordinary market are traded. This creates an opportunity for self-affirmation by the self-evaluation of each participant's own labor. By accepting one's own work, rather than relying on the evaluation and oversight of others, it harnesses the power of people to become their own evaluators. The local currency market becomes a space to experience labor that is not valued in the ordinary market and enables the overcoming of the denial of one's existence that dogs so many people who are either excluded from the labor market or are thrown out through such experiences as redundancy or unemployment. It is possible that the sense of alienation and inferiority that is planted can be overcome by solidarity provided by volunteers and public assistance, which promotes the beneficiary's status and the demonstrates the benefits of overcoming a unilateral model of market transaction with a more mutual one. Gesell's emphasis on the self-esteem of independent small producers and the individual issuance and acceptance of labor notes would be obviated if the Pare-Warren model could be achieved.

Still, even in a system of exchange relations where everyone is a self-evaluator, the question of quantitative validity remains an unavoidable feature. This introduces a temporal element that separates the moments of application, acceptance, and approval in order to complete the exchange. This requires a level of monitoring, as evaluation takes place to judge if different labors are commensurate. Yet, while it may be possible to establish a standard to compare different acts of labor based on skill, time, impact on the laborer's health, etc., the question of establishing absolute criteria for the evaluators is a separate matter. Warren and Pare raised the issue of whether it is possible for such an individual to exist, questioning some of the assumptions about the matter in Owen's system, which tended toward a paternalist model in which Owen as the owner of the system could adopt this role. The Warren-Pare model was keenly aware that this could create two kinds of asymmetrical relations: the first between the patron and the laborer, and the second between the abstract system and the individual laborer. By investing evaluation in the exchangers as individuals directly, the Warren-Pare model sought to provide a solution. Given that one must confirm one's absoluteness and acknowledge it in others as well, Warren and Pare hoped that this equality gave everyone an equal right to determine the value of their own labors and evaluate the labors of others when entering into an exchange relation. The aim here was to avoid establishing a hierarchy of labor, by investing the power of evaluation at the level of the individuals engaging in exchange. Although it may be a hindrance, LETS schemes are based on the premise that the freedom of individual pricing would diversify the price and bring about the individualities of a measure that has becomes multi-valued for a particular thing. But it is difficult to think how such an approach to measuring value will arise inside a monetary system. Rather, the achievement of such a model will require breaking out of the system or breaking the system in such a way that would enable either a new system or multiple systems, thus raising a variety of questions related to political strategy.

Bibliography

Yuki, T. 2009. Motto Jiyū de, Motto Byōdō na: Yūtopia Shakaishugi nyūmon [More free and more equal: Introduction to Utopian socialism]. *Gendai Shisō* [Revue de la pensée d'aujourd'hui], *37*(10), 224–237.

Afterward

As the reader can imagine, this book has been something of a life journey for me. I think it was when I was an undergraduate student that I first became interested in the theory of labor notes. At the time, I had a keen interest in the fundamental contradictions of the capitalist economy, and I randomly picked up books and read them excursively. It is hard to recall why I had such an interest, but I perhaps it was because of my impulsive personality when I was a high school student.

For me at the time, the basic perceptions of the Marxian school did not seem to be theoretically false, but I can recall a sense of discomfort with the ideologically distorted way in which Marxian ideas were discussed in the public sphere. I was also struck by the overall failure of reflection in the wake of the end of the Cold War, which should have provoked consideration of an array of logical and systemic issues. However, I was pursuing a faulty logic, too, in part due to the allure of Tokyo at the height of postmodernity, which I experienced without a pang of discomfort or alienation. However, thinking that there may have been something that the Marxian school had overlooked, I found myself reaching out unaccountably to those utopian socialist writings of the period of the early Marx in the hope that they harbored something that could enable me to revive Marx from the inside, so to speak.

I was fortunate to have been able to study at the Faculty of Economics at Kokugakuin University, which was full of eminent scholars

© The Editor(s) (if applicable) and The Author(s), under exclusive license to Springer Nature Switzerland AG 2021

T. Yuki, *Socialism, Markets, and the Critique of Money*,
Marx, Engels, and Marxisms,
https://doi.org/10.1007/978-3-030-80408-4

whose influence on my thinking should not go unmentioned: Professor Ryōji Takayanagi introduced me to German philosophy, while Professor Katsujirō Fujita opened my eyes to French socialism, and Professor Hiroshi Arata gave me a grounding in Russian-Soviet economic history. Above all, my future path was shaped by the course on the "principles of political economy" taught by Professor Makoto Itoh, who had just retired from the University of Tokyo. When I was allowed to participate in Professor Itoh's seminar in my third year, I was strongly attracted to his thoughts, especially his view that the role of academia is to clarify the objects we determine as facts in terms of their underlying logic. His ideas had a clarity and a rigor that escaped me, and I found myself attending the same lectures twice to grasp the truth of what he was teaching. As with many students, it was often through extra-curricular intellectual activities that I was able to deepen my ideas, and I cannot forget my foundation in Marx by attending a reading group of all three volumes of *Capital* organized by Professor Itoh and reading groups of Kozo Uno's *Principles of Political Economy*. It was also by a stroke of luck that Professor Itoh gave me the opportunity to study at the undergraduate seminar of Professor Michiaki Obata at the University of Tokyo. I faced challenges at the time and nearly lost my intellectual motivation for pursuing the study of political economy upon finding it nearly impossible to grasp the theoretical ideas in Professor Shigekatsu Yamaguchi's *Lecture on the Principles of Political Economy*, which I was studying at that time. However, in retrospect, I can see how that experience exposed me to many new ideas whose value became clearer to me later. Above all, it was a valuable experience to come into contact with Professor Obata's approach to academic study, and the forcefulness of his logic power still reverberates with me to this day.

Despite this background, I was still taken aback by Professor Itoh's recommendation that I work on a graduation thesis on the topic of labor money theory. This spurred me to produce a thesis titled *Two Theories of Labor Money*, for which I was delighted to receive the Aoki Award and the top essay prize from the Faculty of Economics. Producing this essay gave me a deeper appreciation of the benefits of studying under Professor Obata and the need for me to direct my attention toward a specific applied area rather than working on the principles of political economy *in abstracto*. This gave me the edge I needed to cut a swathe for myself in the field of academic research that lay before me.

It was in 2001 after five years of slogging it out in research, that I was allowed to join the Obata seminar at the Graduate School at University of Tokyo. I was given the freedom to pursue my interests and to live a truly enjoyable intellectual life. Perhaps there is something in the saying that "man is condemned to be free," and it seemed no accident that many of the international students who came to study with us would declare how free it feels to work within a graduate Japanese school. Certainly, the discussions that took place in informal seminar on the principles of political economy were both enlightening and exciting. Indeed, I may not have been able to overcome many of the stumbling blocks I encountered later had I not been able to access a space where I could engage in such free and reflective discussion. It would be remiss here to not thank Yasuaki Tsukamoto (Aichi University) for his role in organizing these sessions. I also cannot forget the discussions with Hiroshi Seino (Johoku High School), who was a graduate student at the Graduate School of Literature at Seijo University at the time. Through our conversations, I was able to discover both the joy of learning and the cultivation of skepticism toward mainstream economics. I have often wondered whether ideas that I have passed as my own are not really his, though he has been kind enough not to upbraid me. The philosophy reading group that I have continued with my friends should not go unmentioned. This group, began when we were students, continues to provide helps and illumination.

During the doctoral dissertation review process, Professor Michiaki Obata, Professor Tokutaro Shibata, Professor Makoto Maruyama, Professor Masaki Takenouchi, and Professor Shunji Ishihara helped me. The various issues pointed out in the *viva* and the contents of the examination findings were very helpful for reviewing the structure of my doctoral dissertation. This book is a largely a response to the issues that came up in the *viva*, although some issues may remain unanswered. I also received guidance from Professor Takashi Aosai (Shinshu University), Professor Kazuhiko Okada (Takasaki Keizai University), and Professor Haruo Takeuchi (Aichi University). Let me also note that I benefited from the free and open discussion at the Robert Owen Association, which served as a good mental exercise. Naobumi Hijikata, a member of the association (professor emeritus at Chuo University), taught me the importance of coming to grips with the basics of the historical study of economic thought and international academic exchange. I would like to thank everyone else involved with the association.

The original Japanese version of this book was made up of a compilation of eight papers that I had written over five years, along with the addition of the introduction ("Issues and Methods: The Invisibility of 'Labor Notes'") and the final chapter ("Some Visions on Money and the Market: Possibilities of the Theory of the Labour Note") as new material. For this edition, many of the original papers have been rewritten, with some barely revealing a trace of the original, which reflects how my ideas have further evolved.

Below is a brief bibliographical list of the original essays:

Chapter 2

Yuki, T. (2006). Proudhon no Shakaishugi to Marx no Shijōriron: Mushō Shin'yōron to Kachi Keitairon [Proudhon's socialism and Marx's market theory: Proudhon's theory of free credit and Marx's theory of value forms]. *Hikaku Keizai Taisei Kenkyū* [The Jounral of Comparative Economic Studies], *13*, 91–105.

Chapter 3

Yuki, T. (2004). Marx niyoru Rōdō Kaheiron Hihan no Saikentō: Chiikitsūka heno Shatei [Reconsideratoin of Marx's critique of the theory of labor money: Toward a local currency]. *Robert Owen Kyōkai Nenpō* [Annual Report of Robert Owen Association], *28*, 29–42.

Chapter 4

Yuki, T. (2006a). Josiah Warren no *Kōsei Shōgyōron* [Josiah Warren's *Equitable Commerce*]. *Robert Owen Kyōkai Nenpō* [Annual Report of Robert Owen Association], *30*, 45–61.

Yuki, T. (2006b). R. Owen to J. Warren no Rōdō Shōkenron [Labor notes in the socio-economic theories of Robert Owen and Josiah Warren]. *Keizai Gakushi Kenkyū* [The History of Economic Thought], *48*(2), 19–35.

Chapter 5

Yuki, T. (2007). William Pare no Rōdō Shōkenron: Kahei no Shokinō kara Shijōzō he [William Pare's theory of labour note: From monetary functions to market vision]. In T. Aosai, M. Obata, & A. Shimizu (Eds.), *Marx Riron Kenkyū* [Studies in Marxian theory] (pp. 181–193). Ochanomizu Shobo.

Chapter 6

Yuki, T. (2004). Chiikitsūka to Robert Owen no Rōdōkahei no Hikaku Kentō: Kahei no Hakkōkonkyo Hōshiki wo Shijiku toshite [A comparative study of local currency and Robert Owen's labor money: From the perspective on the grounds and methods of issuance of money]. *Hikaku Keizai Taisei Kenkyū* [The Journal of Comparative Economic Studies], *11*, 80–96.

Chapter 7

Yuki, T. (2007). John Gray no Rōdō Shōkenron: Kahei to Rōdō no Kanrensei [John Gray's theory of labour note: On the relationship between money and labour]. *Kokugakuin Keizaigaku* [Kokugakuin University Economic Review], *55*(3–4), 307–349.

Chapter 8

Yuki, T. (2008). Silvio Gesell no Shihon Riron [Silvio Gesell's capital theory]. *Asia Japan Journal*, *3*, 69–90.

In the process of conducting this research, I received the grant from JSPS KAKENHI Grant Number JP23730204 in 2011–2013, JP245164 in 2012, and Saitama University's Project Research Fund (Project Number A11-09) in 2011, for which I would like to express my appreciation.

Finally, I would like to present this book with all my heart to Chie, Chifuyu, and Shifumi who have supported me when I did not have the means to make a living.

January 26, 2013
Tsuyoshi Yuki

Index

© The Editor(s) (if applicable) and The Author(s), under exclusive license to Springer Nature Switzerland AG 2021

T. Yuki, *Socialism, Markets, and the Critique of Money*, Marx, Engels, and Marxisms,
https://doi.org/10.1007/978-3-030-80408-4

The manufacturer's authorised representative in the EU is Springer Nature Customer Service Centre GmbH, Europaplatz 3, 69115 Heidelberg, Germany. If you have any concerns regarding our products, please contact ProductSafety@springernature.com

Printed and bound by CPI Group (UK) Ltd, Croydon, CR0 4YY
06/10/2026
02228468-0001